# THE STOLEN PRINCE

# THE
# STOLEN PRINCE

Gannibal, Adopted Son of Peter the Great,
Great-Grandfather of Alexander Pushkin,
and Europe's First Black Intellectual

## HUGH BARNES

HarperCollins books may be purchased for educational, business,
or sales promotional use. For information, please write:
Special Markets Department, HarperCollins Publishers,
10 East 53rd Street, New York, NY 10022.

First published in Great Britain in 2005 as
*Gannibal: The Moor of Petersburg,* by Profile Books Ltd.

FIRST EDITION

Printed on acid-free paper

Library of Congress Cataloging-in-Publication Data

Barnes, Hugh
[Gannibal]
The stolen prince : Gannibal, adopted son of Peter the Great, Great-Grandfather of
Alexander Pushkin, and Europe's first black intellectual / Hugh Barnes.
p.   cm.
1. Gannibal, Abram Petrovich, 1697?–1781.   2. Generals—Russia—Biography.
3. Russia. Armëia—Biography.   4. Pushkin, Aleksandr Sergeyevich, 1799–1837—Family.
5. Africans—Russia—Biography.   6. Russia—History—Peter I, 1689–1725.
I. Title: Gannibal, adopted son of Peter the Great, Great-Grandfather of
Alexander Pushkin, and Europe's first black intellectural.   II. Title.

DK130.G3B37 2006
947'.06092—dc22
[B]            2005055299

ISBN-10: 0-06-621265-0
ISBN-13: 978-0-06-621265-4

06   07   08   09   10   ❖ / RRD   10   9   8   7   6   5   4   3   2   1

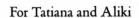

For Tatiana and Aliki

# Contents

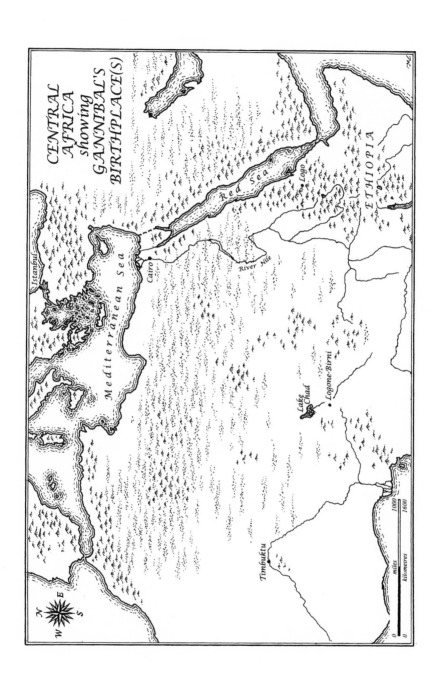

CENTRAL
AFRICA
showing
GANNIBAL'S
BIRTHPLACE(S)

Istanbul

Mediterranean Sea

Cairo

Red Sea

River Nile

Logo

ETHIOPIA

Lake
Chad

Logone-Birni

Timbuktu

N
W      E
S

miles          0    1000
kilometres     0    1600

# THE RUSSIAN EMPIRE AT
## PETER THE

North
Sea

Baltic Sea
Reval
Pernau
L.Ladoga
POLAND
Pskov
St Petersburg
Arkhangelsk
Vilnius
Moscow
Jassy
Kazan
Dnieper
Poltava
Volga
Edirne
Crimea
Ural
Tobolsk
Ob
Istanbul
Black Sea
Azov
Ural Mountains
Omsk
Irtysh
Caspian Sea
Aral
Sea
Amu Darya
AFGHANI-
STAN

N
W E
S

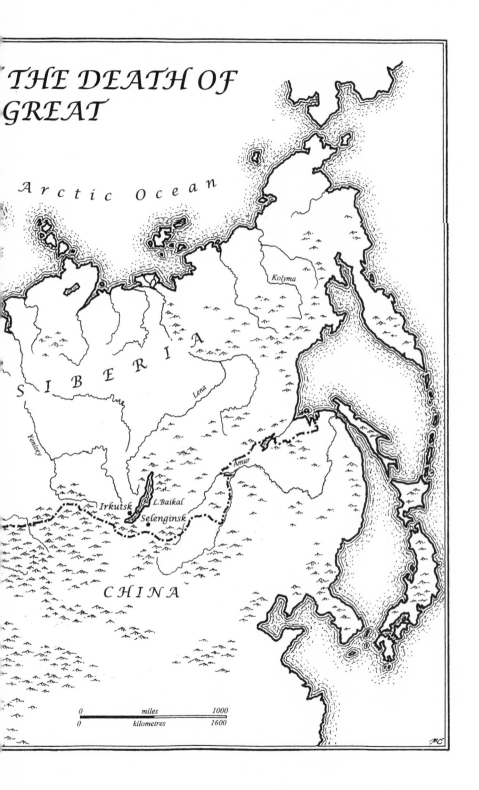

# THE DEATH OF GREAT

Arctic Ocean

SIBERIA

Kolyma

Lena

Yenisey

Amur

Irkutsk

L.Baikal

Selenginsk

CHINA

| 0 | miles | 1000 |
| 0 | kilometres | 1600 |

## Gannibal and his family

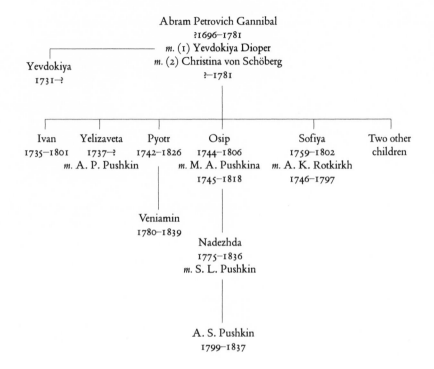

Abram Petrovich Gannibal
?1696–1781
*m.* (1) Yevdokiya Dioper
*m.* (2) Christina von Schöberg
?–1781

Yevdokiya
1731–?

Ivan
1735–1801

Yelizaveta
1737–?
*m.* A. P. Pushkin

Pyotr
1742–1826

Osip
1744–1806
*m.* M. A. Pushkina
1745–1818

Sofiya
1759–1802
*m.* A. K. Rotkirkh
1746–1797

Two other
children

Veniamin
1780–1839

Nadezhda
1775–1836
*m.* S. L. Pushkin

A. S. Pushkin
1799–1837

# The Romanov Dynasty

*italic* = Tsars, Emperors and reigning Empresses

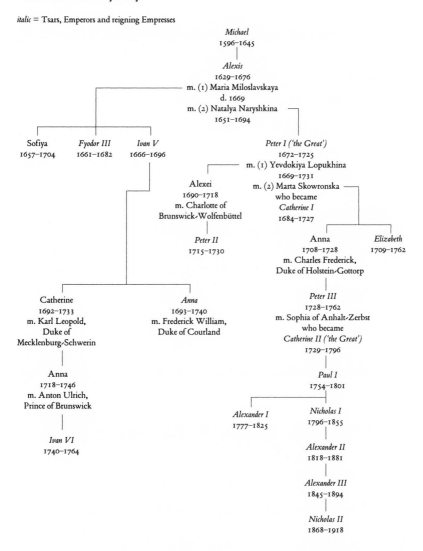

Michael
1596–1645

Alexis
1629–1676
m. (1) Maria Miloslavskaya
d. 1669
m. (2) Natalya Naryshkina
1651–1694

Sofiya
1657–1704

Fyodor III
1661–1682

Ivan V
1666–1696

Peter I ('the Great')
1672–1725
m. (1) Yevdokiya Lopukhina
1669–1731
m. (2) Marta Skowronska
who became
Catherine I
1684–1727

Alexei
1690–1718
m. Charlotte of
Brunswick-Wolfenbüttel

Anna
1708–1728
m. Charles Frederick,
Duke of Holstein-Gottorp

Elizabeth
1709–1762

Peter II
1715–1730

Catherine
1692–1733
m. Karl Leopold,
Duke of
Mecklenburg-Schwerin

Anna
1693–1740
m. Frederick William,
Duke of Courland

Peter III
1728–1762
m. Sophia of Anhalt-Zerbst
who became
Catherine II ('the Great')
1729–1796

Anna
1718–1746
m. Anton Ulrich,
Prince of Brunswick

Paul I
1754–1801

Ivan VI
1740–1764

Alexander I
1777–1825

Nicholas I
1796–1855

Alexander II
1818–1881

Alexander III
1845–1894

Nicholas II
1868–1918

# List of Illustrations

*Picture credits*

Author photograph: 1, 2, 16, 22; Ron Eglash, 3; Moscow, Lev Tolstoy Museum: 8; St Petersburg, Pushkin Museum: 13, 21, 26; St Petersburg, State Museum of Pavlovsk Palace: 9; Stockholm, Nationalmuseum: 4; Tallinn, Estonian Historical Archives: 18, 19; Tallinn, Tallinn City Archives, 24

While every effort has been made to contact copyright-holders of illustrations, the author and publishers would be grateful for information about any illustrations where they have been unable to trace them, and would be glad to make amendments in future editions.

# Preface

Alexander Pushkin was not only Russia's greatest poet. He was also the great-grandson of an African slave. The slave, whose godfather was Peter the Great, claimed to have royal blood of his own. Certainly his Russian descendants believed that he was a prince of Abyssinia. His English descendants have included Mountbattens and others close to the royal family. So the legend goes on.

Pushkin told the story of his black ancestor in *The Negro of Peter the Great*, but this is a different version. The main difference is between fact and fiction. The poet hoped to discover a biographical truth by sticking to the facts, only to discover that facts are slippery and not always true. His biography turned into a novel. Even then, it was left unfinished after six and a half chapters. The scrawled manuscript comes to a halt with a line of dialogue – 'Sit down, you scoundrel, let's talk!' – and a line of dots.

He could be speaking to himself. In any case, it's now time to stand up and carry on with the story. I have tried to join up the dots.

This is a book, then, about a missing link between the storyteller and his elusive subject, between the various branches of a family and its roots, between Pushkin and Africa, Africa and Europe, Europe and Russia, black and white. It is the story of a remarkable life and it poses the question: how is such a life to be explained?

My own explanation began in 2001, while I was living in Russia and working there as a journalist. The first draft was written during the war in Afghanistan, on the road to Kabul, and in the footsteps of the Taliban, but it describes other journeys, other pursuits. One led me to the frontline of a different kind of war, in Abyssinia, or at least to the fifteen-mile no-go zone separating the armies of Ethiopia and Eritrea. According to legend, Pushkin's ancestor was born here, on the northern bank of the river Mareb, where I was arrested for taking photographs and compass readings, on suspicion of being an Eritrean spy. Understandably my captors declined to believe that I was merely a journalist researching the ancestry of Russia's greatest writer, hoping to prove a negative. At the military camp, where I was held for a number of hours, the commandant looked me up and down when I asked, in my plummiest accent, 'I say, my good man, can you tell me, basically, what is going on here?' 'Basically,' he replied, with distaste, 'you is in *pree-zan!*'

The incident taught me something about the imprisoning facts of biography. Journalists, like biographers, are meant to respect facts, and by retracing Gannibal's footsteps, I hoped to find a true story.

Some of those journeys lie behind the book, and intrude whenever it is helpful to show that the past often retains a physical presence for the biographer – in landscapes, buildings, portraits, and above all in the trace of handwriting on original letters or journals. But my own journeys are not the point of the book. It is Gannibal's story. I am only following him.

Descriptions of Africa and the slave trade are drawn from my journeys, but this is not a book about a 'stolen legacy', nor certainly about the intellectual wars that have dogged black history in recent years. Biographers, like novelists, should tell stories. I have tried.

The book was mostly written between 2001 and 2004, but its themes have been in and out of my mind for over a decade. As a result there are long-standing debts. I wish to thank my editor Peter Carson for commissioning the book. I am also grateful to Derek Johns, Joanna Zenghelis, Anne Barton, John Kerrigan, the late Dmitry Likhachev, Sergei Fomichev, Dieudonné Gnammankou, Rachel Polonsky and Kyril Zinovieff, who is a descendant of Gannibal and, at ninety-five, one of the last survivors of the old Russian nobility.

I am grateful to Nicolas Miletitch, of Agence France-Presse, for employing me in Russia, and to his colleagues, David Millikin and Michel Viatteau, for their help and advice; and to Scott and Alexandra Peterson for giving me a quiet place to work in Sad Sam.

# A Note on Dates,
# Currency and Transliteration

Dates are given according to the Julian calendar used in Russia until 1917. It was eleven days behind Europe in the eighteenth century and twelve days in the nineteenth. However, dates referring to events in Europe are given according to the Gregorian calendar.

The monetary unit in Russia was the rouble, which contained 100 copecks, and was worth approximately a quarter of one pound sterling, or six French *livres*, in 1781, the year of Gannibal's death.

Russian spellings have been transcribed using a modified Library of Congress system but, in the case of names, I have sometimes used a more recognisable English form.

The translations are my own.

Russian archival references follow Russian practice: f. = fond (collection), op. = opis (section), d. = delo (file), kn. = kniga (book), l. = list (folio) (ll. = listy).

'A Negro!' Nikolai finished with a smile of delight. 'Of course I remember. But I still don't know if the Negro really existed, or if we just dreamed it or heard a story about him.'

—Leo Tolstoy, *War and Peace*

# 1

# Hermitage

Under the sky of my Africa
To sigh for gloomy Russia.
—Pushkin, *Eugene Onegin*

On 9 June 1762, during the 'white nights' of midsummer in Saint Petersburg, Russia's black knight left the Winter Palace in a huff. He was African and the son of Peter the Great, or so he claimed in a letter to Catherine the Great. (The epithet was bestowed somewhat liberally in eighteenth-century Europe.) 'Sacked!' he wrote in disbelief, 'after 57 years of loyal service, without reason or reward.'[1]

It had been a day of snubs and humiliations. The last straw came at a banquet given by the tsar, Peter's grandson and Catherine's husband, Peter III, to mark the signing of a peace treaty with Frederick the Great, king of Prussia. It was a gala occasion – the first of its kind in the new palace – and the whole of Petersburg was there. Built 'for the glory of Russia' by the Italian architect Francesco Bartolomeo Rastrelli, the magnificent structure cast a spell. Diversity and scale, the icy turquoise façade stretching two hundred yards down the Neva embankment, gave its baroque detail a heavy, almost barbaric flavour. In the half-light of the northern solstice, the vast bulk of the palace seemed to float upon the water. An optical illusion perhaps, or just the visible manifestation of an incomprehensible mystery: Dostoyevsky's 'invented city', its existence seeming to defy the physical and moral order of things.

Other guests noticed the African's moody demeanour. He was peevish and irritable, according to Baron Nikolai Korf, the head of the secret police, who described the outcast 'smiling like a wounded monkey' as he turned his back on the crush of senators, diplomats, ladies-in-waiting, aides-de-camp – even members of the imperial family just arrived from the tsar's native Holstein – and vanished into thin air.[2]

It was the usual racist slur. Not that his was the only black face in the crowd. Negro slaves were a common sight in Petersburg. In the grand salons of Millionnaya (or Millionaires') street, they appeared in a variety of roles, such as pets, pages, footmen, mascots, mistresses, favourites and adopted children. At the Winter Palace, so-called court Arabs – usually Ethiopians dressed à l'orientale in turbans and baggy trousers – stood guard like stage extras in the wings of marble and lapis lazuli. Recent events were the other backdrop. The African was not the only disgruntled soldier who opposed the end of Russia's victorious involvement in the Seven Years' War. Talk of conspiracy was rife. A hotchpotch of disaffected courtiers and adventurers loyal to Catherine were said to be plotting a coup d'état. Even Korf, the tsar's chief dissident-hunter, was thinking of changing sides.

It is often said that the African took part in the overthrow of Peter III. But Korf's anecdote is all that remains of his brief days as a revolutionary. Police reports show he left Petersburg after his untimely departure from the Winter Palace. The only other documentary evidence is a stationhouse register in the province of Pskov. An entry for 5 July – the day of Peter's murder – finds him returning from his country estate at Mikhailovskoye, 285 miles south-west of the capital, and inscribing his name and rank, as well as the date, for communication, in accordance with the law, to the secret police: 'Abram Petrovich Gannibal – General-in-chief – Landowner – Travelling on Private Affairs.'[3]

The story of Abram Petrovich Gannibal, and how he got that name, is the stuff of epic drama or romantic legend. It begins, in 1703, with a journey out of Africa. The young Moorish prince, aged seven, did not leave of his own free will. According to legend, he was kidnapped by pirates off the Barbary coast and sold as a slave to the Sultan of Turkey. Before long, however, a Russian spy in Constantinople rescued the exotic-looking child and dispatched him to the Kremlin as a present for Peter the Great, who became his godfather, and later adopted him. As for the riddle of his 'mysterious origin', which prompted Vladimir Nabokov to write a 60-page essay on the subject, as an appendix to his controversial edition of *Eugene Onegin*, new evidence has emerged in the last decade, and more will come out in the course of this book. By coincidence, in the year of Gannibal's enslavement, Russia's westernising tsar abandoned Moscow to build his new capital on a Baltic swamp. This 'Venice of the North' was founded on malaria-stricken bogs, and built by hundreds of thousands of serfs, many of whom died of disease and malnutrition during its construction. Saint Petersburg and the freed slave grew up side by side. The city with its Italianate architecture and stuccoed façades rose out of nothing on the banks of the Neva. The tsar's black favourite also scaled the heights of European society. He was fêted in salons from the Winter Palace to the court of Louis XV. Women were spellbound by his sexual charisma; their husbands marvelled at his nonchalant wit. At the same time, his military exploits from northern Spain to the icy wastes of Siberia – to say nothing of his marital problems – sealed Gannibal's reputation as the Russian Othello. His life rang with praise and applause, but so far he has been the subject of a disproportionately small amount of biography – none of it in English. The oracles have been dumb, and sometimes surly. Today he is remembered, if at all, only as the great-grandfather of Russia's finest poet, Alexander Pushkin, who portrayed his black ancestor in an unfinished novel, *The Negro of Peter the Great*.

Truth is stranger than fiction. The life of the Moor of Petersburg was not just adventurous; it was also evolutionary. Peter's Russia had always welcomed outsiders. Ever since the time of his first Grand Embassy to western Europe a decade earlier, the reforming tsar had brought back architects and engineers, craftsmen and artists, furniture designers and landscape gardeners. Scots, Germans, French and Italians all settled in large numbers in Petersburg. Under his godfather's watchful eye, Gannibal reversed the experiment, moving in and out of royal favour, but also soaring to dizzy heights as a soldier, diplomat, political factotum, and spy – not only for Russia, but also in France for the duc du Maine and opponents of the Regency.

In Paris, where he studied mathematics as well as military engi-neering, Gannibal played a key role in the exchange of ideas and technology that helped to modernise Russia. At the same time his friendship with Montesquieu and Voltaire, who praised him as the 'dark star of Russia's enlightenment', highlighted the Negrophobia of the contributors to the *Encyclopédie*. For his role as the first black intellectual in Europe, Gannibal was uniquely fitted by his varied experiences and abilities. But the nature of that experience, some of it clandestine and dangerous, has meant that although the African was a figure of substance, his total achievement has always seemed less than the sum of its parts. Not that we really know what all the parts were, since he revelled in the contrasts and conjunctions of his different pursuits: the philosopher and the man of action, the soldier-scholar, the plain-speaking courtier, the 'pensive' Moor, the same word Pushkin used for Rousseau in his discussion of the Noble Savage.[4]

Significantly, perhaps, it was during his sojourn in France that the interloper began signing his name 'Gannibal', a variant in Russian (with its aitchless Cyrillic alphabet) of Hannibal. A *nom de guerre*, it evoked not only the ancient Carthaginian general, his African precursor in the heart of Europe, but also (with a minor consonantal shift) a deep-seated racial prejudice in French thought, from Montaigne's 'On Cannibals' – the singular noun, in Russian, is *kannibal* – to a heading in the *Encyclopédie*: 'Vicious Character of Negroes'. Out of this etymological jumble comes one aspect of the European reaction to Gannibal: fear, a clinging to the idea of back-wardness, of monstrousness. Yet opponents of slavery used Ganni-bal's achievements to point out how wrong it was to enslave such talented people. Given pro-slavery arguments, which rationalised black servitude in terms of African baseness, it was inevitable that abolitionists would see in the Moor of Petersburg a counter-myth of African nobility. Certainly, with his natural gift for mathematics and his unrivalled skill as a field engineer, Gannibal more than repaid his debt to the tsar. Russian despots from Catherine the Great to Josef Stalin have owed stout defence to the line of fortifications he built from the Arctic Circle to the frontier with China. To quote Shakespeare on Othello, he had done the state some service, and they knew it – or, at any rate, Peter's daughter, the Empress Elizabeth, did. In 1741, she rewarded his efforts by granting him the estate at Mikhailovskoye, with its thousands of acres of pine forests and its hundreds of serfs. It was the ultimate irony in a bizarre life: the African slave had become a Russian slaveowner.

But who was Abram Petrovich Gannibal? And where did he come from? Was he really an Ethiopian prince, as the social-climbing Pushkins liked to claim? Or was he purchased by a drunk Russian skipper at the Ottoman Porte for a bottle of rum, as the poet's enemies believed. Here the romantic legend gives way to a detective story. It begins to unravel in Catherine's reign, as soon as he disappeared from the Winter Palace to a well-appointed exile in the Pskovan woods.

Gannibal's opting for hermitage became a legend in his family. 'In the reign of Emperor Peter the Third,' wrote his son-in-law, 'he went into retirement and lived like a sage in a peaceful and untroubled country life.' Rusticity was the feel of Mikhailovskoye, a kind of pastoralism. The manor house was small – fifty-six feet by forty-five – with an open porch looking out onto meadows, the picturesque Sorot river, the Svyatogorsky monastery, founded in 1569 by Ivan the Terrible, and two beautiful lakes, Kuchane and Malenets, surrounded by pine trees, hemp fields and corn stacks. Here Gannibal sat for days on end, in an old armchair in the study, with its smell of kvass and tallow candles, a table piled up with papers, and a glass-fronted bookcase full of volumes of the *Encyclopédie*, cobwebs, and dust.

Pushkin neatly captured the paradox of Gannibal's retirement when he wrote, in a note to *Eugene Onegin*, that 'the black African who had become a Russian noble lived out his life like a French *philosophe*.[5] To see it in this way is not to deny a more down-to-earth explanation. The decree signed by Peter III cited 'old age' as the reason for his dismissal. In other words, as a military commander, Gannibal was over the hill – which is probably true – and his retirement to a 'nest of the gentry' was overdue: it is just a question of scale, of extremity. This is a human story. But there is also an archetypal or legendary aspect to Gannibal which magnifies his gestures and loads his curtest utterances. And if, at times, this construction seems a bit novelistic, that is because the habits of the landed gentry (as we know them from Turgenev or Tolstoy) did not have to be invented, but were simply there: the summer mushroom hunts, the troika rides, the same, roughly predictable cast of characters – the faithful peasant, the unruly steward – as well as the general-in-chief celebrated in *War and Peace* in the figure of Prince Nikolai Bolkonsky.

It was no coincidence that, in 1762, Gannibal helped to invent a new Russian archetype. That year was a turning point in the history of the Russian countryside and a milestone for those 'travelling on private affairs'. It marked the beginning of a golden age for the country estate, which lasted a century until the abolition of serfdom in 1861. During the brief six months of his reign, Peter III made a very significant breach in Russia's system of *noblesse oblige*. Until 1762, the bondage of Russian society extended to the very top. Each individual was assigned to a particular rank – noble, townsman, priest or serf. Since 1722, a Table of Ranks instituted by Peter the Great had obliged even the nobility to serve the state. By issuing a decree that released the aristocracy from military and civil service, his grandson inadvertently enabled the idea of the 'private' individual to develop. The reform of 1762 turned backwaters such as Mikhailovskoye into the patriarchal fiefdoms or bucolic playgrounds – depending on your point of view – that led to the cultural flowering of the nineteenth century.[6]

This was his new life, then: the country gent, the retired soldier cultivating his garden, the philosopher-king, whom Pushkin describes in a poem written at Mikhailovskoye:

On the estate, where Peter's adopted child,
The beloved slave of tsars and tsarinas,
The forgotten one, who lived with them,
My ancestor the Blackamoor hid,
And where, having forgotten the court
And the splendid solemn promises of Elizabeth,
In the shade of lime-tree arbours,
He thought in cool summers
Of his far-off Africa.[7]

In other words, all the while, virtually from the moment Gannibal settled in the country, his mind was reaching out for somewhere else. At first it may have been, as Pushkin suggests, for his African homeland. That sense of nostalgia is evident in the family coat of arms emblazoned on a flag flying from the roof: the image of an elephant, with its hint of the ancient forerunner, and the enigmatic motto FUMMO, to which no satisfactory meaning has ever been ascribed. The most plausible effort to date is a non-existent proverb, *Fortuna viam meam mutavit oppido*, or 'Fate changed my life completely', which is certainly ingenious yet fails to convince, if only because Gannibal knew almost no Latin.

From the summer of 1762, perhaps even from the second week in July, when news of Catherine's coup against her husband reached Gannibal at Mikhailovskoye, the African was taking stock, hatching plans, thinking of revenge. On his desk, among the bric-à-brac of estate papers, were the maps, the charts, the campaign journals of the Seven Years' War. It was the first truly global conflict in history, ranging from Ohio to the Philippines, from Havana to Berlin. The war also highlighted the extraordinary reform of the Russian military that had taken place since the reign of Peter the Great, a reform in which Gannibal himself, both as theorist and practitioner, had played a significant role.

In the edgy aftermath of revolution, Gannibal wrote to Catherine requesting a promotion (to the rank of field marshal) and the financial reward he felt that Peter III had unjustly denied him. During the early weeks of her reign, Catherine lavished such rewards on those who had helped her to the throne. Grigory Potemkin, her future lover and consort, but someone who played only a minor role in the uprising, received 300 serfs, for example, while others got a life pension. So this is probably the true context of his letter to Catherine, which quickly dispenses with the usual expressions of fealty ('Your Venerable Majesty', 'Your Most Virtuous Highness', 'All High and Mighty Great Empress, All-Gracious Autocrat of Russia') to speak of his 'actions' — a clear reference to the plot against her murdered husband, whom he pointedly slights:

> I served the glorious memory of Your Majesty's beloved grandfather without interruption for 57 years, and without faults, but now on the ninth of June, unexpectedly, and without there being any crime on my part, I have been banished from service, and without the usual rewards.
>
> In return for my actions and unstinting service to Your Majesty, I beg you to grant me from the lofty nature of Your Imperial High-ness the ownership, for the sake of my poor family, of the estate in Ingria and Korpusk and the houses and estates of Old Siverko, New Siverko, Bolshevomezhno, Vyra, Rybitsa, in which there were at the last count five hundred and seven serfs, as well as one estate in Kuro-vitskaya.
>
> All-gracious Tsarina, I beg Your Imperial Majesty to judge this petition in my favour. Your entreating general and knight, Abram Gannibal, son of Peter, July 1762.[8]

This bold entreaty was a last desperate throw of the dice. It didn't pay off. In the month of July 1762, Catherine had urgent business in hand. She had no time to waste filling the pockets of a retired general. His petition was quietly dropped. The African didn't even get a reply from the hot-blooded empress. He was already a yesterday's man, a bizarre relic, an unwelcome reminder. In a scribbled postscript to Gannibal's letter, an unknown clerk has written 'no resolution' at the bottom of the sheet of paper, which now languishes in a dusty archive.

It is hard to improve upon the verdict of the anonymous bureaucrat. Such inconclusiveness was typical of Gannibal. From its very beginnings somewhere in Africa, his whole life was almost heroically *unresolved*: a story of departures and flights, of disappearances and reappearances. As a result, one can argue that his years of retirement, of hermitage, of disappointment, were not, as they are often taken to be, some kind of long blank coda at the end of a brilliant career, but an expression of something that was always there, in his life and in his alienation – a desire for self-removal, a dream of leaving and also perhaps of leaving no trace.

Nobody can reconstruct the linear narrative of Gannibal's life. It is full of gaps, of undecipherable clues, of mysteries and riddles. He often falls out of the historical record, goes missing for years, only to crop up again in a different place, in a new role, as a fresh imposture. Little has been written about him. The sources – letters, memoirs, official documents – are tantalisingly thin. The shortage of intimate papers makes it hard to hear the voice in which he spoke to himself and his closest friends. Even when the facts, the bare outlines, of his life are clear, the interpretation of them is very difficult. This difficulty is increased by Gannibal's own reticence about himself. Most of his correspondence has disappeared, and the surviving letters are astonishingly uncommunicative of his character. Their clipped, nonchalant tones, explanatory but somehow evasive, approximate to his conversational style. 'He spoke little,' said his friend Ivan Cherkasov. 'His comments were brief.' This is amply confirmed by others.

The atmosphere of political repression during the early years of Catherine's reign was not favourable to speaking out of turn. Having seized the throne by colluding in the murder of the Romanov tsar, she – his widow, a minor German princess by birth – understandably feared a challenge to her new status as empress, particularly as her son and heir Paul had no Romanov blood, being almost certainly the child of her lover Sergei Saltykov. That fact, though far from public knowledge, might have been known to Gannibal, and may explain the strange formalisation of himself as Peter's 'son', in the letter to Catherine, when the more usual word for 'godson' would have done. Nevertheless, in day-to-day conversation, the African wisely held his tongue. And there was a reason why he took no chances. It was the brutal repression of dissent under a law passed in 1763, called the Manifesto of Silence, which outlawed 'improper discussion and gossip' on political subjects.

His own silence was already manifest. It wasn't the African's way to give himself away on paper. He was not a confessional writer. 'During the reign of Peter III, Gannibal retired,' Pushkin adds in the note to *Eugene Onegin*. 'He wrote his memoirs in French, but in a fit of panic, to which he was subject, ordered them to be burned in his presence, together with other precious documents.'[9] But what caused him to panic? What exactly did he fear? The knock on the door in the middle of the night or a round-the-clock surveillance by Catherine's network of police spies known collectively as the Secret Expedition?

Pushkin wanted to know. In a series of visits to Mikhailovskoye as a young man, he mounted a kind of paper chase for any surviving documents. (Anyone trying to reconstruct Gannibal's story is always trailing in the footsteps of the poet and his detective work.) For example, Pushkin made regular visits to see his great-uncle, the African's second son, General Pyotr Abramovich Gannibal, who lived on the neighbouring estate of Petrovskoye, which Gannibal had built a few miles away. In 1817, soon after graduating, Pushkin went to see Pyotr, hoping to get some family documents from him. The old man was known in the district for his unconventional private life. In his youth, he had, like many another Russian landowner, kept a harem of serf girls. By the time Pushkin came to visit, however, Pyotr's pleasures were more or less confined to drink. 'He ordered a vodka,' the poet noted in his diary,

poured out a glass for himself and told the servant to offer me a glass.
I emptied it at a gulp without pulling a face, a fact which, it seems,
greatly pleased the old Negro. A quarter of an hour later, he again
called for vodka and repeated this five or six times until dinner.[10]

Yet the visit bore fruit. Pushkin left with a handful of papers, including
an unpublished 4,000-word biography of Gannibal written by
his Estonian son-in-law, Adam Karpovich Rotkirkh. The text, in
German, contains a number of absurd fantasies, including the claim
that Gannibal was directly descended from his ancient Carthaginian namesake, as well as some facts that only Gannibal could have
remembered. Based on notes the son-in-law jotted down in the final
years of the African's life, the book's fabulous narrative is not so much
a substitute for the destroyed memoirs as a kind of self-rejoinder, a
complicating of the story told by an old man whose memory was
fading. He was forgetful as well as 'forgotten'. Indeed Pyotr's elder
brother Ivan recalled that, 'at the end of his life, [Gannibal] seemed
to view his former career as in a dream'. The German biography, too,
has a dreamlike quality – unsurprisingly perhaps, since Rotkirkh is
describing events in a remote past, which he knows of only indirectly
and from a source of doubtful reliability. Out of this thin fabric, the
son-in-law builds up an epic story that at least coheres with itself, even
if it doesn't always with the rest of history or geography.

Pushkin, who translated Rotkirkh's biography into Russian,
made several attempts of his own to write about his great-grandfather,
first in a straightforwardly historical vein – and then, out of despair, in
the form of a novel *The Negro of Peter the Great*, which he left unfinished. In 1825, he jotted down what he called the 'notes' to the first
chapter of *Eugene Onegin*, an encyclopaedia of Russian life, but also,
poignantly, a treatment of his own years in exile at Mikhailovskoye.

That same year, he seems to have resumed the scholarly detective
work. In a letter of 11 August, to his friend and neighbour Praskovya
Osipova, then in Riga, he wrote: 'I am counting on seeing my old
Negro of a great Uncle, who I suppose, is going to die one of these

fine days, and I must get from him some memoirs concerning my great-grandfather.'[11]

Pyotr did indeed die shortly afterwards, on 6 June 1826, at his other estate of Safontyevo, forty miles from Mikhailovskoye. It seems Pushkin never learned the identity of the author of the German biography, and his great-uncle was too ill to tell him. Pyotr had suffered a serious stroke and was unable to remember the name of his own son Veniamin.[12] Pushkin, however, took possession of the document, which now lies in the archive of the Russian Institute of Literature in Saint Petersburg, and he used its characteristic phrases, beliefs, misunderstandings and clues left inexplicably behind to write *The Negro of Peter the Great*. There can be little doubt that Pushkin's novel makes Gannibal in some ways a more complex, sympathetic and indeed a more modern figure. Yet there are also conflations and blurrings, imaginary links placed in the narrative, a merging of history and legend that has bedevilled Gannibal biography ever since, obscuring the actual life and crushing it under the weight of scholarship.

The irony did not escape Pushkin. The poet's fame overshadowed, as it were, the invisible facts of Gannibal's life. His story, instead of being properly investigated, was told and retold without any regard for its truth. Pushkin seems to have anticipated and wanted to remedy this fate. 'In Russia,' he wrote,

> where the memory of eminent men is soon obliterated by the absence of historical memoirs, the strange life of Gannibal is known only through family legends. We hope to publish in due time his complete biography.[13]

That biography was never written. But the 'forgotten one' was never quite forgotten.

# 2

# The Mask of Blackness

A Negro can be white, or a Siberian black.
—Tatiana Shcherbina, *Life Without*

The portrait hangs in the attic. It is kept up there, in a locked room, out of the way of prying eyes, like a guilty secret. Few of the visitors to the house on the Moika canal, number twelve, just around the corner from the Winter Palace, even know that a disputed picture of Abram Gannibal exists. They come to see the apartment where Pushkin lived unhappily during the last few months of his life, and where he died one frozen January morning in 1837 after being wounded in a duel. They are literary pilgrims, anxious to pay homage to a famous poet who has become Russia's totem. The subject of the portrait is taboo.

The building is used to secrets. For twelve years, from 1905 until the Russian revolution, Moika 12 served as the headquarters of the Okhrana, Nicholas II's secret police. From these premises govern-ment agents, spies and informers carried out surveillance on the Bolsheviks, and plotted the downfall of Lenin, who was driven into exile in 1907 by their attentions. Secrets were hoarded in these rooms where Pushkin lived and died. They were processed on an industrial scale in the ultimately futile effort to prevent an uprising. So it is hardly surprising if a trace of something disreputable hangs over the place.

Sergei Nekrasov, the Pushkin museum's director, adopts a mock-conspiratorial tone when he raises the question of the building's unsavoury past. That same tone, slightly cloak-and-dagger, can be heard in his pronouncements about the portrait. 'So you want to expose the true face of Pushkin's African ancestor?' he says. 'You think it's in the attic, do you? Perhaps you have been reading too much Oscar Wilde.'[1]

A shambling, scholarly man in his mid-fifties, morose, but with a sparkle in his eyes, Nekrasov takes a key from the cabinet in his study and leads me through the museum's showpiece – a set of rooms on the *piano nobile* furnished handsomely with Pushkin's belongings, even if the family actually lived in rather shabbier quarters below – up four flights of stairs to a doorway tucked under the eaves, and intensely evocative of that locked schoolroom where Dorian Gray hid the eponymous portrait.

The 'true face' of Gannibal is a mystery. The visual record is non-existent: no verifiable likeness of Gannibal as an adult exists. However, some experts argue that the tsar's favourite can be glimpsed as a child in the background of several pictures of Peter himself. Until the end of the Soviet era, such odds and ends were routinely served up in biographies next to the Moika image, which Nekrasov finds stacked away with other questionable pictures of Pushkin family members and forgotten academics after unlocking the room.

There are many reproductions, but you need to see the portrait: see it for itself and for its setting. The first thing you notice is the size of the oil painting – much smaller than expected, perhaps 28 × 20 inches, the colours faded, the surface scored, its details hard to make out in the background gloom.

It shows a lean, uniformed man, probably in his sixties, looking askance but self-assured. He stands erect with his arms by his side in a military pose exuding confidence and perhaps even a certain impatience with the whole business of sitting – or standing – for a portrait. The stance is almost a manifesto, a philosophy of life. It requires no props and neatly serves to show off the medals pinned to his chest and the military cross on a ribbon round his neck.

The reproductions are usually cropped. The actual portrait goes nearly down to the waist, and gives the impression of someone tall and rangy, the head rather small perhaps for the wide muscular shoulders highlighted by the immaculately laundered tunic. The outfit and its badges of honour are superb, and in normal circumstances would amount to a thumbnail sketch of the sitter, pointing to his achieve/ ments and to military campaigns. Russian tsars and commanders had a variety of ways to encourage their subordinates. Peter the Great set an inspiring example when he showered his armies with commemor/ ative medals and chains – and when he instituted the first of a new generation of orders of chivalry designed to reward military valour in the style of the French Order of Saint/Louis. This was the Order of Saint Andrei, created in 1698, with the award of an enamelled dark blue Saint Andrew's cross, on a light blue ribbon and cordon, to officers who had distinguished themselves in the Turkish war and in the quelling of the revolt of the *streltsy* regiments. In 1725, Peter's widow, Catherine I, brought another of his schemes to fruition when she founded the second great Russian order, the Saint Alexander Nevsky – a red enamelled cross, on a bright red ribbon and cordon – named after a medieval prince who had defeated the Swedes in a famous battle on the river Neva.

Unfortunately the condition of the portrait now in the Moika attic had deteriorated so much by the time the picture fell into the museum's possession after the revolution that it was no longer possible to make out the colours, let alone the details of insignia. So already we have to speculate, to fill in the spaces with some guesswork.

The officer's uniform should disclose vital facts about his military record. But the surrounding gloom makes the clues hard to decipher. So, for example, the uniform, often described as red, but actually more of a golden brown, is clearly that of a general. But the rank of general had its own intricate hierarchy within the Russian army, with steps up from major/general to lieutenant/general before reaching general/in/chief, which Gannibal achieved, and field marshal, which he didn't. (The supreme title of *generalissimo* was bestowed just twice in the eighteenth century – on Peter's favourite Menshikov, and on Suvorov, Gannibal's protégé, in 1799.) For each, the uniform was subtly different: red collar with gold lace, red waistcoat with gold lace but black collar, red breeches, hat with gold border, white cockade and white feathers.

'The uniform, the uniform', as Pushkin's friend Griboyedov wrote in his play *Woe from Wit*, speaks volumes. Above all, it speaks of the highly stratified society that developed in Russia in the century after Peter introduced the Table of Ranks. Each detail comes with its own biographical revelation that goes beyond protocol or fashion. Take the black velvet of the military collar, something that was seen on regimental tunics only during the reign of Catherine the Great, and thus dates the portrait to the years between 1762 and 1796. The lapels embroidered with gold thread also hint at the subject's self-importance, while the sash across his chest tells us that he was of noble rank in civilian life – which had a parallel hierarchy – and was thus wearing gala uniform as a mark of distinction.

In other words, the portrait is a statement of prestige, of courtliness. Here is a successful high-ranking officer, possibly one of those who took part in the coup against Peter III. That he is someone who can afford to congratulate himself on picking the winning side is apparent not only in the very fact of the portrait, but also in its hauteur. There is in his gaze the same mood which Nabokov found in Gannibal's life, when he described him as 'a sour, grovelling, crotchety, timid, ambitious, and cruel person; a good military engineer, perhaps, but humanistically a nonentity, differing in nothing from a typical career-minded, superficially educated, coarse, wife-flogging Russian of his day, in a brutal and dull world of political intrigue, favour-itism, Germanic regimentation, old-fashioned Russian misery, and fat-breasted empresses on despicable thrones'.[2]

Other parts of the statement are harder to read. The face is slightly blurred – and in the face, though blurred, is a haggardness. The mouth too is a problem. You cannot say if that is the wounded monkey's grin Korf saw at the Winter Palace on the day of his dismissal. He seems about to break into animation: a smile, a demurral, a cutting riposte. He looks back out at the artist, at the world, with a quizzical gaze.

Perhaps the moody demeanour lends credence to the belief that the portrait was painted slightly earlier than art experts claim – in the 1760s as opposed to the 1770s – and therefore dates from the years of Gannibal's disgrace, and his seclusion from public life, the period of hermitage in the country, when he was writing his memoirs as a way of getting back at the world.

To be scrupulous about it, one should not attribute so much of Gannibal's extraordinary career to the physical characteristics shown in an unknown portrait. To do so would be to repeat the errors of the Soviet Pushkinists who took it for granted that the figure was the *arap* – the Negro – of Peter the Great, simply because an inscription on the back said so.

But who wrote the inscription? In fact, the early history of the portrait is a blank. Nothing is known of its whereabouts between the end of the reign of Catherine, when it was painted, and the mid-nineteenth century, when an old friend of Pushkin's saw it exhibited at the Peterhof palace. In 1899, by which time the portrait had been deposited in the archives of the Russian foreign ministry, where it remained until 1917, a journalist by the name of Dmitry Anuchin wrote a controversial article, or 'anthropological exercise', in which he claimed, among other things, that the picture had been given to the ministry in 1873 after the death of Prince Mikhail Obolensky, a well-known art collector, who had bought it, according to Anuchin, from 'the antiquarian Yuni'.[3]

Vasily Yuni was a Muscovite connoisseur, the son of an officer in the Preobrazhensky regiment, who collected military portraits in the first half of the nineteenth century. A contemporary account suggests that Yuni believed the portrait was of Gannibal, and thus inscribed it with the words 'Annibal, general-in-chief, in the 92nd year after his birth'.[4]

The identification was widely accepted, even though the biographical facts were askew – a direct borrowing from Pushkin's erroneous note to *Onegin*, as the aitchless proper noun makes clear:

Annibal died in the reign of Catherine, relieved of important duties of service with the rank of general-in-chief, in the 92nd year after his birth.⁵

In fact, Gannibal died in 1781, at the age of eighty-five, but that anomaly was not the focus of the doubters' arguments. Instead objectors said the figure in the portrait did not look like an African, or indeed like a black man. They complained that, quite apart from the pigmentation of his skin – almost impossible to assess, given the picture's tenebrous condition – this high-ranking officer, with his aquiline features and Roman nose, did not have the *look* of a 'Negro', that now suspect anthropological term.⁶

Ironically, the same argument was deployed by those who believed that the figure in the portrait *was* Gannibal. The picture was displayed at an exhibition in 1880, to coincide with the unveiling of the Pushkin monument in Moscow. The show provoked a heated exchange about Pushkin's ancestry, with much importance being attributed – or misattributed – to the dubious portrait. The poet's friend of the 1830s, Alexandra Smirnova-Rosset, cited the pictorial evidence, and her own familiarity with Pushkin, to deliver a verdict on his genealogy. 'There was nothing of the Negro in him,' she wrote in her memoirs. 'People say he must definitely have resembled a Negro, because his ancestor Gannibal was a Negro. (I saw his portrait at the Peterhof.) But Gannibal was not a Negro. He was Abyssinian. He had regular features, a long and *dry* face, with a cruel but intelligent expression.'⁷

Sergei Nekrasov, the director of the Moika museum, views the whole problem with jocular disapproval, noting that Pushkin was hailed as a 'Creole' poet by leaders of the Harlem Renaissance in the 1920s and 1930s. 'His mother Nadezhda, who had yellowish palms, according to Yelizaveta [the poet's sister-in-law], was known as the "beautiful Creole",' Nekrasov adds with a mischievous smile, as if sensing a link between the scandalous portrait and the 'black-Creole face' of the first Mrs Rochester, a brooding presence in Charlotte Brontë's *Jane Eyre*: the mad woman locked in the attic.

But Smirnova-Rosset was not Pushkin's only girlfriend to dwell on the subject. Anna Olenina, who captivated the poet at a Petersburg ball in the winter of 1828, praised his 'unique genius', but regretted that it did not 'grant as a bonus an attractive exterior', adding: 'A Negro profile, deriving from his mother's family, did not improve his looks.'[8] Pushkin used a variant of her phrase in a poem to the English portrait painter George Dawe, chiding him for wanting to draw his *arapski profil* instead of Olenina's beautiful face:

Why is your marvellous pencil
Sketching my blackamoor profile?[9]

Certainly it is hard to imagine the Moika portrait as it must have appeared to its nineteenth-century viewers. Murkiness shrouded the outline of the face as much as the uniform and the orders of knight-hood. Russians lacked experience in defining racial types, in piercing through the 'black masks' worn by Negroes or Moors.[10] Out of ignorance, they saw only what the ancient Greek writer Philostratus called the 'strange colour' of the Ethiopians.[11]

Blackness, in Gannibal's eyes, was 'the badge of hell', not something to be worn proudly, like a medal. In Russia he felt not only isolated, but also *incriminated* by the colour of his skin. And he goes further: on 8 April 1745, in a letter to his friend Cherkasov, he talks about blackness as the colour of sin:

Because I am loyal and work hard, and never cheat, due to my fear of God, that's why I am poor and owe money. I wish everybody else was like me: conscientious and honest, as much as possible. Apart from my blackness, that is.[12]

It is a rare moment of plain speaking, or plain letter-writing. But then he checks himself. 'Ah, *batyushka*! [roughly, 'little father']' he writes and immediately changes the subject. His meaning is unclear. Here, as in much that follows, we have to live with unclarity, with uncertainty, with the absence of final proof, or even of terminology.

Neither Pushkin nor his contemporaries made any distinction between the meaning of 'negro' (in Russian, *negr*, French *nègre*) and 'moor' or 'blackamoor' (in Russian, *arap*), although 'mulatto' (*mulat*, *mulatka*) sometimes came into play. Oddly, the poet used both *arap* and *negr* to describe Gannibal, but not the word Russian borrowed directly from 'Moor' (*Mavr*), which he used in other contexts, for instance when discussing Europe's historical debt to Islamic culture: 'The Moors gave us passion and the softness of love, a taste for strange-ness and the gorgeous eloquence of the East,' he wrote in a draft essay of 1824.[13]

In Russian, the word *arap* is derogatory and has racial connota-tions of blackness, but it is as different from *negr* as it is from *arab*, a word also applied to Gannibal on numerous occasions. Pushkin was evidently intrigued by the orthographic differences of a verbal correctness which has not always been observed in memoirs written about him or his great-grandfather. So, in late 1835, or perhaps early 1836, we find the poet setting the record straight in a letter to his friend Prince Pyotr Vyazemsky:

> *Arab* (does not have a feminine), a dweller or native of Arabia, an Arabian. *The caravan was plundered by the Arabs of the steppes.*
> *Arap* [Moor], feminine *arapka*: this is what negroes and mulattoes are usually called. *Palace arapi*, negroes serving in the palace. *He is leaving with three finely dressed araps.*[14]

Such wordplay makes it clear that, for many Russians, the *arap* of Peter the Great was, like Shakespeare's Moor, a stranger, an alien, a newcomer. Strictly speaking, ethnic Moors were Berbers who lived in the Roman province of Mauretania, a region of northern Africa corresponding to parts of Morocco and Algeria, and who conquered Spain in the eighth century. The ancient Greek *mauros* became *Maurus* in Latin, a proper noun that identified a particular ethnic group and, like its Greek predecessor, came to mean 'black', although the existence of 'white Moors' was also recognised. The primary usage of the term 'Moor' in Russian, as in English, was as a religious, not a racial identi⁄fication: Moor meant 'Muhammadan', that is, Muslim. In Gannibal's time, the word was frequently used by Russians as a general term for 'not one of us', non⁄Christian, pointing to their antithetical relation⁄ship with the 'Moorish' subjects of the Ottoman Empire. In other words, the word 'Moor' gradually slipped its mooring under pressure from the centuries⁄long conflict between Islam and Christian Europe. The same thing happened in English, where the first meaning given to the word 'Moor' in the Oxford English Dictionary is *Muhammadan* (up to 1629). But in many of the cited examples, the word seems to mean no more than infidel, or even stranger: an inhabitant of those peripheral regions in the *mappae mundi* where Moors live, according to Othello, together with 'Anthropophagi and men whose heads/Do grow beneath their shoulders'.

The word meant different things to different people. The African explorer Mungo Park described the Moors as 'a nation of lunatics ... combining in their character the blind superstition of the Negro with the savage cruelty and treachery of the Arab'.[15] To others, they were no more savage than a troupe of handkerchief⁄waving Morris dancers in rural England: the word is probably Moorish in origin, from the Spanish *morisco*. It was a catch⁄all term for outsiders who rubbed shoulders (such as these were) with satyrs, hermaphrodites, savage men and others of the species *semihomo*. But it also referred to a more sinister threat, to an object of fear. Discussing Shakespeare's *Othello* at a reunion with old schoolfriends from the Lyceum at Tsarskoye Selo, near Petersburg, Pushkin compared the banishment of Jesuits from Russia to a proclamation by England's Queen Elizabeth, in 1601, ordering the expulsion of the 'great number of negars and Blacka⁄moores which are crept into this realm'. But the Negro who crept into England in *The Masque of Blackness* by Shakespeare's friend Ben Jonson did so only because he'd heard a rumour that the sun, in the personage of King James, had the power 'to blanch an Ethiop white'.[16]

Some Pushkinists have embarked on a similar quest to remove the stain of Gannibal's blackness. Smirnova-Rosset, for example, recalled seeing the portrait at the Peterhof in order to make a dubious, even racist point. But ultimately it was pointless trying to bleach Pushkin's black ancestor. The same lesson can be gleaned from the bizarre denouement to the story of the picture in the attic. In 1976, the Pushkin museum agreed to send the portrait to an art restoration centre in Moscow in a bid to clarify some of the details on the general's uniform.[17] The picture was later sent to the Hermitage, in 1980, and then to another Russian museum for more specialised treatment.

But when the restorers began their work, they got an unexpected shock – or a series of unexpected shocks. To begin with, the application of cleaning materials to the area taken up with the medals and the cross around the general's neck immediately ruled out the Order of Saint Anne and Saint Alexander Nevsky as possible candidates. In fact, it was the cross of Saint Andrew revealed in all its glory hanging from the ribbon round his neck. That order of knighthood could have been awarded to Gannibal, but never was. More worryingly, the medal now brightly disclosed on the upper half of the subject's tunic was unmistakably that of the Order of Saint George, to which Gannibal could never even have aspired, since it was instituted by Catherine the Great only in 1769, seven years after the *arap* had so ignominiously retired from service.

Military experts were called in to advise about the braiding on the uniform, which suggested that the general in the portrait had served in an artillery regiment, not in the engineers like Gannibal. It was agreed that there were only four candidates who held at the same time the Order of Saint Andrei of the first rank and that of Saint George. Three of the candidates could be ruled out immediately because their likenesses were already known from other paintings. Only Ivan Ivanovich Meller-Zakomelsky was left: a Lutheran officer, born in 1728, and a hero of the second Turkish war, according to the *Military Encyclopedia*, he became acting Master General of the Ordnance in 1783, two years after Gannibal's death.[18] His Teutonic relatives duly celebrated this triumph in a foreign land by commissioning the disputed portrait.

Nekrasov laughs, recalling the consternation in Pushkin circles, when the subject of the portrait was unmasked. Because it wasn't only the pigment of the uniform or medals that was altered by the clean-up. His skin also changed colour. Too late for the dozens of Soviet articles and monographs on the picture of Abram Gannibal, now caught in the backlash of de-attribution – the unavoidable truth: the blackamoor of Peter the Great had become a white man.

# 3

# Prince of Abissinia

True Paradise under the Ethiop line.
—Milton, *Paradise Lost*

Gannibal was probably born in 1696, though it might have
been seven years earlier. His biographers are generally rather
confused about exactly when or where he first saw the light of day,
and Gannibal's few utterances on the subject do not exactly dispel
the confusion. His son-in-law Rotkirkh claimed that the Moor, who
died on 14 May 1781, lived to the age of ninety-two. Such a proposition is unlikely because it would mean that he was fifteen at the time
of his arrival in Russia in 1704, instead of eight, as Gannibal clearly
states in the preface to the unpublished textbook *Geometry and Fortification*, written in 1724, long before his memory started to play tricks. In
Russia, Gannibal always celebrated his birthday on 13 July, the day
he was christened by Peter at a church in Vilnius in 1705. Significantly perhaps, on that date in 1776, Gannibal gave a lavish eightieth
birthday party at Suida, his estate just outside Petersburg.

The chronology of his birth may be unclear. Its geography is
totally mixed up. Little is known about his background. No reliable
information exists. To all intents and purposes, Gannibal emerged
from nowhere, or at least out of a gap in our knowledge. Over
the past three centuries, that gap has been filled with all kinds of
speculation. It has been claimed, for example, that Gannibal was
Spanish, or that he was Moroccan, or even that he was a Falasha
Jew from the north-west of Ethiopia, a descendant of the Queen of

Sheba and King Solomon. He was born in the east of Africa but also in the west.

Pushkin wrote that the details of Gannibal's strange life were known only 'through family legends'. So let's begin with that version of events, with the unlikely stories he must have heard as he was growing up in Petersburg. 'The author on his mother's side is of African descent,' he explains in the note to *Onegin*. 'His great-grandfather, Abram Petrovich Annibal, was kidnapped in his eighth year on the coast of Africa and brought to Constantinople.'[1]

It wasn't only the life of Gannibal that was a subject of legend. Pushkin's phrase 'coast of Africa' tells us a lot about Russian ignorance of African reality. Until the nineteenth century, Africa was still hardly more than a coastline, a picturesque shore lacking depth or interior. North Africa was part of the Muslim world, which was still almost closed to Europeans. The Barbary states, famed for piracy, were known mainly through the accounts of the few Christian slaves who had been captured by corsairs and then had escaped or been ransomed. One such was Daniel Defoe's fictional hero Robinson Crusoe, who is on a mid-seventeenth-century slave-trading vessel bound for Guinea when he is captured off the north-west coast of Africa and enslaved by a 'Turkish rover of Sallee', or Sale. Pushkin read *Crusoé* in a French translation by Petrus Bobel, and Rotkirkh mentions a 'Turkish' vessel in his account of Gannibal's enslavement. The family biographers were happy to plunder other legends, as well as their own, in the absence of hard facts.

The ignorance of Russian geographers should be equally unsurprising. The coast of Africa was the edge of the known world. Only a handful of Europeans, usually disguised in Arab dress, had travelled up the Nile from Cairo. One or two, such as the Scottish laird James Bruce, may have penetrated to the Ethiopian capital at Gondar or to the Funj kingdom at Sennar on the Blue Nile. But news of their discoveries was often received with extreme scepticism in their own countries. Fashionable opinion dismissed the mass of new and often deeply shocking information as fantastical nonsense. The dandies of Petersburg and Moscow derided Bruce as a Munchhausen and a fraud.

Early maps of Africa and its coast show the literally marginal knowledge Russians had. For many cartographers it was as if the dark continent did not really exist, but was merely a landscape of the mind. The same mystification of the African continent that manifested itself in Fyodor Tyuchev's 1848 work *Russian Geography* – and went so far as to include the Nile among Russian rivers – saw the land of Ethiopia stretch westwards from the Red Sea not only into equatorial Africa but as far as the Guinea coast. Beyond these second-hand nibblings of reconnaissance, the heart of darkness remained untouched: a land of travellers' tales and medieval bestiaries inhabited by chimeras, pygmies and ponces who had genitals in the middle of their chests.

In racial matters, too, nineteenth-century Russia was a redoubt of ignorance and prejudice, for which history was partly to blame. Seeking to reclaim Pushkin as a black writer, African-American critics have understandably viewed the life of his ancestor, with its background in slavery, from an Atlantic perspective. The leaders of the Harlem Renaissance returned Pushkin's salute to his 'Negro brothers'. The poet Langston Hughes hailed the Russian as the first black writer to scale 'the mountain standing in the way of any true Negro art in America'.[2] Yet the mountain looked rather different to Pushkin's compatriots. Arriving late in traversing the high seas, and though gaining territory in North America, Russia did not achieve a large maritime empire like the western European powers. As a result, it did not participate in the terrible pillage of the African slave trade. Instead, Russia's experience of black people derived from its relationship with the Islamic slave trade, which was quite distinct from the Atlantic model.

Slavery in the west produced racism. Its Oriental counterpart produced a kind of evasiveness about race and the moral questions inherent in the treatment of blacks. Nevertheless the weight of evidence suggests that racial slavery, as the modern world has come to know it, originated in medieval Islamic societies. Tatars and other Black Sea peoples sold into bondage millions of Ukrainians, Georgians, Circassians, Armenians, Bulgarians, Slavs, and Turks living near the Caucasus mountains. As early as the fifteenth century, Italian merchants were selling such 'Slavs' (the medieval Latin *sclavus* is the root of the English word 'slave', *esclave*, *escravo*), along with Greeks and Turks, in Muslim markets as well as in Christian Crete, Cyprus, Sicily and Spain. After the Ottoman Turks captured Constantinople in 1453, slave traders redirected their attention from the Caucasus to sub-Saharan Africa.[3] Blacks and Moors were transported to the Mediterranean, or purchased by the Portuguese along the coast of west Africa. By 1500, Sicilian notaries were recording the arrival of *sclavi negri*, or 'black Slavs', by desert caravan. They were sold to Jewish and Arabic slave traders or found their way across the Black Sea to the Caucasus, where a handful of Negro communities existed right up to the First World War.

It is a neat semantic irony that news of these improbable black Russians first surfaced, in 1913, in an article by the nationalist V. P. Vrady, published in *Kavkaz* (*Caucasus*), a newspaper in Tiblisi. The eighteenth-century German naturalist Johann Blumenbach, who was responsible for naming the white race 'Caucasian', did so at least partly because he thought that the Caucasus mountains produced 'a most beautiful race of men', and that they were, so to speak, the ideal of the white race. Nowadays most ordinary Russians take a xenophobic view of the dark-complexioned Muslim peoples of Chechnya and the other north Caucasus republics. Indeed, they are known disparagingly as the *chorniye*, or blacks, of Russia.

The African background of plunder and licensed cruelty haunted Pushkin throughout his life. His often apostrophised 'my Africa' or 'his Africa' – meaning Gannibal's – and the yearning for a ship to return to his ancestor's birthplace reached a pitch of intensity during his brief exile to Odessa in the early 1820s. At first Pushkin disparaged this new city on the Black Sea for its 'boring' atmosphere. In fact, it was quite an exciting place to be at the time: a polyglot centre, a cosmopolitan city full of Greek revolutionaries and foreign merchants speaking Italian or bad French. The poet recalls the rich mix to be found at the opera or seafront restaurants in a stanza from 'Onegin's Journey', describing the 'proud Slav/the Frenchman, Spaniard, Armenian/and Greek' among his friends before giving special mention to 'that son of Egypt, the retired Corsair Morali', a Moor from Tunis who acted as a Turkish spy.

But there was also somebody else. In a cancelled draft, the poet adds to the list: 'And a black stranger from my homeland.'[4] No more is heard of this intriguing figure. The outcast doesn't even make it into the published version of the poem. Nor do we glean any information about the homeland. Its precise or even approximate location remains a mystery.

Yet Gannibal did leave a clue to the whereabouts of that African homeland. Or was it a riddle, as Nabokov complained: an unreliable memory locked away by a 7-year-old child and recollected almost half a century later? Either way, it occurs suddenly in an official document that Gannibal submitted to the Empress Elizabeth in 1742 while petitioning for the rank of nobility and a coat of arms, the right to use a family crest emblazoned with an elephant and the mysterious word FUMMO.

Reading a copy of the petition in the heraldic archive is as close as we can get nowadays to perusing Gannibal's lost memoirs. Oddly, though it was framed within the meritocratic guidelines of Peter's Table of Ranks, the document does not stake Gannibal's claim for ennoblement on his status as a Russian general. Instead it refers to the precedence of sons of princes, counts, barons and other members of the aristocracy. In other words, Gannibal stresses the nobility of his African origins. He never forgot that, despite the interlude of slavery, he could, to quote Othello, 'fetch [his] life and being/From men of royal siege'. This scion of an African dynasty saw himself as equal to Russia's boyars, or noblemen, in terms of social rank, as he informed the tsarina:

I, your humble subject, am a native of Africa, of the high nobility there. I was born in the land ruled by my father, in the city of Lagone, apart from which he had two other cities under him.[5]

He goes on to explain that he cannot produce documentary evidence to support his claim due to the passage of time and his enslavement, adding: 'Unfortunately I do not have a nobleman's diploma from my homeland or a crest, nor did I ever have such things, because we do not have these traditions in Africa.'

The petition is the only surviving document in which Gannibal refers to this ancestral background, so the question immediately arises: where was Lagone?

The first and sensible answer is, nowhere. Lagone did not exist. But that hasn't stopped literary critics and historians from posing the question again and again. In Russia, the search for Gannibal's birthplace has come to resemble the force-field of a cultish religion. There are sudden converts and hostile sceptics, an intense rhetoric of signs and revelations. There are joyful glimpses of the promised land, though always – as the sceptics point out – at second hand. But despite the indefatigable efforts of several generations of experts, no record of a city such as Lagone has ever been unearthed. As a result, much of the emphasis, indeed the energy of the quest has shifted from the geographical to the anthropological, or even into the realms of a latter-day mythology, whose devotees place the lost city in the empty spaces on a map, like the dragons of medieval cartography.

But the tantalising detail in Gannibal's petition continues to vex and fascinate. The first problem is grammatical and stems from the use of the Russian locative case – meaning 'in the city of' – into which Gannibal puts the word *Lagone*. This is compounded by the uncertainty of the aitchless alphabet. 'The locative case does not disclose the *ultima* of the nominative,' commiserates Nabokov, who adds:

The ridiculous Russian custom of transliterating both *h* and *g* by means of a Russian gamma does not tell us whether this African name in a Roman transcription should be 'Lagon', 'Lahon', 'Lagona', 'Lahona', 'Lagono', or 'Lahono'.⁶

The exasperated grammarian throws his weight behind 'Lahona' as the most likely candidate, but thereafter refers to the mysterious city only as 'L' just in case.

Africa is a big place. Unfortunately in the petition Gannibal gives no further hint as to the location of his fatherland. Nevertheless it seems that he may have discussed the matter privately towards the end of his life, either with his daughter Sofiya, or with her husband Rotkirkh, because the Estonian biographer gives the impression of certainty in his opening sentences. He omits to mention Lagone, or anywhere else, by name. Yet he does enough in a few sentences to unleash a cult of Ethiopianism into Russian literary history. More than two centuries later, it is still going strong. Here is the Rotkirkh version:

> [Abram Gannibal was] the son of a local ruler, powerful and rich, who proudly traced his descent in direct line from the house of the famed Hannibal, the terror of Rome. [Abram's] father was a vassal of the Turkish emperor or the Ottoman Empire, who by the end of the preceding century, because of oppression and molestation, had revolted with other Abyssinian princes, his countrymen and allies, against his overlord, the Sultan; whereupon various petty but bloody wars followed, in which, however, the stronger force eventually triumphed and this Hannibal, still a boy, the youngest son of the ruling prince, with other high-born youths, was sent in his eighth year to Constantinople as a hostage. Although, given his youth, the fate should not have befallen him so early, still, owing to the fact that his father, according to Muslim custom, had very many wives (even up to about thirty, with a correspondingly large progeny), the numerous old princesses and their children joined forces in the common intention of protecting themselves and their offspring; and since Abram was the youngest son of one of the youngest wives, who did not have at court

as many supporters [as the elder princesses], these contrived through trickery and intrigue, almost by force, to put him on a Turkish vessel and turned him over to the fate that had been assigned him.[7]

So here, in the unpublished biography, written in 1782, shortly after Gannibal's death, is the first mention of Abyssinia as the Moor's birthplace. Admittedly, Rotkirkh's Abyssinia is somewhat bare of any topographical details that might be useful in pinpointing Lagone. Yet it is rich in imaginative, or what you might almost call novel-istic touches that help to establish a kind of psychic geography. It also contains, significantly, the assertion that Gannibal's father was a Muslim chieftain in late seventeenth-century Christian Ethiopia – which is plausible if unlikely – and the idea that he traced his lineage back to the Carthaginian leader Hannibal – which is not. 'The statement is of course nonsense,' writes Nabokov. 'It is impos-sible to conceive that an Abyssinian of the seventeenth century should have known anything' of Hannibal.

Pushkin delivered his own verdict in *The Negro of Peter the Great*. Shocked by the prospect of an African becoming his son-in-law, the nobleman Gavrila Afanasyevich seeks to comfort his family with the knowledge that the tsar's favourite is 'the son of a Moorish sultan'. 'Yes, yes,' replies his sister Tatiana impatiently. 'We all know the fairy tale.'[8]

The whimsical allusion to Hannibal of Carthage highlights another problem with Rotkirkh's version of events. Not only is his text infuriatingly at one remove from Gannibal's own words, it constantly requires a kind of double-take as the story oscillates between the legendary and the real. So, for example, if Gannibal's father had indeed been a Muslim ruler in northern Abysinnia, that would have placed him within the orbit of the Christian emperor of Gondar, Jesus I, who reigned from 1682 to 1706. The only European traveller with any knowledge of the region at the time was a French chemist by the name of Charles Poncet. A resident of Cairo, he was invited to Gondar, in 1698, to treat the emperor for a bad case of conjunctivitis. During his two-year sojourn in the Horn of Africa, Poncet explored the different kingdoms, such as Tigray and Shewa, that owed allegiance to Jesus, but made no reference to there being any Muslim rulers. On the contrary, he described the oppressed state of the king's non-Christian subjects. 'Mahometans are tolerated at Gondar,' he writes, 'but it is in the lower part of the town, and in a separate quarter. They are called *gebertis*, that is to say, slaves.'⁹ Both Muslims and Christians traded in slaves, according to Bruce, who marvelled on his first day in Abyssinia that 'the only trade of either of these sects is a very extraordinary one, that of selling children'.¹⁰

Was Gannibal one of them? Rotkirkh claims that his father-in-law was dispatched to the Ottoman sultan as a hostage. Yet the only foreign ruler to whom King Jesus is known to have made a present of slaves was Louis XIV of France. Perhaps the boy was taken hostage or lost by misadventure on the way? In 1701, Poncet set out on the return journey to France. His caravan included the king's gifts of an elephant, some Arabian horses and the *jeunes enfants*, but the elephant died before it reached the old Tigrayan capital of Debarwa and, as soon as they crossed the Red Sea, the governor of Mecca seized the high-born Ethiopian children. Perhaps he forwarded some of them, including Gannibal, to Constantinople as his own tribute. If so, the dying elephant helps to explain the family's mysterious crest because it would have been the child's last memory of the African continent.¹¹

Nobody knows if Rotkirkh read the story of Poncet's travels, but he followed avidly the reports of Bruce's 'discovery' of Gondar, and it is clear that his interest in Ethiopia, once aroused, did not feel constrained by historical or geographical truth. For Rotkirkh, as for Bruce and many other Europeans, Abyssinia was a place full of biblical associations with Solomon and the Queen of Sheba. Not only was there a tradition placing the Garden of Eden in Ethiopia, it was the only Christian country outside Europe until modern times. Such thoughts inspired Bruce, who landed at Massawa in 1769 and reached Gondar the following year. A true son of the Scottish Enlightenment, and an ardent freemason, he was fascinated by the legend of Prester John, a descendant of the Magi and a Christian emperor in Ethiopia, with putative links to the Knights Templar, the Temple of Solomon and the missing Ark of the Covenant (which some people believed had been taken for safety to Aksum, a hundred miles north of Gondar, in the fifth century BC).

*** 

Rotkirkh, who was also a freemason, carried the legend into his account of Gannibal's early life. Details were added and subtracted. The outlines of the story were smoothed and modified and reiterated. Soon his biography had acquired the texture of a folk tale. The description of young Abram's enslavement is particularly heartwrenching:

> His only sister, Lahann, who was some years older than he, had yet sufficient courage to oppose this act of violence. She tried everything but without success as she was heavily outnumbered. Finally, she accompanied him to the very deck of the slave-ship, still nursing the hope that she might obtain by entreaties the freedom of this much beloved brother or purchase it with her jewels. But when she found that her tender efforts remained fruitless to the last, she cast herself in despair into the sea and was drowned. To the very end of his days, the venerable old man would shed tears of the most tender friendship and love as he recollected her; for although he was still very young at the time of that tragic event, yet whenever he thought of her this vague memory would become new and complete for him – and the memory of his sister was so vivid not only because she had tried so hard to rescue him, but also because they were the only siblings from the same mother.

The tone of Rotkirkh's narrative suggests that his Abyssinia was a mythological scene, not a real place. His retelling of Gannibal's enslavement borrows details from *Paradise Lost*, Voltaire's *Candide* and the biblical story of Joseph, who was sold into captivity but later rose to great eminence under a benevolent pharaoh – or, in this case, tsar.

Its tortuous style did not convince Pushkin. In his own version of the myth, he takes Rotkirkh's overheated fantasy and improves it by adding distance, so that Gannibal's remembrance of things past now includes a belief that the only true paradise is the lost one. But if the poet's treatment is more sophisticated, as you might expect, it is hardly less fanciful. In the note to *Onegin*, for example, Pushkin writes:

> Up to an advanced age, Annibal still remembered Africa, the sump-tuous life of his father, and nineteen brothers, of whom he was the youngest; he remembered how they used to be led into his father's presence with their hands bound behind their backs, while he alone remained free and went swimming under the fountains of the paternal home; he also remembered his beloved sister Lagan, swimming in the distance after the ship in which he was receding.[12]

This image of Gannibal as the unshackled favourite son derives once again from the story of Joseph, and leads neatly into an evocation of the Abyssinian idyll. But where did Pushkin get his information? Is it based on any reality? Did such a paradise exist? Bruce mentions the 'fountains of the Nile' in a passage from his travels which seems to have directly influenced Coleridge's dream of an 'Abyssinian maid' in *Kubla Khan*.[13] Poncet also notes that 'in Gondar, the capital of Aethiopia, we found a world of pleasant fountains'.[14] Yet the direct precursor to such utopian imagery was the Happy Valley of Samuel Johnson's *Rasselas, The Prince of Abissinia*, a novel that appeared in English in 1759, and the following year in a French translation which Rotkirkh boasted of reading at Mikhailovskoye. Few scholars deny that he plagiarised Johnson's romance. The temptation was obvious. *Rasselas* updated the legend of the earthly paradise, but it also provided the narrative with a convenient structure, while satisfying Rotkirkh's own fashionable taste for the picturesque description of antique land-scapes and ruins.

To mark Pushkin's centenary, in 1899, the journalist Dmitry Anuchin published a long article in *Russkiye Vedomosti* (*Russian News*) that helped to revive the Ethiopian legend of Gannibal's birthplace. But whereas Dr Johnson's Abyssinia was based on Portuguese sources centuries old, and Rotkirkh's version was timelessly unreal, Anuchin's vivid portrait of L claimed to have the up-to-date authority of a modern anthropologist. His strenuous efforts to locate the fabulous town begin with the assertion that Debarwa, then under Italian occupation, was included in a district known as Logon-Chuan. (Logo was situated on the northern side of the Mareb river in what is now Eritrea.)[15] Yet there is a problem here. In his letter to Elizabeth, Gannibal referred to his birth 'in the city of Lagone', not in *Logon*. The grammatical extension of a word in the locative case is one thing; the switch of a vowel from *a* to *o* is altogether different. The difference troubled Anuchin. 'There is no town in Abyssinia called "Lagone" or anything like it,' he protested, 'apart from this Logo, and so it follows that Gannibal's homeland must have been located there, on the right bank of the river Mareb in the Tigrayan province of Hamasen.'[16]

Nabokov declared that Anuchin's 'geo-nomenclatorial' research was 'below criticism'. So how strenuous were the journalist's efforts, after all? The question is worth asking because his 'anthropological exercise' has cast a baleful influence over Pushkin studies. Unsurprisingly, he never set foot in Tigray – or anywhere else in Africa for that matter. But he was driven by enthusiasm for the wave of so-called Ethiopianism in the second half of the nineteenth century. The mystique of the term derived from its occurrence in the Bible (where Ethiopia is also referred to as Kush, or Cush) and was enhanced, in 1896, when the ancient independent Christian kingdom of Ethiopia defeated the Italians at the battle of Adwa. Writing in the aftermath of that victory, Anuchin succumbed to then fashionable racist theories which distinguished northern Hamitic peoples, such as the Ethiopians, from the 'backward' Negroes of sub-Saharan Africa, contrasting the supposedly superior craniology of 'Nilotic types' with the prognathism and facial angle of 'pure Negroes'. Such thinking is, of course, a 'mismeasure of man', to use Stephen Jay Gould's phrase. But here it is important to remember that, in the second half of the nineteenth century, even members of the Russian intelligentsia, from Westernisers to Communists, accepted this kind of pseudo-scientific nonsense without question. 'We do not think it is necessary to deal with the differences between the skulls of Negroes, and of other lower races of man, and those of people among civilised nations,' wrote the radical Nikolai Dobrolyubov. 'Who is unaware of the strange development of the upper part of the skull among these lower races?'[17]

Not Anuchin, that's for sure, and such an awareness must have contributed to the development of his thoughts about Gannibal and Ethiopia as he sat in Petersburg reading the newspaper reports from Adwa. There, on the front page, looming large in the midst of legend and troop movements, lay the solution he was seeking. His Logo is something that proceeds from the mind of its searcher, and from his European culture. In other words, Anuchin's 'anthropology' was no more than a clumsy ethnological attempt to prove that Pushkin was unsullied by Negroid ancestry. Racism was its motive – and its logic was circular: Pushkin was a genius, and genius is a mountain too high for Negroes to climb, therefore Gannibal cannot have been a Negro, and must have been an Abyssinian prince. Quoting Philostratus, he compares Gannibal to a legendary Homeric warrior, and says approvingly that 'before Memnon's time, black men were a myth only'.[18]

*** 

Gannibal's Ethiopia is a mirage, but it is also a story. Sometimes it degenerates into soap opera or rivalry. No one is ever above or below criticism. Just as the nineteenth-century English explorer Henry Salt, travelling on behalf of his aristocratic patron Lord Valentia, arrived in Abyssinia, in the spring of 1810, with instructions to check Bruce's ethnographic 'facts', I crossed the river Mareb almost two hundred years later in search of Anuchin's Logo.[19]

Salt was a native of Lichfield, in the county of Staffordshire, the same town where the author of *Rasselas* was born. He relished the coincidence. On the road to Logo, as he called it, Salt observed the mountain caves inhabited by sons of the ruler, known as the *Baha-rnegash* (lord of the sea). The sighting led to a moment of Rotkirkh-like reverie. 'My thoughts immediately recurred to the beautiful and instructive romance founded on this custom by Dr Johnson,' wrote Salt.[20] He soon came to appreciate the gap between romance and reality because, in fact, Tigray was far from idyllic. It was dangerous then, and it was still dangerous when I visited the area, now part of a United Nations no-go zone in the wake of a long-running and brutal border war between the Ethiopians and the Eritreans.

The road snaked through humpy mountains. Outcrops of rock pockmarked the distance between emptied villages – a bleakness interrupted only now and then by herdsmen browsing goats and black-faced sheep. In the ruins of Logo, which lies forty-five miles north-west of Aksum, and fifty miles south of Debarwa, some women gathered firewood. The dry stone walls of the huts had been reduced to a heap of rubble. Only displaced strangers lived here now, in this shanty town of twisted metal and tarpaulin. The rest was abandoned or destroyed by the Eritreans as they retreated. Two years earlier, dozens of Ethiopian tanks and tens of thousands of men had advanced across the valley towards the Eritrean trenches, where they met a barrage of artillery, mortar and machine-gun fire. It had been the worst conflict since the fall, in 1991, of the Dergue (the Soviet-backed military dictatorship led by Mengistu Haile Mariam). The war may have claimed as many as 50,000 dead. The battles were few but the casualties many. The death toll was high because the combat-ants were using the weaponry of the Korean War, the tactics of the First World War and the medical treatments of Henry Salt's time. Now the rival armies were separated by a UN-brokered ceasefire and a fifteen-mile buffer zone.

On Salt's map, the village of Logo is situated 39 degrees east and 14 degrees north. It occupies the same few acres of barren mountain and desert where much of the fighting in the civil war took place. The border, established a hundred years ago between Ethiopia and the Italian colony of Eritrea, has never been marked on the ground, even in the 1960s and 1970s when Logo became a centre of Muslim opposition to Haile Selassie, alias Ras Tafari. In 1997 a map appeared in Ethiopia, apparently commissioned by the Tigrayan provincial administration, but actually much older. It showed large chunks of Eritrea belonging to Tigray province. The Eritreans said the map proved the Ethiopians had designs on their territory, including the districts of Hamasen in the north, Serawe in the south and finally Logo itself. Yet the cartographer was no Ethiopian bureaucrat. The blurred signature of Henry Salt could still be deciphered in the bottom right-hand corner.

On 7 March 1810, Salt crossed the dry riverbed of the Seremai and continued 'about a mile eastward to a large town called Logo. It was at this time commanded by a rebellious chieftain styled Baha-rnegash Arkoe, who in the campaign of the preceding year had been reduced to obedience by the *Ras* [or prince].'[21] Fifty of the rebels – 'the most desperate and rascally-looking fellows I ever beheld' – tried to stop and rob Salt's caravan, but the English party escaped. Yet the episode recalls Rotkirkh's sketch of Gannibal's father as a rebellious chieftain. The governor of Tigray at the turn of the eighteenth century was Ras Fares, who ruled for eleven years under King Jesus and may have been Baharnegash Arkoe's great-grandfather. 'For all we know,' says Nabokov of Salt's adversary, the rascally bandit leader of Logo, 'he may have been Pushkin's fourth cousin.'

Pushkin never referred to Abyssinia or Ethiopia in connection with his great-grandfather. He seems to have preferred to think of Gannibal on a more fundamental level as the *Afrikanets*, a Russian general who was 'of African descent'. Admittedly he preserved the Abyssinian details in his Russian translation of Rotkirkh's biography. Yet he never lent them any credence in his own work, a fact that has been exploited by opponents of the Ethiopianist theory. Neverthe-less the poet must have discussed his ancestor's background, however sceptically, in private because his friend Alexei Vulf knew the story long before publication of *The Negro of Peter the Great*. Vulf was Pushkin's neighbour at Mikhailovskoye. He recalled interrupting the poet, on 15 September 1827, while he was at work on the manuscript. In his journal, Vulf glossed

> the first two chapters of the prose romance in which the main character represents his great-grandfather Gannibal, the son of an Abyssinian emir, captured by the Turks and sent from Constantinople by the Russian ambassador as a gift to Peter I, who had him educated and grew very fond of him.[22]

Only two chapters of the novel were published in Pushkin's lifetime. Another five were written but the work remained unfinished. Vulf's reference to the 'son of an Abyssinian emir' comes as a surprise because he can only have gleaned that information from Pushkin himself. In *Onegin*, the poet dreams of Gannibal's homeland 'amid meridional waves', and the fortieth meridian certainly passes through Abyssinia. But the writer was unsettled by the mystery of the Moor's background. It was a gap in his knowledge, a blank that he was unable to fill in. That empty space on the map makes a poignant appearance in the novel itself. In chapter four, the tsar informs his *arap* that he intends to marry him off to the daughter of a nobleman. At first the Moor is surprised by the idea, but then he reflects:

> 'Get married?' the African thought. 'Why not? Why should I be condemned to spend my life in solitude and not know the best rewards and sacred duties of mankind, just because I was born at [...] degrees on the map?'[23]

In the manuscript, Pushkin left a telltale space where the co-ordinates should have been.[24] He couldn't make up his mind – and Vulf was about to knock on the door. In the end there was no definitive answer. Only three dots. Once again Gannibal had vanished into nowhere.

# 4

# Jihad

Listen: far away, far away, on Lake Chad
—Nikolai Gumilev, *The Giraffe*

On 27 July 1827 Pushkin left Petersburg in a huff and went to Mikhailovskoye. A run of bad luck at the card table was the reason for his sudden departure. His gambling debts were the talk of Nevsky Prospekt. And so, utterly broke, the poet retired to the family estate in order to lick his wounds. 'Pushkin has decamped to the country out of annoyance (or perhaps grief), after losing all the money he had to his name: 7 thousand,' reported Andrei Ivanovsky, a secret policeman.[1] But in spite of the gossip, and with the sound of hostile laughter ringing in his ears, the loser put a brave face on his involuntary seclusion. 'I am in the country and hope to write a lot,' he wrote to his friend Baron Anton Delvig four days later. 'No inspiration so far, meanwhile I have taken up prose.'[2]

It was Pushkin's first visit to Mikhailovskoye since the death of his great-uncle Pyotr a year earlier. The house at Petrovskoye felt empty without him, and it may have been sadness at the loss of a direct link with Gannibal – as well as his reverses at cards – that led to writer's block. Significantly, the 'prose' he began, though never finished, at Mikhailovskoye during the summer was *The Negro of Peter the Great*, an historical romance that owes more to Sir Walter Scott than it does to any of the known facts of Gannibal's life. One afternoon his friend and neighbour Alexei Vulf found Pushkin doodling 'at his desk in a red Moldavian fez and dressing-gown ... with the Journal of Peter I, concealed among half a dozen almanacs'.[3] The resulting doodle, which is preserved in the margins of his notebook, provides a fascinating insight into Pushkin's mental picture of his African great-grandfather.

At the left-hand side of a jumbled page, on which Pushkin had been drafting a fragment of 'The Tsar's Moor' – the title *Negro of Peter the Great* was the brainwave of an anonymous editor at the time of its first full publication in 1837, shortly after the poet's death – is a black ink drawing of Gannibal.[4] It is not a lifelike drawing, more a caricature of an African face, with its 'lower race skull' and woolly hair, not to mention the 'goggle eyes' described by Korsakov, the Moor's friend in the novel. But the most revealing thing about the sketch is where it appears in the manuscript, next to the blank co-ordinates for Gannibal's homeland. The counterpoint of doodle and dots helps us to imagine the feverish thoughts swarming through the writer's brain as he tried to conjure up the Moor's yearning for Africa. More importantly, in sketching the likely physical appearance of someone 'born at [...] degrees on the map', Pushkin opts for classic Negroid features as opposed to the Hamitic profile idealised by Anuchin and his fellow Ethiopianists.

But how serious is a doodle? Was the poet merely guessing what the face of his ancestor looked like, or did he have some privileged information about Gannibal's appearance, a hint dropped by Pyotr during their last conversation? It would be only natural if the poet found himself dwelling that summer on the old man's vodka-soaked reminiscences, or hoping that the afterglow of Pyotr's stories would breathe new life into his fictional creation by giving it the kind of detail you seldom find in books. The kind of detail to which Rotkirkh had access, yet squandered with his literary pretensions.

Pushkin had no trouble drumming up his great-uncle's memories. As he sat at his writing table in Mikhailovskoye, he could refer to a 400-word document entitled 'Recollection of A. P. Gannibal', which lay in front of him. This brief *curriculum vitae* had probably been dictated to somebody by Pyotr, because the handwriting is immaculately spaced and ordered, while some of the verbal constructions betray a mild dementia. The last line – 'My father was christened in Poland in the town of Grodno, his godfather was Tsar Peter the Great, his godmother the Queen of Poland' – is not only factually incorrect. It is also quite out of place: a verbatim copy of the first sentence at the top of the page, as if Pyotr's memory had short-circuited, looping back on itself.

However, it may have been an earlier paragraph, dealing with Gannibal's African background and racial type, that led to the caricature. This is how Pyotr's 'recollection' begins:

> My father served in the Russian service, he ended up in one of the top ranks and retired with the rank of general-in-chief, knight of the Order of Saint Anne and Saint Alexander Nevsky. He was a Negro. His father was of noble origin, that is, a ruling prince, and he [Gannibal] was taken hostage. Then my father was stolen from the court at Constantinople and dispatched to Peter the Great.[5]

The word here for 'hostage' is a Caucasian one (*omonat*) still used by Chechen kidnappers in their ransom notes. It is quite different from the standard term *rab*, literally 'slave', which Pushkin used in speaking of his great-grandfather, or from *kholop*, meaning 'vassal', even 'flunkey', as a boyar describes himself in Pushkin's novel. Adam Olearius, the Duke of Holstein's envoy to Muscovy in the mid-seventeenth century, made the observation that all Russians, 'whether of high or low condition, call themselves and must count themselves the tsar's *kholopy*, that is slaves and serfs'.[6] Pushkin, too, was scrupulous in his choice of words – as we saw from the lecture he gave Vyazemsky on the differences between 'Negro', 'moor' and 'mulatto', etc. – so it is not impossible that Pyotr's use of the word *omonat* holds the key to Gannibal's enslavement.

For Pyotr, whom one of his serfs, Mikhail Kalashnikov, described as a 'real Negro', the word *omonat* had special meaning.[7] It evoked what

Pushkin, in a letter of 1824 from Odessa, called 'Turkish slavery', the Islamic slave route to Constantinople via the Caucasus. Two months earlier, in a note to Vyazemsky, he had lamented the same 'fate of my brother Negroes ... in unbearable slavery', transported from their African homeland. The secret of Turkish slavery was the slave caravan: bringing slaves from elsewhere. The *omonat* was 'brought' as well as bought. It is the same word Pushkin uses in his note to *Onegin*. Gannibal was 'brought to Constantinople' by light-skinned Arabs, Berbers and Persians who operated this long-distance slave trade, taking millions of sub-Saharan captives by camel across the desert into the Islamic world, from west Africa to Morocco and Tunisia, from Chad to the Persian Gulf. This trade was still going strong in 1886 when the French poet Arthur Rimbaud described the 'obscure traffickings of the Bedouin' from the Guinea coast to the Red Sea.[8] Visiting Djibouti seventy years later, John Laffin observed a slave auction outside a warehouse near the docks, during which perhaps 200 Africans from the area of Bornu, near Lake Chad (then part of French West Africa), were bought and sold in front of his eyes.[9] Obscure traffic had been leaving Bornu at regular intervals for half a millennium. Leo Africanus gives an interesting description of the trade at the beginning of the sixteenth century, Barbary merchants bringing war horses for the king of Bornu and receiving slaves in return.[10]

The slave network pulled Ethiopians in opposite directions. Once again, they were sundered in twain, heading east and west. It wasn't only Russian cartographers who were confused. Islamic countries imported black slaves mainly for military service, and from the outset Ethiopians were the favoured recruits. Soon the term *habashi* or *habshi*, from the Arabic for 'Ethiopian', came to be used for other black people as well. In slaving circles, Ethiopianism was pan-African. It was hard for outsiders to keep track. Just like the Russians, the English got muddled between their Abyssinians and their Moors. Indeed, as early as the fourteenth century, the author of Sir John Mandeville's *Travels* was confidently reporting that Mauretania was a part of Ethiopia, adding:

> Ethiope is divided into two main parts, and that is the eastern half and
> the western half, which is called Moretane, and the folk of that coun-
> try are blacker than in the other part, and they are called Mowres.[11]

And the confusion spread: at the end of the fourteenth century, in
1395, King Juan I of Aragon reclaimed two 'Ethiopians' (a generic
word he used for all Africans) who had hidden in the monastery of
Santa Maria de Besalú.[12] One of them, who called himself *Gane'ba*,
meaning 'stranger' in dialect, claimed to be the son of the king of
Ethiopia.

Nabokov argued that it would be 'a waste of time to conjec-
ture that Abram was not born in Abyssinia at all; that he had been
captured by slave traders in a totally different place'.[13] Perhaps he
felt that he had already spent too many days and weeks following –
'through the bibliographic dust', as he put it – the mules and camels
of his Ethiopian caravans. Nevertheless, homegrown slaves were only
part of the obscure traffic through Abyssinia. Islamic slave traders
bought and sold between eleven and fourteen million slaves over a
dozen centuries – a sluggish turnover compared to the Atlantic slave
trade, which transported roughly the same number by sea from west
and central Africa to the New World in the course of three and a
half centuries.

Islamic slavery was not only older than its western counterpart; its
purposes were different. Some slaves may have been put to work in the
fields. But more were valued as items of conspicuous consumption.
The Muslim elite wanted slaves as guards and concubines, as cooks
and musicians, or simply to show off how rich they were: a tenth-
century caliph of Baghdad had 11,000 slaves at his palace. Black
military slaves were not unknown, and indeed participated in raiding
and warfare in pre-Islamic and early Islamic times. Histories of the
Prophet Muhammad show that there were several blacks in his army
and in the armies of his pagan enemies. One of them, an Ethiopian
slave called Wahshi, distinguished himself in battles against the
Prophet at Uhud and al-Khandaq in 625 and 627 respectively, and

later, after the capture of Mecca, changed sides and fought for the Muslims. To begin with, Islamic slavers would deal only in unbelievers; no Muslim could be enslaved. Gradually, however, Arabs, Persians, Berbers and Turks succumbed to the lure of profits that could be obtained only by violating Muslim ethical norms. Meanwhile, European slavers began to see that Islamic slavery was not only profitable; it also came with its own anti-abolitionist spin. As one British traveller wrote admiringly:

> Slavery in the East has an elevating influence over thousands of human beings, and, but for it, hundreds of thousands of souls must pass their existence in this world as wild savages, little better than animals: it, at least, makes *men* of them, *useful men* too, sometimes even *superior men*.[14]

In other words, freedom was a small price to pay for self-improvement, though for many slaves freedom wasn't all they lost. Enterprising merchants in upper Egypt made money by purchasing pre-pubescent boys at 300 piastres apiece, having them castrated by Coptic monks, and then selling them as eunuchs for 1,000 piastres.

New fronts opened up in the scramble for African slaves. Inevitably, it was the native peoples who paid for the struggle between Muslim slavers and European colonists. The price was not only enslavement, but also expropriation and sometimes even extinction. This is a bleaker reading of the search for Lagone as Gannibal's birthplace – a colonial propaganda, the gloss on a policy of genocide, a farfetched conclusion: fetched, in fact, from halfway across the continent of Africa. After years of inactivity, the first post-Soviet decade saw Lagone move westward in stages, away from Ethiopia's mountain fastnesses, across the continent, from Legote, near Khartoum, to Lagos in Nigeria, and even Luango, near Timbuktu, a place that was impossibly remote: a byword for nowhere, or anywhere. At times it seemed the first letter L was all a city needed to become a candidate. Then, in the mid-1990s, Dieudonné Gnammankou, a black Russian scholar from Benin, started investigating the background of Bornu – a region where slavery had always been a kind of *realpolitik* – and decided that Lake Chad is where Lagone always was.

Ironically, Nabokov had been the first person to suggest a Bornu ancestry for Gannibal. In a throwaway remark at the end of his trawl through Ethiopian geography, he mischievously wondered if, 'say, the Lagona region of equatorial Africa, south of Lake Chad, inhabited by Mussulman Negroes', might be the lost homeland. Strangely, it took three decades for the hypothesis to be properly investigated, and even now, the case for *Logone* made by Gnammankou is far from conclusive. But it is imaginative, and in his showdown with Russia's diehard Ethiopianists, the African scholar has at least the advantage of being able to cite historical fact instead of legend. Take the nine-teenth-century Hausa, who said, 'The country of Bornu – I am telling the truth – is a country of slaves.'[15] Or Leo Africanus, who described the Bornu slave trade in 1526. Half a century later, the Italian explorer Giovanni Lorenzo Anania described the town of Lagone, the capital of the Kotoko people, as a centre for trading slaves and elephants. It is interesting to note, with regard to Gannibal's mysterious crest and the riddle of the unknown word FUMMO, that the Kotoko, who lived between the Logone and the Chari rivers were 'divided into a number of geographically localised clans, all of whom trace their origins from the legendary Sao', known as the 'elephant people', because, according to Kanemba legend, they inspired terror on arrival from the east (in the tenth century) due to 'their gigantic stature – allowing them to lift elephants'.[16]

The modern city of Logone, also known as Logone-Birni, meaning 'Fortress Logone', is relatively new, dating from around 1700, roughly when Gannibal was enslaved. Its predecessor, occupying the exact same site, was pronounced slightly differently in the past, according to Anania, who gave the first topographical and ethnological account. 'On the shore of the lake is the city of Lagone, and then there are the other Kotoko cities of Uncusciuri [Kuseri] and Calfe [the Kanuri term for Goulfeil],' he wrote.[17]

It seems possible, therefore, that Gannibal was born, shortly before 1700, 'in the city of Lagone' as it used to be called. Moroever, the Kotoko were 'never organised into a single kingdom but rather in a series of walled city-principalities more or less independent of each other and owing nominal allegiance to Bornu. The most important of these were Logone-Birni in the south, Goulfeil in the north, and Kuseri in the centre.'[18] In other words, as Gannibal stated in his nobility petition, the ruler of Lagone 'had two other cities under him'.

European colonists lagged behind the Kotoko's Muslim neighbours in the genocide and slave-trading stakes. Indeed it wasn't until the nineteenth century that the white man's grab for Africa involved real journeys to Lagone which had any serious or practical effects. The first to arrive was Major Dixon Denham, a British government agent, who wrote to Henry Bathurst, the Secretary of State for the Colonies, on 12 September 1823, that he was planning to visit Logone on his way round to the east of Lake Chad – which he named Lake Waterloo – to see if it had an outlet on that side. In his 'Excursion to Loggun', on 23 January 1824, Denham reached the city limits:

> I rode down to the river, which here flows with great beauty and majesty past the high walls of this capital Loggun; it comes direct from the south-west, with a rapid current. We entered the town by the western gate, which leads to the principal street: it is as wide as Pall Mall, and has large dwellings on each side, built with great uniformity, each having a courtyard in front, surrounded by a wall, and a handsome entrance, with a strong door hasped with iron: a number of the inhabitants were seated at their doors for the purpose of seeing us enter, with their slaves ranged behind them.[19]

In Bornu, which Denham described chiefly as a rendezvous for caravans, slaves were exchanged for imports from Barbary. In Logone, where the Miyara (or prince) Salih V received Denham, the major found a more advanced economy, based on the sale of 'tobes, blue cotton in stripes, which the Loggun people make and dye of a very beautiful colour. They have, also, a metal currency in Loggun, the first I had seen in Negroland.' [20]

A quarter of a century later, Denham's successor as British agent, a German by the name of Heinrich Barth, criticised 'his great inac-curacy, both with respect to distances, as well as to the direction of his different routes'.[21] But this was probably just the rivalry – or soap opera – of colonial exploration rearing its ugly head again. It was a diplomatic battle for hearts and minds, as Barth's compatriot Gustav Nachtigal made plain by arriving, in 1868, with presents from the Prussian king to Sheikh Umar of Bornu.

Barth reveals that Prince Bruha, who reigned at the turn of the eighteenth century, was regarded as the founder of the new city of Logone-Birni in 1700. He also explains that the people called the river *laghame na Lagone*, and that one of the princes who succeeded Bruha was known as Ana Logon.[22] In other words, the heir to the throne also inherited the name of the kingdom, as happened with Lahan in Rotkirkh's version:

> The similarity between the name of the sister mentioned in the Ger-man biography and the name of the native town mentioned only in the petition is very disturbing [wrote Nabokov]. I have not found – within the limited scope of my reading – any instance of an Abys-sinian child receiving the name of its birthplace.[23]

But such an instance would have arisen if he had looked beyond Ethiopia – which, of course, he almost did.

Gnammankou knows why some critics are reluctant to abandon the Ethiopianist view of Gannibal's origins, and why the debate has become so heated. 'Some of the criticism I get is undoubtedly racist,' he says. 'For some Russian scholars it is just untenable that Pushkin, their national poet, should have a Negro ancestor. They continue to say Gannibal was Ethiopian because, as far as they are concerned, the Ethiopians are practically white.'[24]

So the dispute is unresolved, like Gannibal's plea to Catherine the Great for a retirement bonus in 1762. It is a stalemate between Gnammankou's Logone in the dark, steamy, profuse interior of equatorial Africa, and the dazzle of Anuchin's east African deserts and mountains. In both cases, it is a question of *jihad*: the stand-off between Muslims and pagans in Chad, between Muslims and Christians in Ethiopia.

Barth argued that Bruha, perhaps Gannibal's father, 'was a pagan, and probably at that time [around 1700] there were only a few Mohammedans in the place; and Miyara Sale, the old prince whom Denham visited ... is said to have been the first among the petty princes of this country who converted to Islam'. Ahmad Baba, a nineteenth-century Berber scholar from Timbuktu, when asked about Muslim slavery, replied that a black African who had voluntarily embraced Islam should not in any circumstances be enslaved. 'The reason for enslavement is unbelief,' he added. 'The position of unbelieving Negroes is the same as that of other unbelievers, Christians, Jews, Persians, Turks, etc.'[25]

Gnammankou says the Bagirmi, a people of mixed Arab, Berber and Negro origins living on the southern fringe of the Sahara, close to Bornu, exercised political dominance over many of the neighbouring cities, including Logone, and that Bornu and Bagirmi had commercial relations with the Ottoman Empire. For a while, Bornu was even considered the fourth power in the Islamic world (after Mecca, Constantinople and Cairo). One of its emperors, Ali Ghazi was invested with the title of caliph by Abbasid Abd al-Aziz bin Yakub at Mecca in 1484. Between 1680 and 1707, Logone and the other non-Islamic cities were attacked frequently by the Sultan Abd al-Kader of Bagirmi.[26] Nachtigal reported that the slaves in the Bornu markets came from raids and 'tribute from vassal princes on the periphery of the country, who likewise carry on continuous warfare for this purpose against their Pagan neighbours'.[27] His words echo Rotkirkh's claim that Abram's father was 'a vassal' of some Muslim overlord.[28] So it is very probable that in the course of one of these incursions against

Lagone, the son of Prince Bruha was among other hostages sold as slaves to Constantinople. Indeed, the state archive in N'Djamena, the capital of Chad, just across the river Logone, has a document from 1714 which mentions Bruha by name, and then goes on to describe a scene not unlike Lahan's unsuccessful attempt to rescue Gannibal. The text in Hausa is only a couple of lines. It is a river scene. It goes like this:

> Now captured and penned inside the boat, the prisoner listened in anguish as his mother and sister wailed and grieved under the vessel's stern. Standing in canoes around the ship, the women enacted terrible rites of mourning, hammering at their own heads with clubs until the blood ran.[29]

But no mention of FUMMO.

# 5

# The Elephant Man

Going up that river was like travelling back to the earliest beginnings of the world, when vegetation rioted on the earth and the
big trees were kings.

—Joseph Conrad, *Heart of Darkness*

The Logone delta covers an area of nearly 7,000 square miles
in the extreme west of Chad. On the outskirts of the capital
N'Djamena – which was still known as Fort-Lamy in 1974, when
Haile Selassie flew here from Addis Ababa on his way into exile
– the great northward flow of the river suddenly falters after 600 miles
and splits into a tangle of smaller branches, such as the Chari, before
emptying into Lake Chad.

Emptying is the right word. When Giovanni Anania mapped
the delta, in 1573, Lake Chad was fifty times larger than it is today.
It is shallow – less than twenty-three feet deep – and its surface area is
still shrinking after decades of drought. As a result, the lake is only
a twentieth of the size it was thirty-five years ago, or so I was told by
Michael Coe, an American scientist in N'Djamena who monitors
the crisis with the help of NASA satellites. He was gloomy about
the lake's future. 'Soon it'll just be a puddle. You'll get crops and
drinking water out of it, but it's game over for the delta's ecosystem.'

Anania did not use the Italian word for 'delta' to describe the
Logone. In his day it referred exclusively to the mouth of the Nile,
whose triangular shape Herodotus compared to the delta of the Greek
alphabet. The *Oxford English Dictionary* says the English word was not

used as a geographical description until 1790 when Gibbon referred to the 'delta of Mesola' at the mouth of the Po river. On the other hand, Anania often used the word 'fummo' – which, in Italian, is just a past tense of the verb 'to be'. Gnammankou has a pet theory that *fummo* is the first person singular of an obsolete Latin verb meaning 'I bombard'. It's a clever idea, and fits neatly with the idea of Gannibal the military engineer. But, as Pushkin says at the start of *Onegin*, 'Latin is out of fashion right now' with Russian historians.[1] Even so, I couldn't help thinking, as I went upriver to Logone in a thirty-foot wooden boat, that surely somewhere there lurked a decisive clue to this verbal enigma. Rowing or paddling against the stream in a narrow boat, similar in many respects to the canoes of the distraught Hausa women, also reminded me of the journey in Conrad's *Heart of Darkness* to meet the 'up-river agent' Kurtz. We passed the big trees on either side: palms, papyrus, ambatch, baobab, jujube and African myrrh.

Dixon Denham reached Lake Chad in August 1823 at the height of the rainy season, when violent storms flooded the delta. Historically, Lake Chad received most of its water from these rains which fell annually from June to August. But at the end of the 1960s the sub-Saharan region experienced a series of devastating droughts. As the rains increasingly failed, local people became more dependent on Lake Chad as a source of water. In the 1970s, irrigation schemes were begun and these, too, contributed to the lake's shrinkage. Then the rains failed again and the water level fell to a point where irrigation could no longer take place. The lake's decline and the years of drought have had a terrible impact on the nine million farmers, fishermen and herdsmen who depend on it for their livelihood. Now the influx of refugees displaced by the civil war in neighbouring Sudan has put the local economy under further strain.

The delta is a strange, shifting landscape: a medieval world of strip-farmers turning up the dark soil. Profuse and luxuriant on the water's edge, the dry fields beyond resemble a desert or a prairie, in that you can travel for hours without much change. Tall, thin walkers stride easily on the riverbank, often carrying a walking-staff horizontally across the shoulders, their arms crooked loosely over it as they follow ploughs pulled by oxen or even donkeys. We passed several marshy floating islands covered with papyrus and high grass, apparently dividing the water into different streams. Soon we noticed a chain of amoeba-shaped blobs in the water. It was a Kotoko farming technique for the cultivation of millet and sorghum, using the river to irrigate the crop.

On the shore a group of refugees strode forward waving sticks in the air. The men wore dirty jellabas, and were chanting slogans in a Darfurian language, but the women hung back in an orderly row, and the collage of their scarves and sarongs, flowing gauze-like robes in vivid yellows and blues and reds, was blinding in the sunlight. Until recently they had lived on the other side of the border, in the savannah of Darfur, grazing livestock on the slopes of Jebel Marra, but they had fled to safety after their village was attacked by the *janjaweed* militia. (*Jaan* means 'evil' in Darfur Arabic, and *jawad* means 'horse', so *janjaweed* means, roughly, 'evil horseman'.) Hundreds of thousands of people had been displaced by the conflict. In Darfur, where the victims were non-Muslims, the official rhetoric justifying the attacks used the vocabulary of holy war, of *jihad*. But the unofficial rhetoric was racial, employing the terms *abd* (slave) and *zurga* (literally 'blue', meaning black, i.e., not Arab, in Sudanese language), words that bear the weight of a history of discrimination and exploita-tion in Sudan, where ethnic groups claiming Arab descent assume a superiority over others. Though named for the *dar* (homeland) of the Fur people, the sultanate of Darfur controlled the desert trade route between west Africa and Egypt. It embraced Islam in the early 1800s, but the history of conflict between its different ethnic groups remained one of Balkan complexity.

It was always like this. The killing in Darfur was only the latest outbreak of violence and exploitation for which many Africans blamed poor harvests and the legacy of the slave trade. The story of Gannibal is timeless. A hundred and fifty years ago, the German explorer Eduard Vogel was murdered in Bornu after intervening in a dispute between slave-traders. He was incensed by the pillage of slavery. 'People here find it more convenient to raid the neighbouring lands than to farm,' Vogel wrote. Instead of tilling the fields, they preferred to 'catch a good number of slaves – mostly children between nine and twelve years old – to barter them with Tubbu and Arab merchants'. Denham reported that slaves were often traded for ivory and tusks. Elephant-hunting was a sacred rite to the people of Bornu. 'The first night [in Logone], we saw forty-seven elephants feeding,' he wrote,

> at first they appeared to treat our approach with great contempt, yet after a little while they moved off, raising up their ears most violently which till then laid flat on their shoulders, giving a roar that shook the ground under us, one was an immense fellow seventeen or eighteen feet high ... one of the Negroes cast a spear at him, which striking him just under the tail seemed to give him as much pain as when we prick our finger with a pin.[2]

Three decades later, Vogel too commented on the 'unbelievable numbers of elephants' at the lake.

It is easier to get to Logone than it was in 1823, but still not very easy. We stopped at the water-gate and climbed ashore, heading for the main street which Denham had said was as wide as Pall Mall. It's not quite that splendid, but the layout of the town, with its massive earthworks deserving of the name *birni*, or 'fortification', is certainly a very unusual one. Despite its size, and the milling crowds of people and horses, Logone retains a secretive aura, a sense of isolation, as if commemorating the many other lives that the young Gannibal might have led. He might, for instance, have returned from Constantinople to Logone and become the ruling prince on the death of his father Bruha. Vogel's guide on his fatal journey to Lake Chad in 1852 was a native of Bornu whom he had rescued from captivity at the Sublime Porte. The guide, who was called Almas, stayed in the region after Vogel's death and later worked as an interpreter for Nachtigal:

Naturally intelligent and unusually energetic and active [wrote the German doctor], he was one of the few Negroes who from a longish stay in Europe still benefit even after their return home.[3]

The export slave trade in Africa, which dates back to the ninth century, continues to this day in some Islamic countries, especially Sudan and Mauritania: as late as 1960, Lord Shackleton reported to the House of Lords that African Muslims on pilgrimages to Mecca still sold slaves upon arrival, 'using them as traveller's cheques'.[4]

I was met by the sultan of Logone, Muhammad Bahar Maruf, the latest in Bruha's line, and – who knows? – a distant nephew of Gannibal's. The sultan has ruled over the Kotoko city since 1965, but had never heard of Pushkin or his great-grandfather until a decade ago when he received a photocopy of a lecture by Gnammankou. Since then Maruf has thrown himself into the role of Pushkin expert, vehemently backing Gnammankou's claims while, typically, adding to the confusion that already exists by proposing a different family tree. '*Ibrahim Hannibal was undoubtedly a prince of Logone-Birni, the son of Mai Djanna I or Abdulkarim I*,' he said, in French, after introducing his several wives and retiring to his palace – more of a tent, really – in the shade.[5] 'Why should I be surprised that a prince of Logone-Birni ended up in Russia?' the sultan added. 'He was a prisoner of war, a hostage. Our people were often kidnapped by our enemies – for money or elephants.'

'Did you say elephants?' I asked, picturing Gannibal's crest, the portly elephant and the word FUMMO – meaning *elephant* perhaps, in one of the approximately 150 languages of the country. 'What's the Kotoko word for elephant?'

He uttered a monosyllabic word: not FUMMO, not even close. I must have looked a bit crestfallen, because he asked what the problem was.

'*Fúmmo*,' I said.

'Fu-mow,' he repeated eagerly, placing the emphasis on the second syllable. 'It's a Kotoko word.'

I looked at him, with astonishment. 'What does it mean?' I asked.

'Homeland.'

# 6

# Sublime Port

Every slave of the Sultan is a spy.
—Voltaire, *Zadig*

The young African slave got his first sight of Constantinople from the deck of a pirate ship as it entered the sea of Marmara on a spring afternoon in 1703. The single-masted Turkish vessel, its square sail hoist to the wind, was hardly the latest thing in ship design. Built like the *Argo*, which had carried Jason through the same legendary waters, the sloop made heavy weather of the voyage. Storms forced it to hug the Mediterranean shore. There was also privation, the diseases and brutalities of life at sea. By the time the slave ship rounded the Dardanelles, a third of its human cargo had succumbed to the 'great and awful dangers' cited by Gannibal in 1722, when he begged Peter the Great to let him return to Russia overland from France.[1] No less pressing were the dangers (and enigmas) of arrival in Constantinople. For Abram, huddling in chains next to the other frightened captives, the end of the voyage was not the end of the ordeal. Sailing to Byzantium was a journey into the unknown. To him the incomparable skyline, blue domes and white minarets framed by dark green cypresses must have seemed a daunting prospect.

Yet the sight of Constantinople was a kind of miracle. Built on a peninsula on the very edge of Europe, surrounded by water and by hills overlooking Asia, the city occupied a triangle of land where the Bosphorus merged with the sea of Marmara and the Golden Horn. From his vantage point on deck Gannibal watched the long, frail Turkish caiques dancing on the waves in front of the sultan's palace. His gaze followed the high wall as it climbed the hill to the High Gate, or Bab-i-Humayun, which the Europeans picturesquely mistranslated as 'Sublime Porte'. Here the severed heads of traitors and rebels were put on display. Gannibal may have described this gruesome spectacle to Voltaire during his later stay in Paris, because it occurs, along with the image of 'Negro pirates', at the end of *Candide*, in a scene where the hero and Dr Pangloss are sitting on one of the Princes' Islands in the sea of Marmara:

> Out of the window boats were often seen passing by, full of effen-
> dis, pashas and kadis going into banishment to Lemnos, Mytilene
> or Erzerum, while other kadis, pashas and effendis took the place of
> the banished, and were banished in turn. Heads, too, could be seen
> empaled on poles and displayed at the Sublime Porte.[2]

To the overheated European imagination the palace of Topkapi, built by Mehmed II after the fall of Constantinople in 1453, was a pleasure dome or a forbidden labyrinth. In the writings of Voltaire and Montesquieu, the sultan's *harem* – a Turkish word meaning 'forbidden' – served as a focus for Enlightenment fantasies: an oriental pageant, a sexual maze, a luxury prison. Its cast of concubines and eunuchs, blind princes and veiled sultanas, manifested the 'otherness' of the Ottomans. Less colourfully perhaps, the *seraglio* was also a place of work, a centre of bureaucracy: the hub of a vast empire stretching over three continents from the Danube to the Euphrates, from the Persian Gulf to Morocco. For the next year or so, it was to be Gannibal's home.

Having arrived, or been unloaded, at Constantinople, a slave's prospects depended on the outcome of an inspection by Ottoman customs officials. Each shipment was divided into two groups: a sixteenth-century port register lists the excise duty on 'commercial' and 'palace' slaves in different columns.[3] The former were sold at the city's slave market, next to the bazaar, in the centre of the city. The latter, handpicked by the chief black eunuch, were delivered to the elite regiment of the sultan's Janissary guard. Eyecatchingly dressed in red caps, yellow boots and blue uniforms with pleated white headdresses like giant sleeves, the Janissaries were slaves brought to Constantinople as part of the *devshirme*, or 'collecting': a periodic levy of non-Muslim children from the Balkan countries under Ottoman rule. These boys were then trained up to become soldiers and bureaucrats, known as Slaves of the Gate, who went on to run the empire. Indeed the power they wielded is a shining example of Ottoman faith in racial variety. (Islamic 'mirrors for princes' taught that slaves made excellent officials because they were dependably loyal, unlike the natives who usually belonged to one rival faction or another. In the sixteenth century a Venetian ambassador wrote that the Janissaries took great pleasure in saying, '"I am a slave of the sultan," since they know that this is a lordship or a republic of slaves.')[4] Drafted between the ages eight and sixteen, the boys were formally admitted to Islam as soon as they arrived in Constantinople. On the dockside they raised their right hands, recited the Profession of Faith – 'I hereby testify that there is no God but Allah. Muhammad is the Prophet of God' – and were then circumcised. The high-fliers served as pages in the *seraglio* until they were old enough to join this fanatical order of military monks: the word 'Janissary' derives from the Turkish *yeni çeri*, meaning 'new soldier'. Such was the fate in store for the 8-year-old Gannibal, according to Rotkirkh:

> Not long after this permanent separation [from his sister Lahan], Hannibal arrived in Constantinople and with the other young hostages was confined in the *seraglio*, to be raised there among the noble pages of the sultan, and there spent one year and some months.[5]

Unfortunately, the German biography has nothing to say about a brother who may have accompanied Gannibal to Constantinople. This mysterious sibling, known as Abdul in some Russian accounts, is never mentioned in any of the 'family legends'. Rotkirkh does refer to 'another black boy – a compatriot of Gannibal's of noble birth' among the slaves in Turkey. But his version of the story ignores their actual relationship. Its usefulness is therefore limited to a matter of chronology. Because we know, from other sources, that two African 'brothers' left Turkey in June 1704, in the company of a Russian spy, it is possible from Rotkirkh's vague reference to 'one year and some months' to guess the date of Gannibal's arrival in Stamboul.

The sea voyage is another blank in Rotkirkh's narrative. Other documents, however, fill the gaps. The first is a report, dated 20 February 1703 and forwarded to the Sublime Porte by the Sultan's dragoman (or interpreter) Alexander Mavrocordato, a Greek from the island of Chios.[6] The founder of an illustrious Ottoman dynasty that later included several princes of Wallachia and a prime minister of Greece, Mavrocordato was also to play a key role in Gannibal's escape from the *seraglio*. By coincidence, the dragoman may have come across the young slave on the eve of his perilous Mediterranean journey. His report concerns the mysterious fate of two young African slaves who vanished in Cairo after a dispute between their 'owner' and a Turkish customs official. The owner was Charles Poncet, the French chemist returning to Paris after his visit to the court of King Jesus I of Ethiopia. In his journal Poncet recalls buying the two *jeunes esclaves ethiopiens* from a Berber slave caravan in Upper Egypt. The boy slaves were rumoured to be the sons of an African prince, and Poncet wanted to give them to Louis XIV as a present. To cut a long story short, the two boys made a scene as they were being loaded onto a Nile barge. One of them was apparently waving the trunk of a dead elephant. The child became hysterical and cried out that he was a Muslim, who was being kidnapped, and that he did not want to go to Christendom. As a result, the Ottoman clerk accused Poncet of seizing the children illegally – since Muslims could not be enslaved – and placed them in the custody of the Turkish *kiaya*, or interior minister, Mustafa Kazdugli.[7]

James Bruce tells a different version of the same story, in which Poncet 'watched helplessly as a bought slave, a poor Abyssinian lad, whom he was bringing to Louis the Fourteenth, was taken out by the Janizaries and made a Mohometan before his eyes'.[8] Bruce is referring here to an act of circumcision. Yet the story only makes sense if the 'Abyssinian lad' was in fact a pagan Negro, since the sons of Christian Ethiopians were routinely circumcised at birth. In his report to Constantinople, Mavrocordato speculates that the *kiaya* sent the missing children to Chios or its neighbour Mytilene. This could be true. Both islands served as depots for the Aegean slave traffic. In 1681, in retaliation for acts of piracy by ships from north Africa, a French fleet bombarded the island of Chios, damaging a mosque and killing 250 Ottoman subjects. The pirate Barbarossa (or Redbeard), who became admiral of the Ottoman fleet and conqueror of Algiers, was a native of Mytilene. Rotkirkh also mentions 'der Expedition von Mittelino' in another context. Unfortunately, once again, truth is shrouded in legend. The only thing we know for certain is that, one day in the spring of 1703, a Turkish vessel carrying Gannibal dropped anchor at sunset in the shadow of the Golden Horn.[9]

We can imagine the scene at the dockside as the young African set foot on dry land. Here were the sights and sounds of the Orient: the loading and unloading, a knot of spice merchants haggling on the wharf, Arabs pushing carts of mastic and antimony, henna, sandalwood and gum, the din of the bazaar, a whirling dervish. On the hill of Tophana overlooking the port, a cannon fired to announce the sunset, and muezzins began to chant the call to evening prayer. Sheikhs delivered sermons, and imams led the worship, at the city's 500 mosques which soon filled with kneeling lines of men rising and falling and crying 'Allah!'

The harbour was a crux, a great traffic junction, a place where east met west. Its strategic position was unrivalled as a gateway between the Aegean and the Black Sea, a bridge uniting Europe and Asia. Overland the great trade routes converged on the city. Sooner or later, if you had something to sell, you ended up on the road to Istanbul. Here the foreign element was not restricted to merchants, craftsmen and travellers drawn to the city by its wealth and fame and opportunities. There were also Christians and Jews left over from Byzantine times, Greek and Armenian priests. Others, too, were drawn to the Sublime Porte. Power was the magnet. Ambassadors came to Constantinople not only from London and Paris, but also from the kingdoms of Africa and as far away as India and China.[10] Lodged in Pera over the Golden Horn, and lacking any daily contact with the palace, English, French and Venetian diplomats spent hours at the dockside on the look-out for information. Under the walls of the *seraglio* they mixed with peddlers, prostitutes and thieves, often training their telescopes on Topkapi.

Constantinople was a nest of spies. Such was the intricate tissue of different offices, religions and nationalities that Lady Mary Wortley Montagu, in her Turkish Embassy letters, described the city as a Tower of Babel.[11] Mozart captured the mood in his opera *Die Entführung aus dem Serail* (*The Abduction from the Seraglio*) in which the disguised hero finds the Ottoman capital bubbling with corruption and intrigue. Significantly, in the spring of 1703, the arrival of slave ships focused diplomatic interest. It was a time of unrest and economic crisis. Inflation played havoc with the fixed wages of Janissaries and government officials. There was a series of revolts. Shortly before Gannibal's ship sailed over the horizon, Sultan Mustafa II had raised political tensions (and the hackles of his enemies) by splashing out on the dynastic weddings of three daughters. Unfortunately, after building a sumptuous palace for each bride, the sultan ran out of slaves to fill the new households. So Mustafa ordered the grand vizier, the head of the Ottoman government – his prime minister, as it were – to find some extra recruits in a hurry. The vizier, Rahmi Mehmed Pasha, immediately wrote a circular letter to provincial governors and other contacts in the slave trade. A copy of one of the letters now lies in the Topkapi Palace archives, dated February–August 1703. 'Whereas in the past it has been customary for you to send men for the army,' Rahmi writes to the pashas of Bosnia, Erzerum and Akhiska, 'be advised that now the Sultan needs only slaves.'[12]

So the docking of the Turkish vessel was an event watched closely by the shadowy figures on the waterfront. But what of the faces that populate the scene? Three men stand out: two Russians (one 'turned Turk') and a Bosnian. Each would play a decisive role in Gannibal's life. Who were these men? The evidence is sketchy, but something of their careers and characters – and, in one case, even a face – can be discerned.

The Russian was Pyotr Tolstoy, the newly arrived ambassador from Moscow, but a veteran of spycraft. An ancestor of the novelist Count Leo Tolstoy, he was sitting in a coffee house at the port, with a large entourage of attendants and servants, on the day Gannibal arrived.[13] Here, straightaway, is a fascinating character who steps right out of the shadows. A portrait of him, painted in 1712 by the German artist Johann Gottfried Dannhauer, depicts a man with shrewd blue eyes, bushy black eyebrows, a high forehead and a grey western wig. Contemporary memoirs, however, often portray him as sinister, unscrupulous and crafty. In any case it is rather surprising to find Tolstoy in Constantinople in 1703 – or indeed still in favour at all, given his chequered history and several run-ins with Tsar Peter.

Born in 1645, Tolstoy was already middle-aged by the time he backed Peter the Great's older half-sister Sofiya, in May 1682, in a power struggle that put her temporarily on top and made her the regent. The child of his father's second marriage, Peter seems to have borne a grudge against Tolstoy, because one of his first acts on seizing power from Sofiya in 1689 was to banish him from Moscow. Out in the cold, literally, the disloyal subject became governor of the Ustyug province in the far north of Russia. Yet Tolstoy was a survivor by nature, and he bided his time until he got a chance to redeem himself. In the summer of 1693, and again the following year, Peter happened to visit Ustyug on his way to and from Arkhangelsk. Tolstoy lavished hospitality on the tsar, and the two men sat up drinking together in the long Arctic evenings. No doubt Peter discussed his plans for war against the Turks – and perhaps Tolstoy, who knew the Black Sea, offered useful advice. The tsar's first aim was to secure Muscovy's southern borders against the threat of raids by Crimean Tatars backed by the

Ottoman Empire. When he failed at the first attempt, in 1695, to gain a foothold on the Sea of Azov, leading to the Black Sea, he retreated up the Volga to build himself a navy. He was the first Russian ruler since early Kievan times to do so. He also gave the man from Ustyug a recall. The next year, with Tolstoy's help, Peter captured the Turkish coastal fort of Azov at the mouth of the river Don.[14]

Shrewd and opportunistic, Tolstoy was determined to make the most of his second chance. He realised that the Azov experience had convinced Peter of the need to improve Russian technology by securing tools and personnel from the west. Tolstoy also clocked the tsar's admiration for those few Russians who had a genuinely international outlook. So, in 1697, at the age of fifty-two, he volunteered to go to Venice to learn seamanship.[15] His timing was immaculate. That same year Peter visited western Europe – something no Muscovite tsar had ever done – on a 'Grand Embassy' to acquire maritime skills and hire experts in various fields, while also drumming up support for a crusade against the Turks. Often travelling incognito under the name of Sergeant Pyotr Mikhailov, the tsar worked as a ship's carpenter for the Dutch East India Company at Saardam, before going to London where he took a job at the Royal Navy's dockyard in Deptford.

Peter wanted allies. He was always looking for reform-minded officials to help modernise Russia. So when Tolstoy returned from Venice not only a competent ship builder but also speaking Italian, and able to understand something of western life and culture, Peter soon dispatched him as Russia's first permanent envoy to Constantinople. It was a frontline posting. The tsar's foreign minister (and spymaster) Count Fyodor Golovin had just negotiated a thirty-year armistice with Turkey. His special envoy, Yemelian Ukraintsev, signed the peace deal in Constantinople in 1700. Yet the Black Sea remained an Ottoman lake. Turkish fortresses on the Sea of Azov blocked Russia's way to the Mediterranean. Here was a stalemate, not the endgame: Tolstoy was merely a pawn in the spymaster's next move. Golovin, the 'most *intelligent* man in Russia', according to England's ambassador Charles Whitworth, regarded the armistice with Turkey as no more than a truce.[16] Ominously, the sultan took a similar view. 'A temporary peace is no different from *jihad*,' warned Rahmi Mehmed, the chief Ottoman negotiator.[17]

So Tolstoy drank a lot of coffee in the line of duty. His orders were to stir up trouble without jeopardising the truce. Golovin asked him to gather information about the internal politics of the regime, and to provide Moscow with analysis of the viziers in power and those most likely to come into power, while also learning what he could about Turkish military and naval tactics and the strength of their fortresses on the Black Sea.[18] It was dangerous work. The Ottomans took a strange if logical view of diplomacy. Ambassadors were seen as hostages: when Turkey finally broke the truce, in 1710, and declared war on Russia, the Ottomans imprisoned Tolstoy in the Seven Towers just to show they meant business. Nevertheless he proved to be an accomplished intriguer, recruiting spies and playing off the various factions against one another. News of the dispute involving the sultan's daughters had prompted Tolstoy to keep a check on the influx of slaves. He was looking for a mole inside the troubled regime, a source of intelligence and a way of damaging Russia's rivals.

Also standing on the dockside that evening was a handsome, thin-faced Balkan adventurer in his mid-thirties, who was to become one of Gannibal's intimates. He arrived at the scene with the Russian ambassador and is described variously as Tolstoy's 'servant' or 'man'. He too is a shadowy but engaging figure, an unsung cosmopolitan known as Savva Raguzinsky. (The name in Russian means simply 'Savva the Ragusan', because he came from the city of Ragusa, now Dubrovnik, in Croatia.) A secret agent of great verve and courage, Raguzinsky unexpectedly found a niche – and a career – in the great game of Black Sea espionage. He was ambitious as well as brave, and his ambition paid off. That much should be obvious from the fact that while Raguzinsky crops up only intermittently in Gannibal's life, each time he does he is one or two rungs higher up the ladder. Thus, for example, in the wake of the Turkish adventure he vanishes almost without trace until 1717 when the Ragusan's name occurs in the roster of 'special envoys' accompanying Tsar Peter to France. Soon afterwards he disappears again, and his where-abouts remain unknown for almost a decade until, by chance, he meets Gannibal in Siberia. Now *Count* Vladislavich-Raguzinsky, and Russia's ambassador to China, this time he is on his way back to Moscow from Peking.

In *The Negro of Peter the Great* Pushkin describes Gannibal, back from Paris in 1723, as having an emotional reunion with 'the young Raguzinsky, his former comrade'.[19] In fact, Raguzinsky was no longer young by then: he was fifty-five. Even so, it is intriguing to speculate about the precise nature of their comradeship. Little is known of the Ragusan's background, except that, as early as 1699, Ukraintsev had recruited several Illyrian secret agents, one of whom was a Bosnian merchant named Savva Lukic Vladislavic. Born in Popovo in Herzegovina in 1668, the son of a pirate named Luca who claimed to be a descendant of Bosnia's Vladislavic princes, at the age of twenty-five he had moved to Constantinople, where he bought a grand house in Pera and made an effort to go straight. In other words, the pirate became a Perote, as inhabitants of the diplomatic quarter were called: '*Pera, Pera, dei scelerati il nido*' ('Pera, Pera, the nest of scoundrels') went a popular Italian song.[20]

Tolstoy inherited Raguzinsky from Ukraintsev, and soon came to rely on the scoundrel's cunning. The Bosnian was deployed as a courier taking secret messages back and forth to Moscow in the guise of an ordinary Black Sea trader 'in olive oil, red calico and cotton', to quote an official document.[21] In a letter to the Russian foreign minister Golovin, written a fortnight after his arrival in Constantinople, Tolstoy is already singing Raguzinsky's praises. He describes him as 'a good chap who has been working zealously until now on affairs of high state importance, and bringing all sorts of information to me, and who wishes to serve loyally henceforth'.[22] The scoundrel used his cover as a respectable merchant to play the go-between. And Tolstoy kept up the subterfuge in his correspondence with Golovin, in case the Turkish police intercepted the letters. On 25 September 1702, he writes to the spy chief:

> A Ragusan dwelling in Constantinople, Sava Vladislavov, who as you know is a good man, has now, by my advice, set out with wares for Azov and from there will proceed to Moscow. He is an infinitely useful person for His Muscovite Majesty to have here.[23]

Tolstoy doesn't make the point explicitly, but one of Raguzinsky's uses was linguistic, of course. Though he also spoke Turkish, Greek, Albanian, Romanian, French and Russian, as well as a smattering of Arabic, the Bosnian shared a mother tongue with the Janissaries, and with the other Balkan 'slaves of the sultan' who had control of the government apparatus. Even Sultan Mustafa spoke Serbo-Croat; it was the palace's second language. Indeed, a sixteenth-century French traveller noted that 'Sclavonian' (i.e. Serbo-Croat) was the language 'most widely used and understood at the Topkapi Seray ... not least because it is common to the Janissaries'.[24]

Peter must have read Tolstoy's letter to Golovin, because he gave Raguzinsky a hero's welcome, in the autumn of 1702, when the Bosnian finally reached Moscow with his secret dispatches. A state document of 1717 notes that Peter 'destined the Ragusan for the civil service'. Certainly the ex-pirate was a cool customer. In his *History of Peter I*, Pushkin implies that Raguzinsky may even have persuaded the tsar to write *affidavits*, or references, on behalf of other Illyrians spying for Russia at the Porte:

> A certain Savva Vladislavovich, born in Ragusa, made himself known to Peter at that time. He was in Constantinople – an agent of Tolstoy's. Peter took kindly to him. Raguzinsky advised him to stand as a witness for other Montenegrin Christians – and Peter sent him a document, recommending them to the Ottomans.[25]

But Raguzinsky did not waste any time in Moscow. As soon as he had received fresh orders from the tsar – including a request for a black African slave perhaps – he was back on the road, bringing sable and ermines (and secret messages) to Constantinople, where he arrived shortly before Gannibal in the spring of 1703.

Tolstoy and Raguzinsky were two sides of the Russian intelligence effort – the ambassador and the spy. The third important figure was a high-ranking Ottoman bureaucrat who had his own reasons for waiting on the dockside as the slave ship sailed into view. Short and fat, with jet-black eyes, Kavanoz Ahmed Pasha wore a turban and bright green satin robes. Several times as he paused to drink a glass of sherbet he stroked his turned-up beard. A Turkish stereotype perhaps, yet Kavanoz was not exactly what he seemed. He was Russian, for a start, though he had lived in the Ottoman Empire all his life, and as a young man had married into the powerful Koprulu dynasty. That marriage to Sherife, daughter of Amcazade Huseyin Pasha, changed everything. It is hard really to exaggerate the power of the Koprulus during the half century that began in 1656 with a Janissary uprising. In that short period, they produced four grand viziers, while a further two were close relations. Statistically, at any rate, that achievement makes the Koprulus the most successful political dynasty in the history of Europe. The grand vizier was the very apex of the Ottoman hierarchy. He was the sultan's 'absolute deputy', though he was actually much more than that: in practice, the vizier ruled the empire, and led its armies into war, while the sultan lolled on cushions in the harem.

The Koprulu power outgrew the bureaucracy. As much a caste as a clan, it seized control of the Ottoman Empire in the half century after Koprulu Mehmed, an Albanian recruited by the *devshirme*, became the family's first grand vizier.[26] In 1683, it almost seized control of the Habsburg Empire, when an army led by Kavanoz's cousin Kara Mustafa surrounded Vienna. The Austrian capital was saved only by a European coalition of the Holy Roman Empire, the Papacy, Venice and Poland. For six years, until the eve of Gannibal's arrival in Turkey, Kavanoz's father-in-law had been grand vizier. It was a system of organised nepotism, literally: Amcazade, meaning 'son of the uncle', was so called because he was the son of Hasan, the younger brother of Koprulu Mehmed.

Kavanoz was no prodigy, however. If Amcazade Huseyin Pasha had earned the epithet Koprulu the Wise, while his predecessors were variously Koprulu the Cruel, Koprulu the Politic and Koprulu the Virtuous, and the Ottoman troops acclaimed Kara Mustafa at Vienna as a *ghazi*, or 'holy warrior', eager for 'the honey of martyrdom', Kavanoz was known simply as Koprulu the Corrupt. During the years he served as governor of Basra, Mosul and Beirut, the Russian acquired a reputation for venality. His first response to any event or proposal, according to a contemporary source, was to ask himself, 'Is there money to be made out of it?' His nickname *kavanoz*, meaning 'fatty', or even 'beehive', pays ironic tribute to the way he accumu-lated riches like honey. In his youth, however, the Beehive had been expelled from the palace in murky circumstances by Sultan Mehmed IV, the father of Mustafa. Everyone knew he bore a grudge. So it was hardly surprising that he accepted Tolstoy's bribes to spy at the Porte. Kavanoz was Russian, after all. How could he resist the opportunity to plot his revenge against the sultan – and make a profit at the same time?

The chief black eunuch led Gannibal and his brother, with the other slaves, up the muddy side streets from the port to the Porte. The *seraglio* was a city within a city. Outside the palace gate a crowd jostled the two boys. A train of camels went past laden with weapons, food and taxes for the imperial coffers. The slaves followed the eunuch into a courtyard decorated with ceramic tiles painted blue and green and white. It was full of magnificently dressed officials and a corps of palace guards standing in front of a square tower with a conical roof. Inside was the Ottoman council, or *divan*, where the grand vizier held court four times a week. Suddenly a hush went round and the rotund figure of Sultan Mustafa appeared, walking briskly in a long robe of purple cloth and a golden turban with a large emerald. He was preceded by a dozen Janissaries with big white feathers on their heads. As he passed on his way, several members of the crowd pressed forward and waved petitions at the sultan, who indicated to a cham- berlain to put the folded papers in a silken bag. Mustafa stopped in front of the chief black eunuch and looked briefly at Gannibal and the other slaves before entering the *divan*.

Overawed as they were, the boys must have noticed how the Turks deferred to this 'black old neutral personage/Of the third sex'.[27] Such was the hierarchy in their unfamiliar new environment. One of the most powerful men in the Ottoman Empire – arguably fourth in line, after the sultan himself, the grand vizier and the mufti of Istanbul (the head of the Muslim judiciary) – he too was an African. He controlled the finances of not only the harem, but also the imperial mosques in Constantinople, as well as the shrines at Mecca and Medina. Between 1645 and 1760, whoever was chief black eunuch ruled the city of Athens. One of them became so rich he built a new port at the mouth of the Danube.[28]

The African was an emblem of oriental despotism. More impor- tantly, he controlled access to the sultan by policing the harem, a sanctuary of women, a closed world of veils and gossip and intrigue. The only passage of entry from the *divan*, where the grand vizier held court, to the sultan's harem was through two consecutive pairs of doors, one set of iron, the other of brass. Each night the eunuch, known as the *kizlar agasi*, or 'aga [i.e. chief] of the girls', received the keys from the watchmen, to whom he returned them when he came off duty in the morning. Nor was the aga of the girls above meddling in politics. The year before Gannibal's arrival in Constantinople, the chief eunuch had been the main plotter of the coup that overthrew the grand vizier, Kavanoz's father-in-law Huseyin. The Bornu aris- tocracy, like the Ottomans, reproduced itself by serial concubinage with slaves. Thus young Gannibal immediately grasped the dynastic principle of the harem.[29] Back in Logone, his father had up to thirty concubines, according to Rotkirkh, who attributed the boy's enslave- ment to the plotting of rival 'wives'. Other details of the Rotkirkh myth came into play. For instance, the eunuch led Gannibal through an intricate maze of luxurious apartments, hammams, corridors, staircases and secret doors to a barber who plaited his hair into dread-locks 'as a reminder that he would always be a slave of the sultan, like Joseph who was the page of the Egyptian pharaoh'.

There were several other African boys among the pages of the harem. Nobody paid Gannibal much attention. He was just the latest arrival, a new face. Soon lessons began. The eunuch ordered a crash course in Turkish for the two princes of Logone. At night Gannibal studied Arabic and Persian, the languages of religion and litera-ture, or listened to readings from the *Arabian Nights* and the Koran. The most important figure in the harem – after the sultan and the chief black eunuch, that is – was the sultan's mother, or *valide sultan*, who was called Rabia Gulnus Ummetullah. Her job was to referee disputes between the sultan's favourites and to organise his love life. In the seventeenth century, however, a series of *valides* had actually wrested political power from the monarchy. (The so-called Sultanate of Women, between 1566 and 1656, is yet another indicator of Ottoman readiness to delegate imperial management to outsiders.)[30] One of the main problems facing these queen mothers was the human wastage inherent in a reproduction factory. Concubinage gave the sultan abundant male heirs, but that very abundance was often a threat. Each time a sultan died there were a dozen claimants to the throne. Hence a law passed by Mehmed II against fratricide, which operated for over a century until, in 1597, at the accession of Mehmed III, nineteen of the new sultan's infant brothers were strangled with a silk scarf. The outcry led to a new policy of imprisoning princes within the harem's 'cages' – effectively, a kind of living death, however comfortable.

Shortly after Gannibal's arrival at the Topkapi Palace, the *valide sultan* assigned him as a page to Mustafa's younger brother Ahmed, who lived in one of the cages. For the most part, Gannibal's tasks were menial. He waited on the prisoner day and night, plumped his cushions, swept his Persian carpets, straightened his Bursa quilts, fed his parrot and polished his silver candelabra. Other chores included shaving Ahmed, clipping his toenails, and accompanying the poor soul on melancholy walks around the fountains in his jasmine-scented garden.

One morning, however, Gannibal awoke to the sound of cannon on Tophana hill. The gunfire signalled the departure of the sultan. Mustafa was decamping from the Bosphorus and heading west to the old Ottoman capital of Edirne, or Adrianople, on what is now the Turkish border with Greece. The *seraglio* was in uproar. The sultan's entourage – not only his eunuchs and concubines, but also his soldiers, sheikhs and secretaries, mutes, jesters and dwarfs, to say nothing of his pet animals – was on the move. A seventeenth-century English ambassador marvelled at such pomp and ceremony. 'One may guess at the greatness of this Empire,' he wrote, 'by the Retinue and number of servants which accompany Persons of Quality in their journeys.'[31] Surrounded by forests, with its sleepy pavilions and kiosks on the banks of the river Maritza, the palace at Edirne offered Mustafa, a keen huntsman, some respite from the pressures of Constantinople. It was a favourite haunt. Suleyman the Magnificent spent winters in the old capital, according to a Flemish diplomat, because 'he has there his *seraglio* which opens upon a chase and he goes hunting almost every day'.[32] In Mustafa's case, however, the exodus was more of a retreat. Though he had begun his reign with bold plans to rid the government of corruption, and to emulate Suleyman by riding into battle with the infidel at the head of his army, the years of plotting inside and outside the Topkapi Palace had eventually taken their toll. Disenchantment had led to aloofness.

Gannibal witnessed Mustafa's last hurrah. It followed a crushing defeat on the battlefield. Troops led by Prince Eugene of Savoy routed the Ottoman army outside Belgrade. The sultan had no choice but to sue for peace, which Alexander Mavrocordato signed at Carlowitz in 1699. Under the terms of the treaty, each side would keep the territory it already held, but Mustafa would have to abandon the dream of conquering Vienna. It was a setback and a turning point in Ottoman history, the beginning of a century of defeats that continued until

Napoleon's invasion of Egypt in 1798.[33] However, Tsar Peter was outraged by the settlement. He felt the Austrians had welched on a deal to banish the Turks from the Black Sea once and for all. 'I've been left with empty pockets,' he complained. 'They take no more notice of me than they do of a dog.'

To the tsar's further dismay, Tolstoy learned that Mustafa was now planning to switch his attack to the Black Sea. Kavanoz handed the Russian ambassador documents outlining the sultan's power play. Mustafa's coup, the so-called 'Edirne Event', aimed to re-concentrate power in his own hands by linking support for the Crimean Tatars to the ousting of the Koprulus from Constantinople.[34] Peter ordered Tolstoy to sabotage the reform – and the plan went like clockwork. Raguzinsky leaked the information to his Balkan contacts at the Porte. On 17 July 1703, 600 Janissaries overturned their cauldrons of pilav in anger at the news and marched to the parade ground in the heart of Istanbul, where they planted their regimental banners, a symbolic act of revolt. 'The folly and madness of the Sultan have put the world in danger,' cried the aga of the Janissaries.

The sound of Janissary pilav hitting the wall, rather like the blanks fired by the battleship *Aurora* in Petrograd in 1917, was a signal for mutiny. The *ulema* backed the insurrection, as did other slave soldiers wanting more pay. Such uprisings were old hat: older than the Ottoman empire itself. In 1250, under the Ayyubid sultanate, Mamluk generals had seized power in Egypt and Syria, where they had ended up ruling for three hundred years. The dynasty originated in a corps of child slaves (or *mamluks*) like Gannibal. This particular Janissary revolt, however, lasted only six weeks, though it nearly degenerated into civil war. It is hard to know how much Gannibal saw of the unrest, most of which took place outside Constantinople: it was the *Edirne* event after all. However, Byron's report of the wreckage from a Janissary uprising in 1807 gives some idea of the mayhem Gannibal would have witnessed a hundred years earlier. On 29 November 1813, the poet wrote to his wife-to-be Annabella Milbanke:

I never saw a Revolution transacting – or at least completed – but I arrived just after the last Turkish one – and the effects were visible – and had all the grandeur of desolation in their aspect – Streets in ashes – immense barracks (of a very fine construction) in ruins – and above all Sultan Selim's favourite gardens round them in all the wild/ ness of luxuriant neglect – his fountains waterless – and his kiosks defaced but still glittering in their decay.[35]

Mustafa sent an envoy to Constantinople hoping to broker a deal, but the Janissaries wouldn't negotiate. Tolstoy followed the sultan to Edirne. Kavanoz joined the rebel muster at the parade ground. Mavro/ cordato took refuge in the French embassy. Raguzinsky vanished into thin air.

On 9 August, some 50,000 disgruntled soldiers began the march to Edirne. Istanbul was in carnival mood. The streets filled with cheering crowds as the long column set off for the Marmara coast. When the sultan heard of the rebel movement, he sent the grand vizier, Rahmi Mehmed, with an army to block its progress on the road from Asia Minor to the Balkans. On 20 August, the two sides came face to face on a plain midway between Istanbul and Edirne. For several days, however, the rebels and the loyalists had been holding 'secret talks', according to one source.[36] An eyewitness, Dmitry Cantemir, who was living in Turkey as a hostage for the good behaviour of his father, the Prince of Moldavia, reports that the Janissaries' mufti pleaded with the sultan's men to lay down their arms. 'We are brethren of the same religion, the same blood, and subjects of the same throne,' argued Nakyb Effendi.[37] Soon the cry went up on both sides: 'Give us Sultan Ahmed!' – and Mustafa's army joined the rebel cause. On his arrival at Edirne, Tolstoy heard news of the rebellion from Kavanoz himself.[38]

Sultan Ahmed! The rebels' choice was still languishing in the cage. His nomination came as a shock to Mustafa and the ruling cabal. The grand vizier fled the battlefield, and was never seen again. His other ministers advised the sultan to kill Ahmed and thereby remove the challenge. Yet Mustafa's spirit was already broken. He couldn't steel himself to give the order of execution. The dissidents urged the *valide sultan* to support the replacement of one son by another. Secure in her own position as queen mother, she replied: 'All of you have requested in concord and unanimity that my majestic son Sultan Ahmed be seated on the imperial throne, and that my other son Sultan Mustafa be deposed. Your petition has been complied with.'[39] On 22 August, Mustafa went to the cage and embraced Ahmed, whom he also saluted as the new sultan. 'My brother, it is you they want for their Padishah,' Mustafa told his sibling.[40] Did Gannibal overhear that exchange? Did the young African page follow his master into the sultan's quarters? Or did he stay behind to welcome Mustafa as the new occupant of the gilded cage? Cantemir, a frequent visitor to the Topkapi Seray, records the brothers' last exchange, a stark warning from the ousted monarch:

> Remember that you justly indeed ascend this throne, as having been possessed by your father and brother; but think that the instruments of your advancement are treacherous rebels, whom, if you suffer to escape with impunity, they will quickly treat you as they do me at present.[41]

The leader of the 'treacherous rebels', Kavanoz had no time to savour revenge. His own advancement was rapid. The next day Ahmed bowed to the soldiers' demands and made the Beehive his grand vizir, much to the satisfaction of the Koprulus and of a certain Russian gentleman drinking coffee in the port.

# 7

# Escape from the Seraglio

How art thou fall'n Imperial City, Low!
—Lady Mary Wortley Montagu, *Constantinople*

The rise of Kavanoz was a godsend for Pyotr Tolstoy. Until the fall of Mustafa, the Russian ambassador had struggled to develop a network of informers at the Topkapi Palace. Naturally suspicious of all foreign diplomats, the Ottoman elite harboured special doubts about the envoy of Peter the Great. In particular, the viziers feared that the Greek-speaking population – many of them Slav in race and all of them Orthodox in religion – would begin to see Russia as a potential liberator. So Tolstoy's presence was often unwelcome at the Porte, as he explained in a letter to the tsar:

> My residence is not pleasant to them because their domestic enemies, the Greeks, are our co-religionists. The Turks are of the opinion that, by living among them, I shall excite the Greeks to rise against the Muhammadans, and therefore the Greeks have been forbidden to have intercourse with me.[1]

The aga of the Janissaries posted a medley of spies outside Tolstoy's door. They watched his every movement, the ambassador complained to Golovin. In fact, the Turks were right to suspect his motives. As they feared, Tolstoy was using the organisation of the Orthodox church to recruit agents such as the Patriarch Dositheus and the Dutch resident, Count Jacob Colyer.[2] Nor was Kavanoz the only

bureaucrat accepting his bribes. The French ambassador considered Mavrocordato sympathetic to Russian ambitions to 'resurrect
the former Greek empire', and ready to serve Moscow 'even to the
detriment of the Porte'.[3] A favourite meeting place for Tolstoy and the
Grand Dragoman was Saint George's in the Greek Phanar district
since the Janissary guards refused to enter a church.

It was a hot peace and a cold war, in which truth was often a
casualty: a victim of propaganda. So, for example, the impious Peter
cast himself as a theocrat, the Orthodox defender of the Christian
faith. The Turks saw him only as a warmonger. Justifying Tolstoy's
imprisonment in 1710, the grand vizier told the English ambassador
that Peter 'promised himself to be one day master of Constantinople
and hoped to be buried in the Church of Sancta Sophia'.[4]

All this cast a long shadow in Russia because the re-conquest of
Byzantium was an old dream, even if that New Rome – known to
the Russians as Tsargrad, or 'city of Caesar' – had been superseded.
When Constantinople fell to the Turks in 1453, the Russian church
proclaimed Moscow the 'Third Rome'. To underline the succession,
Ivan the Great married Zoë Palaeologus, niece of the last Byzantine
emperor, at the Kremlin in 1472. His grandson, Ivan the Terrible,
became the first tsar in 1547 at a coronation ceremony based on its
Byzantine precursor. 'For two Romes have fallen, the third stands,
and there shall be no fourth,' wrote the monk Filofey of Pskov. It
was a prediction that stood until the founding of Saint Petersburg.
In 1721, Gannibal's adoptive father conjured up a new link with
ancient Rome – much as his real father, Bruha of Lagone, had done
– by assuming the title 'Imperator' and by casting his own image on
a rouble coin under the legend 'the new Tsar Constantine for the new
city of Constantinople'. And the double-headed eagle of Byzantium
dominated the tsar's coat of arms.[5]

Tolstoy greeted the Beehive's vizirat with high hopes. Having
a spy inside the *divan* would help Russia press its advantage in the
Black Sea. The first signs were encouraging, too. Kavanoz had no
qualms about taking bribes while in office. He continued to accept

1. The ruins of the village of Logo in the no-go zone between Ethiopia and Eritrea, Gannibal's legendary birthplace, now a heap of rubble in the aftermath of war.

2. The present sultan of Logone-Birni, Muhammad Bahar Maruf, wearing his royal turban and robe. Might he be a distant nephew of Gannibal?

*3. An aerial view of Logone-Birni, south of Lake Chad. The word* birni *means 'fortress' in the Kotoko language. A childhood memory of its geometric pattern may have inspired Gannibal to write* Geometry and Fortification.

*4. The incomparable skyline of Istanbul at the turn of the eighteenth century, with its minarets and pleasure domes, the Seraglio overlooking the Golden Horn. As a seven-year-old Gannibal would have seen it from the deck of a slave ship.*

*5. A glimpse of 'Peter's Paradise', the invented city of St Petersburg: its Italianate architecture and stuccoed façades provided a backdrop to Gannibal's life in Russia. Here, on the south bank of the Neva, is the first Winter Palace, which Peter the Great built in 1718.*

6. *Inside the Kremlin: the cathedral square in Moscow at the time of the Empress Elizabeth's coronation in 1742, and the scene of Gannibal's first meeting with her father, Peter the Great, four decades earlier.*

PETRUS ALEXEWITZ
*Czaret Magnus Dux Moscovia*

7. *The warrior-king: a western view of Peter the Great, the fresh-faced tsar painted in armour by Sir Godfrey Kneller in 1698, during his Grand Embassy to London where he took a job as a ship's carpenter at the Royal Navy's dockyard.*

*8. The tsar's henchmen: Count Pyotr Tolstoy, who rescued the young Gannibal from slavery in Istanbul and later became his friend ...*

*9. ... and Prince Alexander Menshikov, a 'smiling villain' who resented the African's influence over the tsar and banished him to Siberia during the reign of Peter II.*

10. 'Peter the Great has come back to us in the form of his daughter,' wrote a contemporary of Elizabeth, but the empress, who felt a sisterly affection towards Gannibal, did not inherit her father's appetite for hard work. With her ample figure, blonde hair and 'almost English' face, she seemed exotic to the Russians. So did her lifestyle of Frenchified luxury and vice.

11. 'Little Figchen': the young German princess Sophia of Anhalt-Zerbst before she became Catherine the Great and the subject of lurid jokes. Fear of her secret police drove Gannibal to burn his memoirs in retirement.

12. *On a visit to Regency Paris in 1717 Peter the Great meets the seven-year-old Louis XV, still wearing an infant's halter, as if to enhance the symbolism of a puppet regime. To the court's astonishment, the giant-sized Russian tsar lifted the boy into the air and kissed him several times.*

money for information. The leaks, if anything, grew more frequent. 'In fact, during his grand vizirat, [Kavanoz] pushed his cupidity to its ultimate limits, in favour of corruption and the selling of secrets,' wrote one source.[6] He and Tolstoy met clandestinely after dark at the vizier's *yali kiosk*, or seaside house, on the Asian side of the Bosphorus. After a furtive exchange of documents and money, the two men sat on the waterfront, speaking Russian and gazing at the sky until dawn. Sometimes, wearing kaftans, they drank long sentimental toasts to a new era of peace and understanding.

The Russian spymaster Golovin exulted at the outcome of the Janissary revolt. On 28 August, he wrote to the ambassador with a list of instructions for harvesting the Ottoman secrets. His letter soon bore fruit. At its first session the *divan* urged Kavanoz to rebuke Peter for building a Russian fortress at Taganrog, on the Sea of Azov. The double-dealing vizier sent an official protest to Moscow. 'The Ottoman council of his Imperial Majesty informs the Prince of Muscovy that the Sultan no longer trusts Russia's pledges of friendship, and, believing the Sea must remain immaculate, objects to certain measures it fears will rupture the peace,' he wrote. The same dispatch, however, contained unofficially, as it were, outlines of Turkish plans to construct a fortress of their own at Yenikale on the eastern end of the Crimean peninsula.[7]

Rotkirkh suggests that it was Tolstoy who now plotted the abduction of Gannibal from the *seraglio*. But Ottoman sources tell a more intriguing story. Since the fall of Mustafa the African page had seen various changes in his day-to-day life. In Ahmed's wake, for example, the *valide* would have ordered his transfer from the cage to the sultan's quarters at the very centre of the harem. Instead of his former seclusion Gannibal now had some contact with the outside world. To be precise, he entered the orbit of the grand vizier. By coincidence, Kavanoz was coming under pressure from Tolstoy to plant spies inside the harem. His response was to order the aga of the Janissaries to double the number of slaves hovering round the sultan. One day, as Kavanoz sat working in his richly painted rococo office, he heard an angry whisper coming from the grilled window behind his head known as the 'Eye of the Sultan'. Ahmed protested about the number of spies in the harem. 'If I go up to my bedroom, forty Privy Chamber pages are lined up,' he said. 'If I put on my trousers, I do not feel the least comfort.'[8]

Since August relations had soured between the sultan and his grand vizier. Ahmed recalled his brother Mustafa's warning about treacherous rebels and began to plot the Beehive's downfall, though he proceeded cautiously, in the knowledge that Kavanoz would always be ready with secret intrigues to maintain his position.[9]

On the night of 17 November 1703 the axe fell – or perhaps it was a case of long knives. The first to go was the aga of Janissaries. Having been summoned to the Audience Hall on an innocent pretext – an award ceremony perhaps, or the issue of new credentials – the police chief mysteriously disappeared. According to palace rumour, he was thrown into the sea.[10] The sacking of Kavanoz was less brutal yet just as unexpected. The sultan denounced his corrupt ways and misman-agement of Ottoman affairs, and replaced him with his Greek son-in-law, Damad Hasan Pasha, known as 'the dauntless vizier'. The Beehive died in exile in Lepanto.

The ousting of his prized agent dealt Tolstoy a severe blow. He was crestfallen. Not only had his plans come to nothing, but the unknown Damad was a daunting prospect. 'The new vizier is very ill-disposed to me,' he wrote to Golovin in December, 'and my wretched situation, my troubles and fears are worse than before. Again, nobody dares come to me, and I can go nowhere. It is with great trouble that I can send you this letter.' In a glum postscript, Tolstoy added that the downfall of the Beehive meant he no longer had contact with the several 'talented African Negroes' spying in the harem.[11]

The phrase evidently struck a chord in Moscow. It recurs in a letter Peter the Great sent to Constantinople, according to Rotkirkh, who takes up the story:

The tsar came up with the idea of writing to his ambassador in Constantinople to request him to obtain for him and to send him the talented African Negroes. His minister followed his orders with the utmost fidelity: he got acquainted with the supervisor of the *seraglio*, where the sultan's pages were being reared and educated, and then through the intermediation of the grand vizier obtained, in a secret and dangerous manner, three lads.[12]

As usual, Rotkirkh's version of events is far from reliable. His tendency to mythologise the life of his father-in-law obscures vital facts. For instance, Tolstoy professed ignorance of the scheme to rescue Gannibal and his brother until they were actually in the hands of Raguzinsky. 'Mr Savva Vladislavich has told me that you commissioned him to buy the two Negroes. He bought them as you ordered,' the ambassador wrote to Golovin on 22 July 1704, before sketching their onward journey to Moscow.[13] Certainly the involvement of Raguzinsky is more likely, not least because Tolstoy's movements were so restricted under the new vizirat. In retelling the legend the snobbish Pushkins, it seems, merely repositioned Gannibal a few rungs higher up the social ladder: not just an African but an *Abyssinian*, not just an Abyssinian but a *prince*, and saved from perdition by the Russian ambassador, not just his Balkan sidekick.

Gannibal had no such qualms. In his only surviving reference to the Turkish episode, a throwaway sentence in the 1742 nobility petition to the Empress Elizabeth, he nominates Raguzinsky as his deliverer. It's a bald statement of fact, though Gannibal gets the year wrong:

In the year 706 [*sic*] I left Tsargrad for Russia in the suite of Savva Vladislavich of my own accord at a young age and was brought to Moscow to the house of the Tsar Peter the Great of blissful and eternal memory.[14]

It wasn't quite as simple as that. Let's begin with the riddle of his 'abduction'. Was the young slave *bought* or *brought* out of the *seraglio*?

Tolstoy is clear in his letter to Moscow that Raguzinsky was 'commis-sioned to buy' the African children. Both he and the Ragusan go out of their way to stress that the children were obtained by means of a legitimate transaction. Do they protest too much? Gannibal's son Pyotr wrote in the fragmentary memoir he showed Pushkin that his father had been 'stolen from the court of Constantinople'.[15] The poet writes in his note to *Eugene Onegin* that 'the Russian ambassador somehow rescued him' — and then we have Rotkirkh's tantalising reference to a 'secret and dangerous manner' of escape. Finally, it is difficult to know what to make of Gannibal's phrase 'of my own accord', unless his assertion of free will is meant to imply that *he* found Raguzinsky, not the other way round. In a letter of 1707, the French ambassador reveals that he often had to deal with fugitive slaves seeking asylum in his embassy. Sometimes they were smuggled onto ships in the port and then away to freedom.[16]

The dispute about Gannibal's escape will never be settled. Legend now obscures the truth. 'Pushkin's great-grandfather was an Ethiopian, bought in Constantinople by the Russian ambas-sador,' writes a leading historian of Ottoman Turkey.[17] Was it just a straightforward purchase? The question should only matter to us because it mattered to Pushkin. Gossip tormented the poet, and in the end scandal killed him. During the last decade of his life he was put out by a rumour that his great-grandfather's origins were somewhat humbler than his family made out. The rumour originates with Georg von Helbig, who was the Saxon ambassador in Peters-burg from 1787 to 1795. On his return to Germany, Helbig wrote a book entitled *Russische Güntslinge*, or *Russian Favourites*, in which he noted that 'Abraham Petrovich Gannibal was a Moor, whom Peter I brought to Russia as a ship's cabin boy'.[18] This version of the story was taken up, in 1830, by Pushkin's enemy Faddey Bulgarin, a minor writer and police spy, who gave it a malicious new twist. He claimed that the ship's captain had 'bought the Negro for a bottle of rum'.[19]

No such colourful description occurs in the letters of Raguz-insky and Tolstoy. Yet a note of skulduggery persists: a touch of the cloak and dagger, even a nagging sense of guilt. Take the Ragusan's first mention of the affair. On 29 June 1704, he scribbles a quick dispatch to Nicolae Milescu, a Moldavian working at the Russian foreign ministry in Moscow. It is only a filler, perhaps no more than a bulletin. 'The ambassador will write to you in detail about my activities,' Raguzinsky says. However, the fate of Gannibal and his brother is obviously preying on his mind, because he adds that he will be sending 'something extra' with his next delivery of cotton and secret messages:

> With it there will also be two Negro boys as promised, and I hope that soon I'll be able to dispatch them into the Multyansky province [i.e. Moldavia], and that they will arrive safely, and I trust they will be acceptable to His Excellency [i.e. Golovin]. Believe me, my friend, it was a very difficult business to get hold of them, and to smuggle them out of Turkey. As I have told His Excellency, only God and a pure heart made it possible for me.[20]

A 'pure heart' is an intriguing phrase. What is Raguzinsky trying to say? And why is he writing to Milescu instead of directly to Golovin?

A veteran of Ottoman *realpolitik*, Milescu was aged sixty-eight in 1704. He had a brilliant career behind him as a writer of great verve and a diplomat, not only in Constantinople, where his friends included the Patriarch Dositheus, but also in the old Moldavian capital of Jassy. In 1668, hoping to be appointed *hospodar* (or ruler) of Moldavia, he intrigued against Prince Ilias Alexandru, who punished him by cutting off his nose. In disgrace, Milescu went into exile in Moscow, where he became translator to the foreign ministry under the pseudonym Nikolai Gavrilovich Spafary, and then ambassador to Peking. Though he never returned to Moldavia, he maintained a secret network of agents across the region, as Raguzinsky knew from his regular jaunts to Moscow and back.

The purpose of Raguzinsky's letter was to seek help in smuggling

Gannibal and his brother, as well as a third black slave, through Moldavia. The principality was in a state of unrest that summer due to a boyar uprising against Prince Dukas. Sultan Ahmed dispatched an army to restore order and to patrol the main routes north to Kiev and west to Belgrade. He also installed as *hospodar* a son-in-law of Constantin Cantemir. No doubt Raguzinsky feared an Ottoman ambush, and so he appealed to Milescu for safe transit through the country.

But what had Raguzinsky done that weighed so heavily on his conscience? How do we explain the 'pure heart'? These are unanswered, perhaps unanswerable questions. Except that Cantemir's son Dmitry, the eyewitness at Edirne, whom we met in the last chapter, lets slip a delicious morsel in his *History of the Growth and Decay of the Othman Empire* (1716). Cantemir writes that soon after the fall of Kavanoz, the Porte began to clamp down on Russian agents plying the Black Sea. He adds that the admiral of the Ottoman fleet, Abaza Othman Pasha,

> condemned as a spy to the gallies a *Raguzæan* merchant, who after having turned bankrupt, had engaged in the service of the Emperor of Russia, and was hiring some Grecian sailors, whom he intended to conduct to Azov.[21]

Cantemir does not mention Raguzinsky by name, though 'Raguzæan' is close enough. Two other scraps of evidence, however, make it clear that Gannibal's 'young comrade' was the condemned spy. The first is a description by Cantemir of the fearsome tanners of Istanbul, one of the city's oldest and most powerful trade guilds, who settled after the Ottoman conquest at Yedi Kule, also known as the Seven Towers. It was a noisy, low-class suburb, with a famous stench: a quarantine station where travellers along the plague routes had to stay for a week before they were allowed into the main city. Thieves and murderers – to which roll of honour Cantemir adds 'and Illyrian spies' – escaping from the law were seldom pursued into the tanners' quarter.

Indeed, such a pursuit was hardly necessary since the tanners, while harbouring the fugitives, also made them collect dog dung, which was a vital component of the tanning process. It was an ordeal that only Raguzinsky's 'pure heart' — or Milescu's lack of a nose — could endure.

The Ragusan doesn't cast any light on the journey to the under-world. In his official report to Moscow he leaves out — or perhaps leaves to Tolstoy — the smelly details. Nevertheless the other scrap of evidence is his letter to Fyodor Golovin of 21 July 1704, from Constantinople, which does hint at the anguished mission, and at the help he received from Prince Dmitry Cantemir. By this time Gannibal and the other children were already out of the *seraglio*. Raguzinsky ought to have been flushed with success. Yet he seems troubled by something as he plots the next move:

> The present letter will be handed to you by my servant Andrei Geor-giyev, whom I will send with three young Negroes. Two of them are intended for Your Excellency, and the third for your ambassador. It cost me a lot of hardship to buy them and trouble to send them, which I did thanks to the son of Constantin Cantacuzene [alias Cantemir], to whom I explained that they were intended for you. I pray to God that they arrive safe and sound. I hope they will please you because they are very black and beautiful. They are not Turks, they are not circumcised. Your Excellency can keep whichever ones he pleases and leave the third for the ambassador, because he has already paid me money for them.[22]

The date of the letter is somewhat mysterious, because Milescu also writes to Golovin to say that Raguzinsky left Constantinople on 21 June, on a ship heading across the Black Sea to Azov, with cotton and secret documents as well as the live presents for the tsar. So it would be impossible for the Ragusan still to be in Constantinople a month later. Once again, someone must be making a mistake, or forgetting something, or mixing things up.

The answer to the puzzle comes in a letter Tolstoy sends Golovin the day after Raguzinsky's second dispatch. Here the ambassador explains to the foreign minister that Raguzinsky's servant Andrei Georgiyev will escort the slaves, while his master will stay behind. So Gannibal left Tsargrad 'in the suite of Savva Vladislavich' only in that technical sense. Tolstoy also sets out the complicated details of Gannibal's itinerary: the overland route to Edirne and then Jassy via Bucharest, not the sea passage from the Golden Horn to Azov. Eight years after the naval victory at Azov, it seems the Russian fleet was still fearful of pirate raids by the Crimean Tatars:

> I have authorised Savva's servant to leave with them, by land through Wallachia. I have given them passports and made arrangements for carriages to take them from Kiev to Moscow. I have written to the nobles of Wallachia and Moldavia, and to the prince of Wallachia, so that they will make sure their passage is safe as far as Kiev. And I hope that with the Grace of God, they will arrive at yours, my dear sir, safe and sound.[23]

The caravan departed Istanbul in the summer of 1704 at the start of a dangerous journey out of Asia into Europe that lasted almost three months. The first stage retraced the march of the Janissary rebels the previous year. The carriages followed the Marmara's northern shore, to the plain where the two armies had met face to face, skirting Edirne, and then north over the Balkan mountains into Bulgaria, towards Bucharest and Jassy. Progress was slow and hazardous: it was enemy country, after all. But at each stage Georgiyev sent news via Milescu to Golovin, who was absent from Moscow, commanding the troops at Narva in Estonia.

No record survives of Gannibal's impressions of the journey into another country, another life. Perhaps he recalled the experience in the memoirs he later destroyed. Fortunately, other sources help us to re-create the scene. Raguzinsky, for example, had undertaken the same trek in 1702 and 1703, and would do so again the following year. In the old Balkan citadels of Bucharest and Jassy, Gannibal entered a new world at the intersection of three cultures (Catholic, Orthodox and Muslim) and three empires (Habsburg, Russian and Ottoman). In the eighteenth century too, more so perhaps than Constantinople or even Mount Athos, the two cities were important centres of Greek culture now enjoying a renaissance under the rule of Cantemirs. Milescu had prepared the way. In each town the convoy was met by a welcoming committee of Russian-speaking Orthodox. The unusual sight of three black slaves gave the retinue something of the attraction of a travelling circus. The caravan moved slowly, and stopped often; there were unseen delays and accidents and wrangles. On one occasion, according to Milescu, local warlords briefly held the travellers hostage outside Jassy, where progress was halted for three weeks.

That Jassy might be another Capua, the city whose pleasures had diverted Hannibal from Rome 2,000 years earlier, may be the whimsy of its proud native, Milescu. The Russian literary historian Natalya Teletova suggests that Gannibal was christened at the Church of the Three Hierarchs in Jassy on 9 October, the feast day of Saint Abraham.[24] Standing in front of the icons, with sunlight from the tall windows illuminating the gilded walls and frescoes, as if beamed through the eye of God, Gannibal took the name commonly given to black slaves in eighteenth-century Russia. The sojourn in Jassy had its tragic consequences, however. A local report says that the Romanian climate was so harsh and unfamiliar to the exotic travellers that one of the slaves sickened and died from pneumonia or, somewhat implausibly, malaria.

Here, once again, Rotkirkh fails to dispel the confusion. He claims that Tolstoy also sent to Russia the 'other black boy – a compatriot of Gannibal's of noble birth – who, however, died of smallpox on the way, and a Ragusan of nearly the same age, i.e. under 10. The tsar deplored the loss of one of the boys, but was delighted that the other two had arrived safely.' This mention of an infant Ragusan is clearly a garbled reference to Raguzinsky, who was in fact thirty-seven years old at the time – and wasn't even there. It is a confusion that may be explained by a footnote to the escape from the seraglio. Three months later, the Ragusan made a similar journey with his 13-year-old nephew, Yefim Ivanovich, crossing the Black Sea to Azov, and then heading overland to Moscow.[25]

On reaching the Danube basin and moving into the foothills, the caravan turned east towards Kiev, running the gauntlet of Muscovite robbers. In 1699, the Austrian ambassador Johann Korb expressed astonishment at the dangers of the Russian road. Brigands operated in packs. There were mysterious, unsolved murders. A foreign sea captain dining with his wife at a boyar's house was invited for a sleigh ride in the snow. When he returned he found that his wife's head had been cut off, and there were no clues as to the identity or motive of her assassin.[26]

The end was now in sight. On 15 November 1704, Milescu wrote to Golovin that the African slaves had arrived in Moscow two days earlier.[27] The sleighs had reached the 'Third Rome' approximately ten weeks after setting out from the second. Gannibal surveyed his new home from Sparrow Hills overlooking the palaces and golden cupolas which sparkled in the pale winter sun.

The tsar was absent from the Kremlin when the convoy arrived, so Gannibal spent his first weeks in Holy Moscow at Golovin's house in the 'German suburb' of Preobrazhenskoye, on the banks of the Yauza river. It was as if the struggles of Tolstoy and Raguzinsky had all been in vain. Turkey was now old news. Having shored up Russia's southern defences on the Black Sea, Peter embarked on a new military adventure in the north. 'On 18 August we celebrated peace with the Turks, with a splendid firework display, on the 19th we declared war against the Swedes,' he boasted.[28] The breezy tone was a mistake. The Great Northern War would last, on and off, for twenty-one years. It was to be Gannibal's apprenticeship.

# 8

# Old Muscovy

this *giant*-genius sent;
Divinely siz'd – to suit his crown's extent!
—Aaron Hill, *The Northern Star*

Peter the Great is a giant figure in Russian history. Literally. At six foot seven inches tall, he stood head and shoulders above his subjects. In the boyar imagination, too, the tsar was larger than life: a colossus bestriding the narrow world of old Muscovy. He inspired awe and wonder, but also a kind of morbid curiosity. Like Gannibal, he was a 'strange creature' in many people's eyes. 'Between you and me,' Korsakov says to Ibrahim in *The Negro of Peter the Great*, 'the tsar is a very strange man.'[1] Some of his enemies claimed that Peter was mentally unstable because he was descended from the 'blood of slaves', a reference to the obscure Tatar origins of his mother's family, the Naryshkins.[2]

The tsar's long-term absence from the Russian capital bolstered the view that Peter was a freak. 'The sovereign isn't in Moscow,' a peasant woman complained in 1700. 'The sovereign who is now in Moscow, who is he?'[3] The secret police tortured her as a punishment for speaking out. Yet she had a point. It is hardly surprising that the tsar seemed strange to the Muscovites. He *was* a stranger, always off somewhere, fighting wars against the Turks and the Swedes, or building a new city in Petersburg. The Cossacks spread a rumour that Peter was in fact a German impostor, not the real sovereign at all. But even the Germans found him strange. 'It is impossible to describe him, or even to give an idea of him, unless you have seen him,' wrote Sophia, Electress of Hanover, after meeting 'Peter Mikhailov' on his Grand Embassy in 1697.[4] Other foreigners were less reticent. 'Tsar Peter was tall and thin, but rather out of proportion,' recalled Filippo Balatri, a young Italian castrato singer who joined the royal household in 1698.[5] (The Ottoman court didn't have a monopoly on eunuchs.) Since he only stayed for three years and then waited three decades to write up the experience, his recollections are somewhat vague and moulded into clichés. Nevertheless they provide a clue to Gannibal's first encounter with the tsar by helping us to imagine how the odd mannerisms of Peter the Giant may have struck an 8-year-old African boy. 'For his great height, Peter's feet seemed very narrow,' the Italian wrote. 'His head was sometimes tugged to the right by convulsions.' The artist Valentin Serov summarised Peter's appearance in grotesque detail: 'He was frightful: long, on weak, spindly little legs and with a head so small in relation to the rest of his body that he must have looked more like a sort of dummy with a badly-stuck-on head than a live person. He suffered from a constant tic and he was always making faces: winking, screwing up his mouth, twitching his nose, wagging his chin.'[6]

Abram Gannibal first saw Peter on Christmas Day in 1704. The tsar had been absent from Moscow since the height of summer, since before a victory over the Swedes at Narva, in fact. The victory had given Russia a psychological as well as strategic boost. It wiped clean the memory of abject defeat on the same site four years earlier. Now Peter returned to Moscow on 19 December with even more good news. His army had decisively repelled a Swedish attack on the one-year-old city of Saint Petersburg. It was a time of renewed confidence and victory parades. On his return to Moscow the tsar passed under seven triumphal arches. Fifty-four enemy battle flags and nearly 200 captured Swedish officers followed in his wake. Golovin took advantage of the sovereign's ebullient mood. He informed Peter that the black slaves had arrived from Constantinople and, on receiving the tsar's impatient summons, wrapped them in fur coats and packed them off to the Kremlin without delay.

The Russian winter came as a shock to Gannibal. So it has to countless visitors, from Rurik to Napoleon. In chapter ten of *Onegin*, Pushkin recalls 'the threat of 1812', and asks, 'Who helped us then? Winter or the Russian God?'[7] The two were really the same thing. Never before had Gannibal experienced sub-zero temperatures. So biting was the cold, so 'romantic' the weather, it chilled him to the marrow.[8] Yet the frozen landscape was a source of magic, too. Snow and ice and hurtling clouds formed an uncanny backdrop. Crossing the Moskva river by sledge, the young African saw white-stoned cathedrals, with blue and gold onion domes, rising over the Kremlin's red-brick walls. Did he wonder perhaps as he swept into Red Square, past the turbaned fantasy of Saint Basil's cathedral, whether he had been transported back into a scene from the *Arabian Nights*? Such a thought has occurred to other interlopers, and even to the Russians themselves. 'If there were only minarets instead of churches,' wrote the critic Vissarion Belinsky, 'you might think you were in one of those wild Oriental cities that Scheherazade told stories about.'[9] The Muscovite story of Christmas 'holy nights' was different from the *Thousand and One* variety, but its entertainments culminating in Twelfth Night had a wildness of their own.

Between the feasts of Nativity and Epiphany – which were real feasts, served up with vodka and caviar, after the long weeks of pre-Christmas fasting – Red Square played host to a kind of saturnalia. 'Christmas time has come, O what joy!' writes Pushkin in *Onegin*. He goes on to describe his Moscow-bound heroine's delight in old Slavic rituals of fortune-telling and magic:

Tatiana, being Russian in her soul,
Loved the Russian winter,
With its cold beauty ...
[And] trusted the legends
Of the peasant olden days,
Dreams and tarot cards,
And predictions of the moon.[10]

By the time Gannibal arrived in Red Square, the crowd was immense. Hundreds of people in garish costumes followed a parade of mummers, shamans and icon-toting priests. Jugglers rubbed shoulders with fire-eaters. The smell of pancakes hung in the frigid air. Even the pie-sellers wore fancy dress. The centrepiece of the festivities was the moment at midnight when a woman dressed in white entered the square on a sleigh pulled by twelve caparisoned horses. The peasants bowed or prostrated themselves in front of this snow queen, whom they worshipped alternately as the Virgin Mary and Kolyada, goddess of the Sun. Here was proof of a contradiction. Holy Russia inherited sacred rites from Byzantium. Its 'holy nights' also grew out of a deeper past, one that blended magic and religion. Yule was a hybrid, like the Virgin Kolyada herself, dating back to the heathen celebration of the winter solstice. Pagan gods had simply evolved into Christian saints. Demons had assumed Satan's likeness. The dread of folklore had given way to the light of the gospel, but only up to a point, and only recently, because Russia's clergy shared that dread. The idea of magic survived in the hocus pocus of the mass. Indeed, for an outsider like Gannibal it was hard to know the difference between the ululating of priests and the shaman's chants. Both shared a primitive belief in the power of rhythmic language. The use of icons was a kind of voodoo, like a witchdoctor's spell, a superstitious reaching after the spirit world that would have reminded the young African of Kotoko ceremonies on the banks of the river Logone.

Nowhere was Moscow's 'incomprehensible blend of superstition and magnificence, ignorance and enlightenment' felt more keenly, according to the poet Konstantin Batyushkov, than inside the Kremlin.[11] Prince Yury Dolgoruky of Suzdal, the city's twelfth-century founder, used the word 'kreml', meaning 'fortress', to describe the stronghold he built out of logs and earth on a hill above the Moskva river. At the time Kiev was the capital of Christian Rus (the old name for Russia), but when it was sacked, in 1240, by a Mongol army under Batu, grandson of Genghis Khan, the hegemony shifted to Moscow.

Soon afterwards the head of the Russian Orthodox church transferred his seat from Vladimir to Moscow, and the growth of the Kremlin came to symbolise the Muscovite ascendancy in religion as well as politics. Ivan the Great hired Italian architects to build sixty-foot-high, sixteen-foot-thick walls, a vast expanse of red-brick crenellations, towers, bastions and fortified escarpments stretching a mile and a half. Within the embrace of these battlements, however, lay an oasis of cathedrals. Half-fortress, half-sanctuary, the Kremlin was another hybrid, a servant of two masters — one temporal, the other spiritual — whose rivalry was evident in the Christmas carols Gannibal heard as he passed through the gateway.

Yuletide bells were ringing inside the Kremlin. A deafening wave of sound passed over Gannibal as the sledge came to a halt in the cathedral square. 'The white-blanketed earth shook with vibrations like thunder', is how one awed visitor described the cacophony.[12] A palace guard led Gannibal through a huddle of black-robed priests to a small wooden building next to the Annunciation cathedral. 'The Moor, the Moor, the tsar's Moor,' he barked to a red-nosed servant guarding the door. Tallow candles were burning dimly inside the hut, which was bare except for a noisily whirring lathe. Out of the darkness stepped a Brobdingnagian figure dressed in a workman's leather overall and holding a chisel in his left hand. The other hand gripped a huge mallet, which he swung over his head, freezing momentarily as he took aim under the gaze of half-amused, half-fearful boyars. It was a pose caught famously in 1723 by the architect and sculptor Carlo Rastrelli in bronze: Peter as Pygmalion carving out a new Russia in the shape of Galatea. Here, in Pushkin's words, is the avatar of kingship, as he appeared to Gannibal:

> Surrounded by favourites,
> Out steps Peter. His eyes
> Shine. His face terrifies.
> Moving fast, he's splendid,
> Utterly, like the wrath of God.[13]

Much can be guessed from this almost allegorical scene. The Danish ambassador Juel once caught Peter working furiously at his lathe 'as though he had to earn a living from this particular form of labour'.[14] The palace flunkey Oleg Belyayev gives a fond description of the tsar's workshop: its rough and primitive grandeur, a carpenter's gothic, the tsar's wild eyes, his unkempt hair, the faintly comic moustache.[15] Semi-divine but self-contradictory, 'Peter is an example to his subjects for he works like a simple man,' wrote the Swiss adventurer Franz Lefort.[16] Yet the face Gannibal saw on his first encounter with the tsar belonged to a younger, less terrifying man than appears in Rastrelli's bronze, even if it had already lost the adolescent dewiness captured in London seven years earlier by the English court painter Kneller. His open expression contradicted the harsh autocratic demeanour Peter sported in middle age, and is unrecognisable in the pasty, drink-ravaged face of the despot staring out of a deathbed portrait. Cheeks have yet to become jowls, or the nose bulbous. His voice is still free of a wheezing rasp as he turns from the lathe and, seeing Gannibal, calls out over the hum of the flywheels: '*Arap!*'

So they meet at last: Peter the Great and his Negro. For Pushkin, the two were indissolubly linked. It was a double-act, like Crusoe and Friday. 'Their story is one of the literal epics of Russia, a journey in the dark labyrinth of a time,' wrote the Soviet critic I. L. Feynberg.[17] Ironically, that epic journey began in 1705 with the fellow travellers moving in opposite directions: in the Kremlin, the founder of Peters-burg seemed like a visitor from Russia's European future, the sultan's former slave a hostage from its Byzantine past.

Time was a paradox in Russia. Until 1700, Russian chroniclers (using not Arabic numerals but Cyrillic letters with numerical equiv-alents) had followed the Byzantine practice of numbering years from the notional creation of the world in 5509 BC. As in Constantinople, the Muscovite New Year had always begun on 1 September, rather than the first of January. On the eve of the new century Peter ruled that official records would henceforth count from the birth of Christ, as in 'many European Christian nations'.[18] Old Believers denounced the tsar for meddling with 'God's time'. Traditionalists condemned such reforms as witchcraft. However, Gannibal's son-in-law took a different view of Peter's meddlesome nature. Rotkirkh notes that the Petrine revolution transformed the army 'from an Asiatic horde into a professional force of the kind maintained by Sweden, France or Prussia', and introduced western standards in government, archi-tecture and education, as well as the Table of Ranks, which helped Russia to emerge as a European nation. Significantly he portrays the arrival of Gannibal in Moscow as a turning point in the tsar's efforts to unlock Russian potential:

> At that time the Emperor Peter the First was introducing the arts and sciences into his realm and endeavouring to spread them among his nobility. He did succeed to some extent in this undertaking; yet considering the gross multitude of nobles in that most extensive of the world's empires, the number of people who showed inclination towards learning proved much too insignificant, a state of affairs that caused the late Emperor much grievous and vexing pain.[19]

Peter's zeal to introduce western habits met with incomprehension and fury among the doltish boyar nobles. For example, he shaved off the beards of his courtiers and forced them to smoke tobacco and wear frock coats instead of kaftans. According to Cornelius de Bruyn, who first visited Moscow in 1702, the tsar's orders were executed by men who went around the street shaving 'all manner of persons without distinction', many of whom 'would not be comforted for the loss of their beards'.[20]

Gannibal defended Peter's actions in a letter to his widow, the Empress Catherine, written shortly after the tsar's death in 1725. 'His Majesty never did anything unless it would be useful to the state, to the welfare of the people and to the glory of his reign,' he recalled, alluding to their first encounter in Moscow twenty years earlier.[21] Certainly Peter's appetite for work made a sobering impression that entered family legend. 'The tsar shut himself in his workshop and occupied himself with affairs of state,' wrote Pushkin in *The Negro of Peter the Great*. 'Ibrahim could only marvel at the quickness and strength of his intelligence, the power and flexibility of his attention, and at the variety of what he did.'[22]

Yet the atmosphere of Peter's court was anything but sober. His Majesty was not just a *work*aholic. He had other appetites that Gannibal fails to mention. Johann Korb refers to life at the Kremlin as a 'sumptuous comedy' of drunkenness and mayhem. At Christmas the tsar presided over a series of wild bacchanalia, known as the All-Mad, All-Joking, All-Drunken Assembly, whose lewd enter-tainments shocked foreign visitors. Korb recalls a mock religious ceremony at which a naked Bacchus blessed the kneeling congrega-tion with two long Dutch pipes.[23] 'A great glass of wine sanctified the occasion,' wrote the English ambassador Charles Whitworth, who also hinted at 'several other gallantrys no less diverting, but they are more proper for conversation than Letter'.[24] The Danish envoy attributed the scandalous behaviour to Peter's freakish personality and his delight in 'turning the world upside down'.[25] For example, his illiterate friend Fyodor Romodanovsky was crowned tsar amid great pomp, and may actually have ruled Russia during Peter's absence in 1697. Other drinking chums such as Ivan Buturlin and Nikita Zotov masqueraded as the king of Poland and the 'Patriarch Bacchus' in long-running burlesques of Muscovite pageantry and church ritual.

The clergy responded by denouncing Peter as the Antichrist. His entourage was a 'swarm of demons'.[26] Some neutral observers, however, gave the monarch the benefit of the doubt. Perhaps his debauchery was just a case of letting off steam. 'The Tsar among all the heavy cares of Government knows how to set apart some Days for the Relaxation of his Mind, and how ingenious he is in the Contrivance of those Diversions,' noted the Hanoverian Weber.[27] Yet the Drunken Assembly went beyond such devilish games. Its jesting had a secret agenda, or at least a coherent theme. Its ingenuity was about poking fun at religion and Peter's boyar opponents. Dressed up as the Archdeacon Peter Mikhailov, and using the obscene slang *mat*, instead of church Slavonic, the tsar gave all the mock-patriarch's servants rude nicknames based on the Russian for 'prick' (*khuy*). Bad language also featured in the punishment of the *streltsy*. 'Peter the Great was a master of *mat*,' writes the novelist Victor Erofeyev. 'While decapitating rebellious Kremlin guards, he let out an immense stream of *mat*, a legendary tapestry of seventy-four words woven together by the force of his wrath.'[28]

This foul-mouthed, vodka-swilling tyrant was 'no mean connoisseur of humankind', according to Rotkirkh.[29] Indeed, Peter's connoisseurship took the bizarre form suggested by his authorship of a 'decree on monsters': 'It is well known that in the human species, as in that of animals and birds, monsters are born, that is freaks,' the tsar wrote in 1718.[30] The object of the decree was to enlarge his collection of such 'monsters' by soliciting donations. It was the next logical step after the Drunken Assembly – transforming the court into a freak show – not for the sake of Yuletide mockery, though Peter did stage a wedding for the royal dwarf Yakim Volkov to coincide with the nuptials in 1710 of his niece Anna Ivanovna and the duke of Courland. The tsar prided himself on the quasi-scientific 'cabinet of curiosities'. Its list of specimens included 'an eight-legged lamb, a three-legged baby, a two-headed baby, a baby with its eyes under its nose and its ears below its neck, Siamese twins joined at the chest ... a baby with a fish's tail, two dogs born to a 60-year-old virgin, and a baby with two heads, four arms and three legs'.[31] But in fact the Kunstkamera, as it was called, was just a colossal freak show, a racist phantasmagoria, its ghoulish 'anthropology' catering to every cheap and lurid prejudice.

Into this menagerie stepped Gannibal, 'the young Negro whom people regarded as a freak', according to Pushkin, 'a kind of rare beast, an unusual and strange creature'.[32] So what exactly were Peter's motives in acquiring the boy? The tsar shared the taste of many contemporary European rulers for human exotica. Nabokov suggests that 'the young blackamoor was no doubt welcomed as an additional curio'.[33] Rotkirkh provides supporting evidence for such a claim, describing the tsar's inspection of Abram and Abdul ('his newly arrived objects') rather as if they were exhibits in a museum. The nineteenth-century historian Shmurlo also refers to some documents in which Abram is mentioned three times in the same breath as the tsar's jester, Jan da Costa.[34] A court ledger of 1709 notes:

> By the tsar's orders, in view of the Christmas festival, kaftans have been made for Yakim the dwarf and Abram the blackamoor, with camisoles and breeches. Moreover, eight arshins [six yards] of scarlet cloth and brass buttons have been purchased for both.[35]

Russian attitudes to black people had yet to evolve. Iconography, for example, depicted evil men as black-faced or Negroid. In royal pageants Negroes often acted as bogeyman figures. Indeed, there is a record of a Kremlin masquerade in which the devil appeared as the king of Ethiopia. Pushkin refers to Ibrahim as a 'black devil' in *The Negro of Peter the Great*.[36] His friend Alexander Griboyedov wrote a play, *Woe from Wit*, in which the heroine's aunt calls her black servant a 'real devil', adding: 'Isn't she black? Enough to frighten you!/How could God have created such a race?' In a sense Gannibal helped Peter find the answer.

Utterly godlike, the tsar hoped to galvanise Russia by creating a new race of citizens with broader horizons and the skills necessary to carry through military, naval and administrative reform. Here is the Pygmalion figure seen in the Rastrelli bronze. 'All Russia is your statue, transformed by you with skilful craftsmanship,' declared the free-thinking cleric Feofan Prokopovich.[37] Peter's own schooling was inadequate but he understood that education, of which the boyars disapproved, was the key to the future. In Gannibal, who was 'quick, keen and fiery', he identified the raw material for one of his most ambitious projects. 'The tsar looked around to find a pupil among the enslaved nations, and to present him to his own people as an example and model.' Meanwhile Peter had Abdul baptised in Moscow as 'Alexei Petrov', and then sent, aged nine, to train as an oboist in the Preobrazhensky regimental band.[38]

\*\*\*

The Petrine revolution was a vast, utopian project in social engi‑
neering. It was an attempt to reconstruct the Russian as a European. In
some respects the life of Abram Petrovich Gannibal served as its pilot
scheme: an attempt to reconstruct the African as a Russian. Rotkirkh
argues that, by educating the young Negro in a style befitting a prince,
the tsar hoped to teach the nobility a lesson, 'and to put Russians to
shame by convincing them that out of every people and even from
among wild men – such as Negroes, whom our civilised nations assign
exclusively to the class of the slave – there can be formed men who,
by dint of application, can obtain knowledge and learning, and thus
become helpful to the monarch'.[39]

Over the winter and into the early spring Peter and the African
boy constructed a friendship. The tsar quizzed Gannibal about the
Sublime Porte and marvelled at his gift for languages (in addition to
a mastery of Turkish, he already spoke Russian with some fluency).
As with Savva Raguzinsky, it was his linguistic ability that singled
Gannibal out. 'Peter the Great took a great fancy to him,' according
to one source, 'and kept him about his person. Always bright, the
boy now developed exceptional cleverness, and Peter, who was not
the man to neglect any intellectual promise, had him carefully taught
under his own eyes.'[40]

In early 1705 the tsar left Moscow and went south to Voronezh to
work in the shipyards. He took Gannibal with him, as well as Fyodor
Apraxin and Zotov and others. It was an early sign of the boy's
favoured status. On the day of departure, a Kremlin clerk made the
following note in the sovereign's income‑and‑expenses book: '1705,
18 February, for Abram the blackamoor, uniform and trimmings,
paid 15 roubles.'[41]

The tsar and his entourage stayed in Voronezh for Easter, before
leaving on 27 April for Moscow. Peter wanted to join his army in
Lithuania, but as soon as he got back to the capital he was struck down
by illness, and had to spend the first three weeks of May recuperating

at Golovin's house in the German suburb. In his nobility petition Gannibal wrote that he was 'brought to Moscow to the house of the Tsar Peter the Great'.[42] It was merely a slip of the pen.

Golovin was very proud of his new mansion, built in 1702, just outside Moscow's walls, among the handsome brick houses and shaded gardens of the European merchants and diplomats. He had already commissioned the Dutch engraver Adrian Schönebeck to produce a series of views of the house before Peter came to stay. The artist had come to Moscow at the tsar's invitation in 1698 and worked more or less constantly at the Armoury palace until his death in September 1705.[43] Schönebeck's last surviving prints were in fact four scenes of Golovin's house, in one of which the young Gannibal can be seen next to a recuperating tsar.

The two lower folios show a number of houses on the banks of the river Yauza, with Golovin's in the middle. Underneath the engraving Schönebeck has written, 'View of Count Golovin's house outside Moscow. Peter I with a Negro boy.' The boy's name is not given, but all the details suggest it is Gannibal, who was indeed staying at the house with the tsar, from 4 to 22 May. 'Schönebeck's expenses for engraving work' is listed among the 'income and expenses for April–September 1705' in the Kremlin ledger.[44]

The portrait shows Peter wearing a richly embroidered kaftan – Nabokov refers to the garment as 'a French king's dress' – with the tiny figure of Gannibal standing behind him and peering over the tsar's right shoulder. All you can really make out is his black curly hair and bright eyes, and the outline of a kaftan. The rest of him is obscured by Peter's body, which may explain why the Schönebeck print has never attracted the same degree of attention as the Meller-Zakomelsky portrait. Nevertheless it is worth celebrating if only because, in the words of one Russian historian, it is 'the only likeness we have of the famous Negro who was Pushkin's ancestor'.[45]

# 9

# Baptism of Fire

I am — or rather *was* — a prince.
—Lord Byron, *Mazeppa*

The medieval city of Vilnius lay 450 miles west of Moscow, across the border that Russia shared with Lithuania and Poland. In the early 1700s, you could look out from the parapet of the castle of Gediminas, high on the hill, over the narrow, winding streets and see the frontline of the Great Northern War in the muddy countryside beyond. A devastated landscape bore witness to the violent history of the conflict. Burned-out villages dotted the wilderness. Smoke clouds hung over the deep glades of oak and fir. 'The land is neglected and untilled,' wrote Ambassador Whitworth, 'because whenever the enemy approaches, the people are warned to move out, taking with them only a few belongings, while the cozacks set fire to the rest, as they have done several times already in sight of the Swedish army, who find all desolate before them, and as they advance will run further into want and cold.'[1]

The border, like the war itself, was a phantom affair. Rival nations claimed the overlapping land. 'O Lithuania, my country,' wrote the Polish patriot Adam Mickiewicz in his epic *Pan Tadeusz*.[2] His friend and rival Pushkin made up other tales from the Lithuanian woods. Here, on 13 July 1705, or so he wrote in *Beginning of an Autobiography*, Peter the Great 'baptised the young Ibrahim in Vilnius, with the help of the queen of Poland, the wife of Augustus, and gave him the name Gannibal'.[3]

Both details – the royal godmother, the *nom de guerre* – add colour, if not accuracy, to Pushkin's claim, in the note to *Onegin*, that it was 'Peter the Great who baptised [Gannibal] in Vilnius'.[4] He seems to have forgotten the earlier ceremony in Jassy – and even the date is unclear. In his painstakingly researched *History of Peter I*, for instance, Pushkin states that the tsar was only in Vilnius between 15 and 30 July. In fact, Peter sent two letters from Vilnius on 9 July, and was still there on 3 August, writing to General George Ogilvie, the ex-Austrian Scot who commanded the Russian army.[5] The discrepancy is interesting because it casts light on a bitter power struggle among the generals.

On 22 May, after the lengthy amusements of the winter and the brief recuperation in the German suburb, Peter's unwieldy circus pulled out of Moscow. In tow was Gannibal, now apprenticed to the Preobrazhensky regiment and proudly wearing its lustrous green uniform. The first stop was the town of Polotsk, in modern-day Belarus, on the western Dvina, where the tsar, reunited with his army, held a council of war. On the surface there was plenty of good news. Much had been accomplished during Peter's absence to improve the efficiency of Russia's military machine. To begin with, the number of troops had increased significantly. Around 40,000 infantrymen and 20,000 cavalry and dragoons were occupying temporary quarters in Polotsk, whose strategic location made it possible to attack the Swedish army on any of three fronts, by moving battalions north into Livonia, on the east coast of the Baltic, west into Lithuania, or south into Poland, then occupied by the Swedes. The influx of soldiers was partly due to a new system of recruitment, which had come into effect in February, conscripting one man from every twenty peasant house-holds. A sizeable auxiliary force was also provided by the Cossacks under the command of the mercurial Ivan Mazepa, the *hetman* (or leader) of the Ukraine. Not everybody shared Peter's delight at the raw recruits. In the opinion of Whitworth, they were 'fitter for surprise and skirmishes than any regular action'. The Austrian ambassador Korb was even less flattering in his appraisal of the 'bandits' now in uniform. 'If we may form an estimate from these fellows from the rash audacity of their crimes, they are fitter for robbery than for rightful war,' he wrote in the first account of the new Russian army to be published in the west.[6] Peter tried in vain to hunt down and destroy every copy.

Halting the rapid eastward march of the Swedish army was the most urgent task facing Russia's generals. Now camped in the fields outside Warsaw, Charles XII must be prevented at all costs from advancing on the road to Moscow, warned Peter. The tsar questioned his generals about the troops' readiness for combat. Field Marshal Boris Sheremetev reported that both infantry and cavalry were plenti¬ fully equipped with muskets and grenades, pistols and swords. News of improvements to the artillery also buoyed Peter's spirits. Bells from churches and monasteries across Russia had been confiscated and melted down for their metal. Thus over the winter Sheremetev had taken delivery of a batch of gleaming new ordnance, in the form of 243 cannon, thirteen howitzers and twelve mortars.

In spite of Korb's criticism, the real trouble with the army was not its rank and file but the leadership. Squabbling and jealousy between Russian and foreign generals threatened to undermine the war effort. In particular, the two field marshals Ogilvie and Sheremetev were engaged in a long¬running feud. Each schemed incessantly against the other, though Sheremetev's background gave him a distinct advantage in the war of words. The wily old boyar was 'the politest man in the country', according to Whitworth, but he was also a cunning politi¬ cian who had weathered the storms of Sofiya's regency by means of shrewd politicking.[7] He was, in other words, a dangerous enemy for an outsider like Ogilvie to make.

The Scot had little understanding of Kremlin intrigue. He had only entered the Russian service in 1702, at the age of sixty, and lacked friends at court. As a result, he sometimes overplayed his hand as the bluff, no¬nonsense military man. For example, he greeted Peter at Polotsk with a thirteen¬point article entitled *Plan and Arrangement for the Army According to Foreign Practice*. Its concern for the soldiers' welfare made the author popular with the army as a whole. Yet the officers rejected the plan because Ogilvie did not speak Russian and therefore had to use an interpreter to outline its main points, which were in any case somewhat technical. The long-winded memorandum outraged Sheremetev, who protested to the tsar about its 'unpatriotic' tone, and apparently won the day. In a bid to end the dispute Peter mothballed the Scot's reforms. 'Because of your distress I have called a halt to this reorganisation and ordered the old arrangement to stand,' he wrote to Sheremetev's deputy, Prince Nikita Repnin. His letter refers to Ogilvie as 'that stupid and vexing person'.[8] Peter also hoped to diffuse the tension by splitting the army in two, sending 10,000 men under Sheremetev's command north to the Baltic coast, while Ogilvie led operations in the south.

Such was Gannibal's baptism of fire. In the aftermath of the quarrel between his two senior commanders, Peter led a convoy into the Lithuanian forest, moving slowly through the woods until he reached Vilnius with a small entourage on 8 July 1705.[9] It was from this moment that Gannibal dated the beginning of his preco-cious military career. Writing to Peter's widow Catherine many years later, on 23 November 1726, the African recalls the upheaval of that summer as a milestone in his life:

> Then most gratefully did I have the honour to serve from my earliest youth – which is to say, I was only seven or eight years of age, to begin with – at the feet of His Majesty, and at Your Majesty's feet too, when out of the holy font of His Majesty, he became my godfather in Lithu-ania in the city of Vilnius in 1705.[10]

Of course the prose style is neither fluent nor elegant. (I have tried to render the unnatural syntax of the Russian original as faithfully as possible into English.) Unfortunately Gannibal's letters are often peppered with these failings of verbal self-assurance. Toadying might be another way to describe the strenuous uncertainty of tone. Yet perhaps the African had reason to adopt such an idiom: it's unwise to mess with autocrats, especially if you are an outsider. Today's protégé can easily become tomorrow's 'stupid and vexing person'. Never backward in coming forward, as Pushkin's detractors were to allege, Gannibal repeated his version of events at Vilnius in the nobility petition he wrote for Peter's daughter in 1742:

> I was baptised by the Tsar-Emperor of immortal memory into the Orthodox Greek confession of faith, and His Imperial Majesty chose to stand as my godfather in his own very high personage, and from that day onwards I was constantly at his side.[11]

No mention here of Elizabeth's mother Catherine, or of the baptism at Jassy. Significantly, also, no mention of the phantom godmother who came to dominate what Pushkin called the 'family legends' relating to the ceremony at Vilnius. Thus Rotkirkh, for example, claims that Gannibal 'was baptised into the Greek religion in Poland', and that 'both the tsar and the Queen of Poland, the wife of August II, graced the baptism with their lofty presence as godparents'.[12] Neither of these statements can be squared with the known whereabouts of the personalities involved. Unless ironic, the son-in-law's reference to Poland as the location was probably just another slip of the pen. A native Livonian, Rotkirkh knew his Baltic geography, and offers a reliable guide to its fluid political boundaries during the first decade of the eighteenth century. It is likely, however, that he gleaned some of his information from Gannibal's son Pyotr, whose unreliable memoir set the template for two enduring family myths. 'My father was baptised in Poland in the town of Grodno. His godparents were Tsar Peter I and the queen of Poland,' Pyotr wrote towards the end of his life.[13] That memoir also serves unwittingly as a postscript to Ogilvie's miserable career as a Russian commander-in-chief. By placing Gannibal inside the fortress at Grodno, which Charles's army surrounded later that year, forcing an ignominious Russian retreat, Pyotr wrongly makes his father a witness to the Scot's final humiliation.

The retreat from Grodno was the end for Ogilvie. His quarrel with the Russian generals had only intensified in the period after Sheremetev's removal. In particular, Repnin and Alexander Menshikov, the tsar's favourite general, declined to obey Ogilvie's orders. It was hard for the Scot to compete with Menshikov, whose victories against the Swedes on the Baltic coast led to the founding of Saint Petersburg and won him the tsar's lasting admiration and friendship. Ogilvie blamed Menshikov for the retreat from Grodno. 'The general of cavalry [Menshikov] without my knowledge in the name of Your Majesty ordered the army to go to Bykhov, and took on himself the air of commander-in-chief, taking no account of me,' the Scot complained to Peter. 'As long as I have been at war, nowhere and never have people treated me as badly as here.'[14] Chastened by the loss of Grodno, the tsar allowed Ogilvie to resign his command on a plea of ill health. The Scot left for Saxony, where he died four years later.

The answer to the riddle of the queen of Poland lies in the drunken background to the Vilnius baptism. It seems the Gannibal family's mythmakers exaggerated the solemnity of the occasion. Other sources describe a rather unholy event: a mock-religious ceremony in the style of the All-Mad, All-Joking, All-Drunken Assembly. Even the venue, the medieval stone church of Saint Paraskeva, was especially chosen to maximise the jest. Once the last pagan nation in Europe, Lithuania had only converted to Christianity as late as the fourteenth century, under the rule of Grand Duke Algirdas, the son of Gediminas. Though he continued to worship his own warlike gods, Algirdas built Saint Paraskeva in 1345 while defeating the Teutonic knights and repelling the Tatars of the Golden Horde a century before Muscovite princes accomplished the same feats. This mixture of paganism and Christianity was undoubtedly a case of Algirdas hedging his spiritual bets. Nevertheless it proved rather effective. By coincidence or not, Lithuania became the dominant power as far south as Ukraine, though it later merged with Poland to form a joint commonwealth. The people's wholehearted embrace of Roman Catholicism was a condition of that union, signed at Krewo in 1385, but nobody ever forgot that Algirdas had built the first stone church in Vilnius on the site of a pagan shrine to Ragutis, the god of beer. The historical link provided a subtext to Gannibal's baptism. Insobriety set the tone. The ceremony, according to Nabokov, 'was conducted in the rowdy and slapstick atmosphere of Peter's court and smacks of mock marriages between freaks or the elevation of jesters to the ranks of Barataria'.[15]

Court records show that Ivan Buturlin, in his usual fancy dress as the king of Poland, was present at the baptism on 13 July. Indeed, his arrival in Vilnius two days earlier with news that the Russian army under General Adolf Bauer had captured the Latvian town of Mitau was the official reason for the celebration. The christening of a 'black devil' was merely a sideshow at a time of public rejoicing, as is made clear by a plaque on the wall at Saint Paraskeva's, linking the victory and the baptism:

> In this church the tsar Peter the Great in 1705 listened to the thanks-giving prayers for the victory reported over the armies of Charles XII, and gave the church the Swedish standard seized in the battle, and baptised here the African Gannibal, ancestor of the illustrious poet A. S. Pushkin.

The presence in Vilnius of Buturlin, with his mock title and his unashamedly lascivious habits, may also explain the legend of the royal godmother. Perhaps the young African, in his bewilderment at the drunken antics of Peter's cronies, assumed that one of Buturlin's mistresses was indeed the queen of Poland. In any case the real holder of that title, Christina Eberhardina of Brandenburg-Bayreuth, the Electress of Saxony, was definitely not among the celebrants at Saint Paraskeva's that day. Her attendance would have been unthinkable, given the collapse of her marriage to King Augustus II, who had converted to Catholicism, in 1696, hoping to improve his chances as one of eighteen candidates to succeed John III Sobieski of Poland. The tactic was successful insofar as the Elector acceded to the throne. Unfortunately the switch of faith alienated his Lutheran subjects at home, and caused his wife, a Hohenzollern princess, to leave him. By 1705, the two were all but separated, Christina sulking at her castle in Saxony, while the king occupied himself on the various battlefields of the Great Northern War. He did a fair amount of sulking himself, especially when Charles installed his own candidate, Stanislaus Leszczynski, on the Polish throne, thus casting Augustus into the political wilderness for several years. Just for the record: Stanislaus's wife – the *other* queen of Poland – was not in Vilnius either. She apparently felt so insecure in her husband's turbulent new kingdom that she never ventured outside Swedish Pomerania.

The naming of Gannibal was equally unstraightforward. Rotkirkh notes that the boy was christened Peter Petrovich Petrov – literally Peter, son of Peter, Peter's son – 'after his godfather, the tsar'. However, the son-in-law then adds that 'because he was known previously in his homeland as Ibrahim, which is to say, Abram as it is written in Arabic, and because he had remained unbaptised for so long, he was allowed to call himself Abram and the new name fell into disuse, and so it was only in the church records that he was named Peter'.[16] Pushkin, whom the poet Marina Tsvetaeva once called 'the great-grandson of the giant's godson', explained that the boy had to throw a tantrum in order to get his way. 'He burst into tears at the baptism and protested that he did not want to be called by his new name,' Pushkin added.[17] It was an old trick. A flood of tears had saved Gannibal once before, in Cairo two years earlier, when a Turkish customs officer rescued the hysterical child from the clutches of Charles Poncet.

The wilderness years of Abram Petrovich began in the Lithuanian forest. Unlike the king of Poland, however, the African boy never fell out of favour. On the contrary, according to his son, 'he was educated personally by the blessed and most glorious tsar Peter the Great, and because he also took part in all the campaigns and battles at which His Majesty deigned to be present, he became a special favourite of the tsar's'.[18]

Life in the wilderness of the Great Northern War shaped his

childhood. For Gannibal, as for Russia itself, the war dominated the environment. 'It determined the order of everything, set its pace and even the methods of reform,' according to the great historian Klyuchevsky. 'Everything that was done was done in the order of the war's requirements.'[19] Not all of these lessons can have seemed 'blessed' and 'glorious' to the 9-year-old. He was a boy soldier. He grew up on the battlefield. Not only was he separated in 1705 from his brother Abdul, now called Alexei, and the last remaining link with his family, but he was seldom given an opportunity to mix with other children. He was always in the company of adults, and rather eccentric ones at that. Many of the tsar's cronies viewed the young African with suspicion as a cross between a jester, an outlaw and a human guinea pig in some bizarre nature-versus-nurture experiment. Nor can it have been easy living at such close quarters with Peter, always moving from camp to camp, often sleeping out in the open, sometimes in foul weather. 'Danger levels man and brute,' wrote Byron in *Mazeppa*, a romantic poem about the Great Northern War. 'But he was hardy as his lord,/And little cared for bed and board.' Hardy he may have been. Yet the brutal experience left its mark on Gannibal's personality, according to a family friend. Ivan Golikov blamed the complicated relationship with the tsar-*batyushka*, the father-emperor, for the African's 'strangeness'. Among a series of notes entitled 'Table Talk, 1836–37', Pushkin tells a story ('not very clean, but it shows Peter's ways') to illustrate what Golikov meant:

> One day the young Moor Gannibal, accompanying Peter I on his daily rounds, stopped for a certain necessity and suddenly cried out in terror: 'Tsar! Tsar! The guts are coming out of me!' Peter walked up to him and seeing what the matter was, said: 'Nonsense, that's not your gut, it's a worm.' And he pulled the worm out with his own fingers.[20]

In Vilnius, Gannibal met Peter's other 'special favourite' Menshikov, who had also risen from humble origins. 'By birth,' wrote Prince

Kurakin, 'Menshikov is lower than a Pole' – in other words, a Lithuanian.[21] His father was a soldier who served under Peter's father and
became a corporal-clerk at the village on the Yauza, near the German
suburb, where Peter lived during Sofiya's regency. Young Menshikov
joined in the boy's war games. He was present, for example, on 30
May 1690 when, as the Scottish mercenary Patrick Gordon recorded
in his diary, Peter spent his eighteenth birthday arranging mock battles
at Preobrazhenskoye.[22] The word *preobrazhenskoye* means 'transformation' or 'metamorphosis', and indeed there was something almost
miraculous about the way this Lithuanian boy rose to become not
a grand master of the Teutonic knights like Mickiewicz's Konrad
Wallenrod, but a field marshal, first senator, a 'Serene Highness' and
a prince of Russia – the first commoner to receive that hereditary title
– as well as a prince of the Holy Roman Empire.

Gannibal's encounter with Menshikov left a deep impression on
him. Now thirty-one, the mighty satrap had retained his good looks
and athletic physique. His rapport with Peter was obvious for all to
see. It even caused tongues to wag. 'Some have thought their intimacy
rather resembled love than friendship, they having frequent jars and
constant reconcilements,' wrote the English ambassador Whitworth.[23]
He means 'jars' here in the sense of 'lovers' tiffs', though Peter and
Menshikov were riotous drinking companions too. In an apocryphal
story Menshikov was the son of a pastry cook who first met the tsar
while peddling his wares on the streets of Moscow. Once, over a jar
or two, Peter reminded his friend that he had the power to return him
to his pie-selling origins. The next day the prince turned up at the
Kremlin dressed in an apron with a tray of *pirozhki*, shouting 'Hot
pies, hot pies' at the astonished tsar.

Menshikov's youthful appetite for self-indulgence had been
replaced by lofty ambition. Nowadays he wore a curly white wig like
a French grandee at the court of the Sun King. Gannibal noticed the
owlish gleam in his unforgiving blue eyes. Henceforth the African
would always refer to Menshikov as the 'shining prince'. Yet there
was vulnerability too in his gaze, and even paranoia. It is apparent in

all his portraits, which have the same enigmatic Mona Lisa smile. As Ogilvie learned to his cost, jealousy was a weakness that Menshikov often disguised with a mask of arrogance.

Menshikov's early triumphs in the Great Northern War set the stage for Peter's giant *mise-en-scène* on the site of an old Swedish fortress, which the Lithuanian occupied in 1702. The Russian tsar gave the fortress on Lake Ladoga a Dutch name before transforming the wilderness of the Neva estuary into the most magnificently appointed city in European memory. On his return from Poland, which he called the 'opposite of paradise', Menshikov wrote to the tsar in glowing terms of Sankt Piter Burk as the 'promised land'.[24] This 'heavenly place' would lift Russia into the ranks of Europe, he added. Utterly godlike – and 'being in this hell', i.e. Lithuania – Peter could not resist using another biblical image to describe his new creation. His reply to the shining prince betrayed impatience at the slow progress of the Great Northern War, and a wish that 'the Holy Comforter in his justice might bring this affair to a speedy conclusion, and allow us quickly to set eyes again on our very own Eden'.[25]

# 10

# Peter's Paradise

By nature we are fated here
To cut a window through to Europe
—Pushkin, *The Bronze Horseman*

The idea of Saint Petersburg as a 'northern Eden' contributed to the legend of Abram Petrovich Gannibal.[1] His early biographers delighted in the apparent symmetry of a life that began in Abyssinia, where biblical tradition placed the earthly paradise, and ended in this Baltic utopia, with its exotic trees and fountains and even a 'gardening bureau' attached to the tsar's cabinet. Stealing a motif from the Happy Valley of Johnson's *Rasselas*, Rotkirkh tells how Peter imported fruit trees from Persia and rare birds from Africa to live in aviaries shaped like pagodas. Outside the city, at Peterhof, he ordered the French architect Le Blond, who had worked with Le Nôtre in designing Louis XIV's gardens at Versailles, to recreate the classical imagery of paradise in Ovid's *Metamorphoses*.[2] Blue monkeys chattering in gilded cages added to what Pushkin called the 'fairy-tale' aspect of Gannibal's new surroundings. Ironically, the same phrase was used by a twenty-first-century tsar, Vladimir Putin, in reviving the Petersburg creation myth.[3]

The 'wounded monkey', whom Nikolai Korf spied leaving the Winter Palace half a century later, first set eyes on Saint Petersburg in the spring of 1706. It was hardly a joyful occasion. Cut off from his army by the Swedish advance on Grodno, Peter retreated with a small knot of followers, including Gannibal, to the settlement on the

Neva while Ogilvie and Menshikov continued to squabble on the battlefield.

This sharp reversal in Russia's fortunes highlighted the gap between reality and myth. Four years earlier, advancing towards the inhospitable shores of the Gulf of Finland, Menshikov had captured a fortress on Lake Ladoga from the Swedes. Deep in ancient Novgorodian territory – a wasteland of thick mists inhabited only by wolves and bears – the lake, which was the source of the fast-flowing Neva river, had inspired Peter to rename the fort Schlüsselburg, meaning 'key to the sea'. On 16 May 1703, he laid the foundations for another stronghold on Yanni-Saari (Hare Island) at the mouth of the river, about fifty miles to the west. Eighteenth-century panegyrists compared the building of Saint Petersburg to the creation of the universe. Mythmakers rewrote the opening chapters of the Book of Genesis, with Peter giving birth to earthly paradise out of chaos and water and void. In a stroke, he willed the new Russia 'from nothingness into being', wrote his minister Gavrila Golovkin. Historians dutifully recorded the primal scene: the godlike tsar walked to the centre of Hare Island, where he saw an eagle hovering overhead, grabbed a bayonet, cut two strips of turf, and arranged them in a cross on the marshy ground. 'Let there be a city!' he intoned.[4] The opening lines of Pushkin's epic poem The Bronze Horseman, subtitled a 'Petersburg fairy tale', crystallise the legend:

On the shore by desolate waves,
*He* stood, full of lofty thoughts,
And gazed into the distance.[5]

The future was the distant object of Peter's gaze. He saw a vision of stuccoed palaces and classical façades. His lofty thoughts were of aristocratic salons filled with European manners. Such futuristic projections are a leitmotif in Russian history. Pristine and pure, indeed utopian – literally so, given that the legend of Saint Andrew's visit to the same coast had partly inspired Thomas More's *Utopia* – the sea bewitched the tsar of landlocked Russia. He named the mosquito-infested colony Sankt Piter Burk because he was fascinated by the way the Dutch had drawn wealth and power from the sea. Yet the name was ambiguous – did it stand for 'Saint Peter's City' or 'the Holy City of Peter'? – and perhaps a blasphemy, too. Old Believers regarded the 'Petropolis' not as Russia's Eden but as an alien kingdom of the apoca-lypse: Babel and Babylon, Sodom and Gomorrah rolled into one.

In the spring of 1706, however, the tsar drew only inspiration from his visit to the Baltic 'holy land'. His plans for the city did not stop at its becoming the new Rome. Peter dreamed also of a new Holland, a new Venice, a new Novgorod, a new Archangel, a new Moscow. He even boasted of its resemblance, though in a harsher, rougher form, to the New Jerusalem described in the Book of Revela-tion. 'I cannot omit to write to you from this Paradise, where, with the help of the Almighty, everything is fine,' the tsar told Menshikov on 7 April, adding: 'We may be living in heaven here.'[6]

The reference to 'paradise', for which Peter used the Latin-derived Dutch word instead of its Russian equivalent, must have puzzled Gannibal. He saw only that Petersburg was hell for its builders. Tens of thousands of serfs died clearing forests, digging canals, laying roads and erecting palaces on the sodden marshes of the Neva. 'It would be difficult to find in the annals of military history any battle that claimed more lives than the number of workers who died in [the building of] Saint Petersburg,' wrote Klyuchevsky.[7] Even the Muscovite nobles who settled in 'this barren corner' did so, according to Whitworth, 'with no small difficulty since the climate is too cold, and the ground too marshy to furnish the conveniences of life, which are all brought from the neighbouring countries'.[8] Peter imported granite from Finland to build the Neva's famous embankment. Its baroque palaces were clad in marble from Italy and the Middle East. Porphyry came from Sweden. The tiles came from Lübeck. Such borrowing was not to everybody's taste. On a visit to Petersburg in 1739, the urban connoisseur Count Francesco Algarotti saw only 'a kind of bastard architecture' stolen from the Italian, the French and the Dutch.[9] 'In Saint Petersburg everything has an air of opulence, grandeur, magnificence,' wrote the Marquis de Custine a hundred years later, 'but, if you judge the reality of this appearance, you will find yourself strangely deceived.'

The strange unnatural beauty of Petersburg struck Gannibal. He was 'a kind of bastard son', according to the Saxon Helbig, and may have identified with the city for that reason.[10] By 1706, a solid row of buildings already lined the Neva embankment. Yet behind the façade the city remained, as one commentator wrote, 'full of log cabins, kitchen gardens, cowsheds, and clutchy mud'.[11] The Russians have a word – *fasadnost*, 'façade-ness'– for this culture of false appearances. It occurs in *The Negro of Peter the Great*, in a passage giving the black hero's first impressions of 'barbaric Petersburg':

> Ibrahim stared with curiosity at the newborn capital that was rising out of the swamp due to the passion of the autocrat. Unfinished dams, canals without quays, wooden bridges bore witness everywhere to the recent victory of human will over the hostile elements.[12]

Here Pushkin lays bare the ambiguity in Gannibal. The Moor of Petersburg was a stranger in a strange land. Yet he too owed his nurture to the experimental passion of the autocrat. The parallel was a common theme in early biographies. Helbig even described the Petropolis and Pyotr Petrovich Petrov, alias Gannibal, as 'unnatural twins'. Both the newfound city and the foundling son were exotic imports, or so he argued in *Russian Favourites*. Both grew up in the name of the father and under westernising eyes: the distant gaze of the tsar-*batyushka*, the father-tsar.

Insofar as Petersburg reflected the un-Russian character its founder prized in Gannibal, Helbig's analogy has the logic of a parable. Unquestionably the boy felt a kinship with the 'northern Eden'. He was, in Peter's theology – as Adam was in Saint Paul's – 'a type of the one who is to come', a forerunner of the new citizenry: literate and numerate, with a knowledge of languages, history, science and geography.[13] Gannibal studied arithmetic, geometry, trigonometry, navigation and astronomy under the tutelage of Fyodor Golovin and various hand-picked graduates of the School of Mathematics. He was briefly apprenticed to the Italian-Swiss architect Domenico Trezzini whom Peter commissioned in 1706 to enlarge the fortress and then to build in its centre the cathedral of Saint Peter and Saint Paul. Builders from Trezzini's home town of Lugano had played a part in shaping baroque architecture all across southern Germany and northern Italy. But, more importantly for Gannibal, the architect brought with him several years' experience as a fortifications engineer in Copenhagen. 'The young Moor had a sharp intellect, and showed a great gift for acquiring knowledge of the science of fortification. His industry was quite exceptional,' wrote Helbig, whose account of Gannibal's education often reads like a Bible story.[14] In September 1706, for example, the young African watched in panic as the Neva burst its banks, inundating the tsar's apartments. Peter likened the sudden deluge to a biblical flood. 'It was amusing to see people sitting on roofs and up trees, not only men but women too,' he wrote to Menshikov from the safety of his yacht.[15]

Some historians tell an apocryphal story of the jester Tyurikov. One afternoon, the tsar retired to his cabin for a nap, leaving Gannibal on deck with Count Jean Armand de Lestocq, a French aristocrat, who played a joke on the dozing jester by gluing his beard to his chest. Awoken by Tyurikov's screams, Peter rushed up on deck only to find his godson standing there, alone. 'Don't ever interrupt my sleep again!' cried Peter before flogging him unmercifully. At nightfall, the tsar was astonished to see the boy still weeping, and so he asked him why. 'Because you have beaten me cruelly and unjustly,' replied Gannibal, before explaining what had really happened. 'Well,' said Peter, 'since I punished you this time undeservedly, the next sin you commit shall be pardoned.'[16]

Slavery was another biblical motif that Peter associated with the Moor. Hoping to introduce a semblance of European-style liberty among his subjects, the tsar saw the freed slave as a perfect avatar of reform.[17] Yet, as so often happens in Russia, the façade of progress masked a contradiction. 'All subjects, whether of high or low condition, call themselves and must count themselves the Tsar's *kholopy*, that is slaves,' Adam Olearius, the Duke of Holstein's envoy to Muscovy, had written in the 1640s.[18] Nothing really changed under Peter. The new citizens were indistinguishable from the old serfs. 'There is no real Advantage to them in it (for they are but Slaves still),' observed the English engineer John Perry in 1716, 'yet the very Sound or Change of the Word has pleased them.'[19] It was a paradox that by institution-alising serfdom Dostoyevsky's 'nihilist Peter the Great' actually made the peasants less free. Of course, the peasantry was enserfed during the seventeenth century. But each individual still retained links to the village and the land. To prevent tax evasion, Peter introduced a new unit of taxation, the 'soul' – i.e. a male peasant of working age – for calcu-lating landowners' payments. The peasant thus became a mere item on the tax roll. Many were sold or exchanged to pay for the building of fine houses on the Neva. Others perished during construction. So it was that Gannibal, in the eyes of Gogol and other nineteenth-century writers, came to symbolise the duality of the Petersburg myth, a whited sepulchre with its 'black cargo' of *Dead Souls*.

In this counter-mythology, the 'northern Eden' was a gloomy arti-ficial place built on tears and corpses, a phantom city haunted by ghosts seeking revenge for the victims of the tsar's architectural folly. Slave labour also cast its shadow. The Hanoverian ambassador described Petersburg as 'a Heap of Villages linked together, like some Planta-tion in the West Indies'.[20] To Custine it was matter-of-factly a 'city of slaves'. Echoing Pushkin, the French aristocrat noted Petersburg's 'real barbarism clumsily hidden under a revolting magnificence'. He compared the city to a theatrical stage set, to a mummer's mask, and to 'a black silhouette on a sheet of white paper'.[21] Some Enlighten-ment *philosophes* interpreted Gannibal's life as an existential journey into this heart of darkness, into all the highly charged ideas and ideals of noble savagery that Petersburg conjured up in certain intellectual circles of the Romantic period. The young African too probed its layers of deception. For all the talk of a stone capital symbolically replacing wooden Moscow, he noticed that even the grandest buildings were mostly constructed of stuccoed brick painted in bright colours. Indeed, it was among the 'damnable opinions' of Abram Gannibal, as reported by the spymaster Korf in 1762, that 'the decorations of Saint Petersburg resemble the warpaint of an African tribe'.[22]

The art of war defined both the Petropolis and its dark twin. Gannibal never forgot the city's origins as a fortress in the Great Northern War. Nor did he forget the importance of the Swedish campaign in his own upbringing. Just as Trezzini and later Rastrelli (among others) transformed a primitive work of fortification into a celebrated work of art, with its mixture of architectural styles, its seductive enfilades of baroque, rococo and classical palaces overlooking granite-paved canals, so the Moor's self-transformation was an extraordinary cultural achievement. The French have a phrase (*l'œuvre-vie*) for the 'work of life' as opposed to the work of art. It might be argued, in other words, that the African's life of science and soldiery was actually Russia's masterpiece: the real window into Europe.

Home to the schizophrenic Raskolnikov in *Crime and Punishment* and to the 'strange creatures' of Gogol's *Petersburg Tales*, Peter's paradise seemed not only to embody the new meritocratic Russia hated by the old boyar aristocracy but also to *dis*embody it, along the lines satirised by Gogol in 'The Nose', where the detached body part acquires a higher position in the Table of Ranks than the person from whom it has been separated. Lowly origins were almost a prerequisite for advancement. 'New men' dominated the court, and Gannibal was perhaps the most successful of these 'fledglings of Peter's nest' – to use Pushkin's celebrated phrase – after Menshikov and the tsar's Lithuanian mistress, Marta Skowronska.

Marta became Peter's second wife and then, as Catherine I, succeeded the tsar when he died in 1725, but up until her coronation she and the Moor had somewhat parallel careers. Her remarkable evolution from Baltic peasant to Russia's empress in her own right began on the Latvian battlefield. Captured by Sheremetev at

Marienburg in 1702, she (like Gannibal) entered the royal household as a present first to Menshikov and then to Peter. Unlike his first wife, Yevdokiya Lopukhina, whom the tsar dispatched to a convent in 1698, Skowronska was the opposite of a boudoir princess. Indeed she was dubbed 'Catherine the sutler' by Pushkin's friend Prince Kozlovsky because of her readiness to follow Peter from camp to camp during the Great Northern War.[23]

Gogol was born in 1809 in the Ukrainian province of Poltava where, a hundred years earlier, Gannibal played his part in a decisive victory over the Swedes, thereby assuring Petersburg's future. Charles XII's march to Poltava in the spring of 1709 is famous as one of the classic invasions of Russia. Unfortunately for the Swedish king, it is also an object lesson in how not to conduct warfare in that country. (Even so, Napoleon and Hitler failed to learn from his mistakes.) Given the vastness of Russia, and the brief campaigning season due to winter, the invader's choice of direction is always critical. With twelve regiments of infantry and sixteen regiments of cavalry and dragoons – a total force of around 35,000 troops – Charles launched his attack on Moscow from Grodno in June 1708. Instead of pressing eastwards at full speed, however, Charles hesitated in the knowledge that Peter had more than twice as many soldiers at his disposal. The king hoped delay would enable him to link up with his second-in-command, Count Adam Löwenhaupt, who was marching south from Riga with 12,500 reinforcements and supplies.

Most of the reinforcements never reached Charles because, on 28 September, Gannibal and 12,000 other troops led by Peter and Menshikov caught up with Löwenhaupt in the village of Lesnaya. The young African was deployed with a regiment of the Preobrazhensky guards to ambush the Swedes as they tried to cross the river Sozh. The battle raged until nightfall, when a sudden snowstorm – unusual for so early in the autumn – brought the fighting to a halt. By then the Russians had lost about one third of their troops, but the Swedes more than half. Löwenhaupt was left with only 5,000 combatants to bring to Charles.

Peter was so delighted with Gannibal's courage during the Russian victory at Lesnaya that he commissioned a portrait of himself on the battlefield, with his black godson in attendance. The painting, by the French artist Pierre Denis Martin, shows the tsar on horseback while the 12-year-old African boy, dressed in the green Preobrazhensky tunic and a white turban, stands in front of Menshikov's grey horse.

Just as the battle of Maloyaroslavets in the autumn of 1812 blocked Napoleon's retreat from Moscow through the fertile south, instead forcing the hungry Grand Armée back through countryside it had devastated on its advance, so the mauling at Lesnaya forced Charles to change direction and turn his army south-east across the Dnieper into Ukraine, there to join forces with the Cossacks led by Ivan Mazepa, who had defected from Peter's side. These unlikely allies laid siege to Poltava, a fortress standing on the Vorskla, and a place which, in Swedish hands, would have given Charles a route back through Cossack territory to the Crimea, and an avenue by way of Kharkov and Kursk to the prize of Moscow. (Ironically, Poltava was also the place to which Hitler flew in December 1941 with an order diverting the German Sixth Army's Panzer divisions from their advance on Moscow and instead opening the way south to destruction at Stalingrad.)

No event was more fundamental in the parallel lives of Petersburg and Pyotr Petrovich Petrov than the catastrophic defeat that Charles suffered on 'dread Pultowa's day', to quote Byron. Indeed Peter wrote jubilantly to Count Fyodor Apraxin in the afterglow of victory on 27 June 1709, claiming it had laid the new city's 'final foundation stone'.[24] On 8 July, he wrote a mock letter to the mock-tsar Fyodor Romodanovsky: 'Now without any doubt Your Majesty's desire to have your residence in Saint Petersburg can be satisfied now that the enemy has met his final end.'[25] In his poem *Mazeppa*, the Russophobic Byron also noted the shift in the balance of power:

> The power and glory of war
> Faithless as their vain votaries, men,
> Had pass'd to the triumphant Czar.[26]

Yet Peter earned his triumph by dint of careful preparation. After hurrying to relieve Poltava in the spring of 1709, he saw immediately that a crucial battle would be fought in front of its walls. The Russian plan of operations was Peter's own, and drew on conversations with Trezzini about the art of siege and fortification. Gannibal's apprenticeship came in useful. Rotkirkh even suggests that it was the boy's idea to use military engineers to transform the battlefield, though he provides no evidence to support the claim. Certainly the building of redoubts in the path of the Swedish troops to break up their combat order was a tactic that Gannibal would discuss at length in his magnum opus *Geometry and Fortification*.[27]

*** 

The battle of Poltava was a defining moment in Gannibal's life, not least because it encouraged him to reflect on the role of science in warfare, and bolstered his desire to study military engineering. With 10,000 Swedes dead or wounded, compared to only 1,345 on the Russian side, the moment was more final than defining for Charles, though he escaped capture by taking refuge with the Turkish army encamped on the banks of the Prut river, and did not reappear in the northern theatre of war until 1714. The view from abroad was as Russophobic as Byron's. In England, Daniel Defoe was struck by what he saw as the frightening combination of Peter's brutal methods and Russia's vast resources, and he maintained that there was something almost unfair about the way the battle of Poltava had gone: 'An army of veterans beaten by a mob, a crowd, a mere militia; an army of the bravest fellows in the world, beaten by scoundrels, old alms-women, or anything what you please to call them.'[28] And 13-year-old children, he might have added.

Romantic poets, musicians and artists fixed on the tragedy of Mazepa, who died in exile in Turkish Moldavia two months after the battle. A hero to some, an opportunist or traitor to others, the Cossack prince none the less inspired Victor Hugo, Liszt and Tchaikovsky,

Géricault and Delacroix, as well as Byron. One day in February 1825, hearing that the poet Kondraty Ryleyev was writing a poem on the same theme, Pushkin wrote to his brother Lev from Mikhailovs-koye: 'Advise Ryleyev to put our great-grandfather in Peter I's suite in his new poem. His ugly Negro mug will produce a strange effect on the whole picture of the battle of Poltava.'[29]

In fact, Ryleyev, who was executed for his part in the Decem-brist uprising later that year, had already finished the poem, which makes no reference to Gannibal. Surprisingly, Pushkin also omitted to mention his great-grandfather in his long narrative poem *Poltava*, written in 1828. However, the African does show his 'ugly mug' in an allegorical painting that represents Peter as the vanquisher of the Turks at Azov and the Swedes at Poltava. Now part of the vast Hermitage collection in Petersburg, the anonymous picture is dominated by the giant figure of Peter, who strikes a rather effeminate pose as he gazes into the future, with his arms akimbo, a sword in one hand, and a foot resting on the chest of Charles. Sitting in front of the tsar, only knee high, Turkish prisoners-of-war look suitably dejected in chains. Indeed the only smiling face in the picture – even Peter seems weighed down by victory – belongs to Gannibal.

Standing at Peter's left shoulder, the African is again dressed in Preobrazhensky uniform. This time, however, he is holding the reins of a horse which rears up as if to salute the triumph of Russia. The literary critic Teletova was the first to identify this boy as Gannibal, and to emphasise the significance of his central placement in the victory tableau.[30] It is indeed an extraordinary apparition: the black groom and the bronze horseman, the tsar-*batyushka* gazing at paradise, cutting his window to the west, an image that belongs more to romance or mysticism than to the history of Europe, though as always in the Petersburg story, we find a blurring between the symbolic and the physical, the mud-stained enactment of empty metaphors and impos-sible desires.

# 11

# Secret Sharer

His real son was the Negro
—Marina Tsvetaeva, *Peter and Pushkin*

Peter used the words 'my poor African' and *Herzenkind*, meaning 'child of the heart', to address Gannibal. The upshot of this familiarity, hovering between truth and metaphor, was to make others wary of the foundling. Of course the ex-slave raised on a battlefield was anything but innocent: like some Hausa prototype of Heathcliff, the interloper upset the balance of the royal household.[1] His nicknames 'Katenka' and 'Lisa' for the future empresses Catherine I and her daughter Elizabeth were another turn of the screw. Conservative boyars disliked hearing Peter's children refer to their 'black brother'.[2] Nevertheless, in the tsar's all-mad, all-joking court, a world as public as a theatre, it was not thought utterly strange that the sovereign should consort with a Negro. Pushkin notes the blockheads' curiosity about what was really an intellectual companionship:

As a rule, people usually looked upon the young Negro as a freak, and always crowded round him, swamping him with compliments and questions. Their curiosity, although it was hidden under a mask of politeness, offended his dignity. Even the delicious atten-tion of women, which is almost the single aim in a man's life, not only failed to make him happy but actually filled his heart with bitterness and indignation. He felt like an outlaw or a prize attrac-tion in the zoo, an exotic phenomenon accidentally transported into this world but having nothing in common with others, a strange creature.[3]

Yet Gannibal had his own way of being – of having to be – this sort of creature, and his way was that of the inhabitant of a court which preferred outlaws to in-laws, being often impatient with its native sons. Certainly there was a stark difference between Peter's affection for the Moor and his coolness towards the Tsarevich Alexei, his son by the discarded Yevdokiya. Born in 1690, Alexei was the natural Romanov heir but he grew up hostile to Peter's reforms. Not only did his conservative outlook lead to an estrangement from his father. In other respects, too, Alexei was the opposite of Gannibal. He was a timid boy who disliked being outdoors. His scant enthu-siasm for military service disappointed the tsar. The Danish commer-cial agent Georg Grund reported that Peter sometimes took Alexei with him on campaign, but the prince could not bear the pressures, and was often ill, so he was sent behind the lines.[4]

The tsarevich may have lacked the warrior-like qualities Peter wanted in a son, but he still played a crucial role in his father's strategy. In the wake of Poltava the tsar proposed a match between Alexei and Charlotte, daughter of the duke of Wolfenbüttel, to seal an alliance with the German prince who disliked Sweden's interference in the Holy Roman Empire. The dynastic marriage of Peter's niece Anna Ivanovna to the duke of Courland in 1710 helped to secure the anti-Swedish coalition. The tsar swept irresistibly through Sweden's Baltic provinces in the year after Poltava. The great city of Riga fell to Sheremetev in July. Three months later Reval (now Tallinn, in Estonia) also capitulated. Among the Swedish officers captured there was one Matvey von Schöberg, who joined the Russian army and later became Gannibal's father-in-law. Peter might have further pressed his advantage had not the Swedish king, still licking his wounds on the shores of the Black Sea, persuaded the Turks to declare war on Russia. The tsar received the unwelcome news in Moscow at Christmastime. Sultan Ahmed III had imprisoned the ambassador Pyotr Tolstoy in the Seven Towers of Constantinople and joined forces with Devlet-Girei, the anti-Russian khan of the Crimea.[5]

The Ottoman campaign of 1711 saw Gannibal return to his old Balkan haunts. In the summer he marched with Peter to Jassy. On the banks of the river Prut, a tributary of the Danube, the two princes of Wallachia and Moldavia, Constantin Brancovan and Dmitry Cantemir (who had indirectly helped in Gannibal's escape from the *seraglio* seven years earlier), now failed to send reinforcements after defecting from the Turkish side. Outnumbered by the Janissaries, the tsar had no choice but to sue for peace, though he was lucky to escape with the loss of only Azov and Taganrog. 'The Almighty drove me out of this place like Adam out of paradise,' Peter said of losing Azov. Once again the Black Sea was an Ottoman lake. The Great Northern War rumbled on, but Peter's southern dream was in tatters.

Henceforward the Russian military concentrated on the Baltic coast. Seen from this perspective, the disaster on the Prut was just a blip. In 1714, for example, Peter won his first significant naval victory off Cape Hangö in Finland. A week shy of his eighteenth birthday, Gannibal helped to capture the Swedish rear-admiral Nilsson Erenschild 'with one frigate, six galleys and two sloops, after much and very fierce fire'.[6] Russian military archives provide other glimpses of the young African in the run-up to this 'naval Poltava'. Peter's campaign journal shows that Gannibal drew up the order of battle after a survey of the Russian fleet. 'His Majesty dined on the battleship *Pernov* and then paid a visit of inspection to a Danish frigate and to the *Victory*, where His Excellence was accompanied by Prince Vasily Dolgoruky, [his chaplain Ivan] Bitka and Abram Petrov,' reads the entry for 2 June.[7]

Sometimes Gannibal acted as the tsar's private secretary, sharing that role with a keen-eyed, long-faced, dour-looking official by the name of Andrei Makarov. A gifted civil servant with a sharp-pointed beard, Makarov had no stomach for danger, and rarely ventured out of Petersburg. In the war zone it therefore fell to Gannibal to be

Peter's 'shadow, his memory, his eyes and ears', and also his spy.[8] The archives of a Russian commodore, Sinyavin, reveal that a few weeks after Hangö, Gannibal embarked on a secret mission to Estonia. 'On 10 August, the Negro Abram came to Reval on a Russian brigantine with messages from the tsar,' Sinyavin reported, without elaborating, though he praised the African's bravery in a storm that almost ship- wrecked the royal frigate on its way back to Petersburg.

The Soviet critic Nikolai Malevanov argued in the 1970s that Peter sent Gannibal to Reval to investigate a pro-Swedish conspiracy among German-speaking aristocrats such as the Rotkirkhs and the von Schöbergs. Russia's acquisition of Ingria and Livonia had brought into the empire a new political minority, the German elites. The tsar admired their western culture. He also shared their distaste for the backward Slavs. Inevitably these Baltic nobles served as a model for his new citizenry. Indeed, Pushkin's friend Prince Vyazemsky wrote that 'many things in our history can be explained by the fact that a Russian, Peter the Great, sought to make us Germans, while a German, Catherine the Great, wished to make us Russians'.[9] As the liberator of Reval, Gannibal welcomed the influence of German science and education. Yet he was appalled by the Teutonic mistreat- ment of the native peasantry. The new order in Estonia was rife with bitterness and intrigue.

The shipwreck drama had far-reaching consequences. Not only did it confirm the African's dislike of navigation. 'I am no man of the sea!' he wrote to Makarov in 1722.[10] The narrow escape prompted the tsar to reflect how easily Gannibal's secret letters could have fallen into the wrong hands. In future, the tsar decreed, intelligence must travel in the expectation of being intercepted. Hence the importance of codes. A skill in ciphering and 'secret writing' became essential to Peter's statecraft: in other words, a storm in the Baltic changed Russian espionage for ever.

Gannibal set out the principles of cryptography in a manual he wrote for Peter. Before drafting the work he studied various methods of transforming a letter to hide its meaning. The bookshelves in his

study at Petrovskoye betray a close reading of such works as Giambat-
tista della Porta's *De furtivis literarum notis* (1563) and Blaise de Vige-
nère's *Traicté des chiffres*, published in 1586, while the dashes of pencil
in the margins of *Poliorceticus*, or *On the Defence of Fortified Positions*,
by the Greek military scientist Aeneas Tacitus, show Gannibal
experimenting with ciphertexts and cryptograms, hieroglyphs and
numerical codes, transposing or substituting letters and mathematical
symbols. Writing in the fourth century BC, Aeneas devoted a whole
chapter of *Poliorceticus* to cryptography.[11] Gannibal followed suit in
1725 with *Geometry and Fortification*, giving a rudimentary account of
the different encryption systems.[12] The book earned the Moor praise
for his 'subtle mind' and 'natural intelligence', according to Field
Marshal Burkhard Münnich, the German strategist who became one
of the major political figures in Russia during the reign of Peter's
niece Anna in the 1730s. 'The secret game of hide-and-seek is one at
which he excels,' Münnich wrote to her,

> and that is why the uncle of Your Imperial Majesty, the Sovereign
> Emperor of Eternal Memory, made sure that at all times, and in all his
> military campaigns – including Dobroye, Lesnaya, Poltava, Hangö
> and Prut – and in a great many trials, that His Majesty always kept
> Abram Petrovich Gannibal by his side.[13]

Of course there was another mundane reason why Gannibal
became indispensable to the tsar. In his testimonial Münnich glossed
over a plain fact that we have already touched on. Somebody had to
write Peter's letters, coded or otherwise. With Makarov back in Petersburg, it came down to a straightforward choice between the Moor and
the illiterate Menshikov. 'I am credibly informed that Menshikov can
neither read nor write,' the English ambassador Whitworth reported
in 1706.

Rotkirkh adds that the young African 'soon became the secret clerk
for the Imperial Sovereign in many very confidential and important
matters'.[14] Yet he was more than just a pen pusher. Still a teenager, but

already a member of the tsar's inner circle, Gannibal played a key role as his political adviser. He was a secretary, in the original Elizabethan sense of the word – a privy councillor – as Pushkin boldly asserted in his poem 'My Genealogy': the African was anything but a flunkey to Peter, who

> was close to my granddad,
> And the purchased blackamoor
> Grew up zealous, incorruptible,
> The tsar's secret sharer, not his slave.[15]

It was not simply a linguistic quirk or romance that led Pushkin to the idea of a 'secret sharer'. His enemies, such as Faddey Bulgarin, scoffed at the poet for upgrading his ancestor's rank in *The Negro of Peter the Great*. Yet the fact remains that Gannibal had a unique relationship with the tsar. The unfinished novel reaches a turning point in chapter five when Peter's matchmaking on his behalf shocks Ibrahim into reconsidering his wifeless future. No doubt Pushkin intended the Moor's realisation that he might swap 'the flinty and steel couch of war' for a honeymoon suite to echo Othello's speeches in the opening act of Shakespeare's play. 'Are you fast married?' asks Iago. '"Married?" thought Ibrahim. "How can one believe in love? I rejected such foolish notions long ago and chose other, more serious affairs instead."'[16] As we have seen, Peter was an incorrigible wedding arranger – and 'freak' weddings were a staple of the all-mad assembly. Two dwarfs and a black couple were sent to Germany for the marriage of Alexei in 1711. A year earlier, Anna Ivanovna and the duke of Courland were the guests of honour at the wedding feast of the royal dwarf Yakim Volkov, which took place at the same time and in the same room of Menshikov's palace as their own. Indeed Gannibal's elder brother, also called Alexei, was married against his will, in 1716, to a serf girl on Prince Vasily Golitsyn's estate during a week of festivities reminiscent of a peasant wedding by Bruegel: drunken, coarse, anarchic.[17]

Pushkin got it wrong, however, in *The Negro of Peter the Great*. The tsar's matchmaking of Ibrahim and Natasha Afanasyevna was just a plot engine, but it overheated, forcing him to abandon the novel. In real life Peter did the exact opposite to his fictional counterpart. He actually vetoed the idea of a wedding. 'Take note,' he wrote in a stern memo to Avtamon Ivanov, secretary of the All-Drunken Assembly. 'The Moor is not to be married.'[18] Presumably the kind of marriage Peter wanted to avoid was the mock ceremony or freak show. It shows how far the 'strange creature' had come since Ivan Buturlin masqueraded as the king of Poland at his baptism in Vilnius. Now the tsar had 'other, more serious affairs' in mind for Gannibal. The Moor had risen from the cabinet of curiosities to the cabinet itself.

The secret sharer found a niche in the circles of courtiers and aristocrats, soldiers and civil servants, politicians and spies. He was a young man of wit and bravery. His fame was beginning to spread. Once-scornful boyars and grandees scurried to ingratiate themselves, waiting for hours in his antechamber, which, said the historian Golikov, was 'never empty of noblemen and foreign gentlemen and even ladies, whose sole occupation seemed to be a desire to pay court to him'. Undoubtedly Peter valued the African on account of his intellectual gifts. Insomnia was another secret of his success, according to Golikov, who heard the following story from Gannibal's own lips:

This Russian Gannibal had among his other talents an extraordinary eccentricity, which meant that he did not sleep very deeply, but always awoke at the first sound or murmur. This eccentricity of his was the reason that the tsar made him a secretary and slept in the same room as him, or in the one right next door.

Gannibal himself told me this anecdote, which he always recounted with tears in his eyes, that there was never a night when the sovereign did not wake him, and sometimes it was more than once. Waking up, the great tsar, shouted for him: '*Arap!*' To which Gannibal would immediately reply: 'What do you want?' 'Give me a candle and a board — by which he meant the slate kept on a hook with a pencil by the bedstead. Gannibal handed over the slate and the tsar proceeded to scribble or dictate his drafts, which Gannibal would then write out in code in the morning in his journal, for the tsar to sort out according to priority.[19]

His clandestine habits raised eyebrows at the Tsarevich Alexei's wedding in Saxony, a lavish event hosted at her castle in Torgau by Christina Eberhardina, queen of Poland and the phantom godmother. The windows of the state ballroom were covered with drapes and the walls hung with mirrors to reflect the light of thousands of candles. The German philosopher and mathematician Gottfried Wilhelm Leibniz dined at the same table as Gannibal, and the two of them discussed cryptography, military engineering and the tsar's education reforms. A friend of the bride's father, the enlightened duke of Wolfenbüttel, Leibniz had a low opinion of Russians, whom he dubbed 'the Turks of the North', even after Peter gave him a life pension. But he had gained from the duke a high opinion of blacks. Since 1707, Wolfen-büttel had employed an African page by the name of William Amo, who was brought to Europe by Dutch slavers. In 1727, Amo went to the University of Halle to study philosophy and jurisprudence, and, in 1734, he earned a doctorate from the University of Wittenberg.

Leibniz was astonished to find that Gannibal knew his work on differential calculus, as well as Newton's treatise *Principia Mathematica*. Indeed eyewitnesses reported that the 65-year-old genius seemed to prefer the company of the softly spoken African, with his grasp of languages and easy understanding of Cartesian algebra, to the drunken antics of the Slavs. 'I shall be charmed if I can help him [Peter] make science flourish in his country,' Leibniz wrote in a letter to an unnamed official at the Kremlin after the wedding. The package also contained various memoirs and documents – outlining plans for secondary schools, industry, agriculture, newspapers, printing presses, research into the magnetic properties of the Russian soil and a proposal for the founding of an Academy of Sciences – as well as an arithmetic textbook entitled *Cyfferinge* by the Dutch mathematician Willem Bartjens. The book, with its new owner's inscription, 'Abram Petrov. Moscow. 1711', still occupies pride of place in the library at Mikhailovskoye.

Over the next few years Gannibal immersed himself in the study of mathematics under the guidance of the Ukrainian cleric Feofan Prokopovich, who taught arithmetic, geometry and physics at the Kiev Academy. The first authentic voice of the Enlightenment in Russia, Prokopovich took Peter's side against Mazepa and delivered a panegyric at Poltava. His knowledge of such writers as Bacon, Spinoza and Descartes helped Gannibal 'to become one of the most educated Russian officers', according to Prince Pyotr Dolgoruky.[20] The Moor's papers from this period, now held at archives in Tallinn and Pskov, are full of scribbled investigations into finite and infinite sequences of numbers. The young African was especially interested in questions of logic and notation – or, as we say now, computing – and since it was derived from Bartjens's work on 'ciphering', his research won Peter's blessing. The tsar was painfully aware of his own inadequate education. His personal seal bore the legend: 'I am a student and I seek teachers'. He admired the African's didactic spirit, and believed his formidable mathematical talents would unlock Russian potential:

> Abram Gannibal furnished the most striking proof of the injustice of that odious prejudice which assigns to the Negro race a reputation of intellectual and moral inferiority. He had immense spirit, a prodigious facility for study, and a rare capacity for mathematics and diverse branches of the human sciences, although mathematics always served as the *science-mère*. He was also blessed with a noble and elevated character and an incorruptible probity.[21]

Sometimes, however, Peter got frustrated at the lack of tangible progress. At Bad Pyrmont in May 1716, on the eve of another meeting with Leibniz, the tsar demanded to see the fruits of Gannibal's study. His godson reached for a notebook and drew a magic square:

|    |    |    |
|----|----|----|
| 11 | 6  | 7  |
| 4  | 8  | 12 |
| 9  | 10 | 5  |

'Why is it magic?' Peter asked, with a frown. 'Because the sum of the numbers is always twenty-four, whether you add them up along a diagonal, a row or a column,' Gannibal replied. The furrows deepened on the sovereign's brow. He began to count out loud, on his fingers, until puzzlement returned. 'Does the magic work for all sums?' The African nodded. For any sum $x$, he went on, if $y = \frac{x}{3}$ you can line up the following numbers: $y+3, y-2, y-1, y-4,$ $y, y+4, y+1, y+2, y-3$. Gannibal wrote out the equation on a fresh sheet of paper. For a moment the tsar looked nonplussed, then grabbed his pipe and stormed out of the room.[22]

It is hard to imagine a more dramatic transformation. Once an alien presence in Russia, Gannibal had become the embodiment of Petrine reform, not only the tsar's adviser, but an intellectual guide, and as natural a participant in the councils of state as Menshikov and Catherine. Yet success came at a price, with strings attached, and the great mystery in Gannibal's life is the disappearance of his brother Abdul/Alexei.[23] How to explain his abrupt removal from the story? Did the Negro of Peter the Great lose touch with his older brother? Did they quarrel? A document from 1716, now held in the Moscow archives, certifies that Alexei 'served as an oboist with the Preobrazhensky regiment since he was eight years old', but there is no military record, nor anything in the Golitsyn family papers, to say what happened afterwards.[24] The brother of the famous Moor simply vanished without trace.

The Pushkin family may have believed that Alexei escaped from his life of serfdom and returned to Africa. Indeed an unexplained stanza in the first chapter of *Onegin* outlines such a fate:

> It is time to leave the dull shore
> Of a country that is hostile to me,

And amid meridional waves
Under the sky of my Africa
To sigh for gloomy Russia,
Where I suffered, where I loved,
Where I buried my heart.[25]

Nabokov suggests that the speaker here is Gannibal, who never returned to Logone, but it might just as well be Alexei. The sheer distance of Lake Ladoga from Lake Chad makes such a journey improbable, even though it would fit neatly into another fraternal legend. Delving once again into the biblical story of Joseph, Rotkirkh's biography describes a conscience-stricken reunion between the Moor and one of the brothers who sold him down the river Logone:

> At that time his ruling half-brother, being pressed, I suppose, by the still living mother of this European Gannibal, about the fact that her son was (or so she thought) languishing in slavery in Constantinople, decided to pay a ransom to free him, and with this idea in mind he dispatched one of his younger brothers to go in search of the second Joseph, who had been sold into slavery by his own kith and kin. This brother went first to Stamboul, but then to Petersburg, from where he imagined he would be able to buy Gannibal's freedom, with the help of a large payment, and bring him back to Africa. But it was no longer possible for Gannibal, a youth with so much promise, who had by now converted to Christianity, to return to paganism and barbarism, because he had already grown accustomed to the European way of life, and in any case had no wish to go back, so he issued a flat refusal to the brother who had brought precious weapons as gifts and Arabic documents proving Gannibal's royal origin. The brother departed empty-handed for his homeland, with many tears on both sides.[26]

Nabokov dismisses the tale as a 'family fantasy', adding: 'There is hardly any need to remark that no Abyssinian seigneur could have travelled to Muscovy via Turkey without being enslaved there, nor

is there any historical information of any free Abyssinian under-
taking such a journey in the first part of the eighteenth century.'[27]
Throughout his life Gannibal dreamed of returning to the homeland
whose symbol, the elephant, adorned his Russian coat of arms. But
the youngest son of Prince Bruha of Logone had undergone a kind
of metamorphosis, an irreversible change, to become 'this European
Gannibal', for whom there was no way back even if he wanted one.

Tsarevich Alexei shared an unhappy fate as well as a name with
Gannibal's brother. Yet *his* removal did not strike Peter's conscience.
The rift between father and son had only widened after Alexei's
marriage to Charlotte. She died in 1715 giving birth to a child, the
future Peter II, by which time the tsar feared that Alexei was plotting
to undo his reforms. In a remark that some attributed to a preference
for Gannibal, Peter declared that he would rather hand the country
'to a worthy stranger than to my own unworthy son'.[28] In 1716, he
ordered the tsarevich to renounce his claim to the throne. When
Alexei fled the country instead, his father vowed that he would be
'eternally damned and pursued like a traitor'.

The pursuer was Pyotr Tolstoy, now back from Constantinople.
He tracked Alexei down to the island fortress of Saint Elmo, near
Naples, and persuaded the tsarevich to return to Petersburg with the
false hope of a pardon. Under torture, in the Peter and Paul fortress,
a broken Alexei confessed to plotting with the Holy Roman Emperor
and was accused of treason. His death, on 26 June 1718, was officially
ascribed to natural causes, but rumours implicated Peter.

# 12

# Nègre du Czar

I'm in Paris,

I've begun to live, not just to breathe.

—Ivan Dmitriev, *Diary of a Traveller*

News of Alexei's death reached Gannibal in Paris, where he was already the talk of the town, visiting the Louvre and the Palais Royal, promenading in the Tuileries and the Luxembourg Gardens. 'The appearance of Ibrahim, his black face, his culture and his native intelligence captured the attention of the whole of Paris,' wrote Pushkin. 'All the ladies wished to see *le Nègre du Czar* at their salons, and vied with one another to catch him.'[1] The French courtier and memoirist Saint-Simon marvelled at 'the singularity of journey into France of so extraordinary a prince' and his black godson.[2]

Gannibal's fame spread beyond the court. He became – in a modern sense of the word – a personality. Bewigged fops hailed the prodigy from darkest Africa as one of the *lumières* of Russia's Enlightenment. Few realised that he was also a spy. Yet the opening sentence of Pushkin's unfinished novel hints at a subtext of espionage. 'Among the young men sent abroad by Peter the Great to gather intelligence necessary for a developing country was his godson, the Moor Ibrahim,' wrote the godson's great-grandson.[3] The Russian word for intelligence, *svedeniye*, bears a complex meaning. It can mean 'knowledge', 'science' or 'education', which is usually how it appears in English translations of *The Negro of Peter the Great*, but it can also mean more than that. Here the word figures as a pun. The education of the Moor was just a cover story. In public, Gannibal kept up the pretence that he had come to Paris to study military engineering under the watchful eye of Louis-Auguste de Bourbon, duc du Maine, a bastard son of Louis XIV. Privately he spent the long ceremonial days at court gleaning as much secret information as he could about the rival claimants to the French throne.

The summer of 1717, when Gannibal arrived in Paris, represented the high-water mark of Bourbon conspiracy. The death of Louis XIV two years earlier had left the court in disarray. For seven decades life had revolved around a Sun King who had alarmed Europe, and bankrupted France, in his quest for military glory. Shortly before the sunset of Louis Quatorze, however, an unpredictable bout of mortality had wiped out three heirs in the space of three years: the king's son, his grandson and his great-grandson. A series of defeats in the war of the Spanish Succession complicated the tragic sequence. In 1713, the peace treaty of Utrecht confirmed the king's younger grandson, the duc d'Anjou, as king of Spain – though only in return for Philip V (as he became) renouncing any claim to the French throne. Thus, in the aftermath of the princely holocaust, the Sun King was succeeded by his younger great-grandson. A 5-year-old child became Louis XV, though poor health made it seem unlikely he would outlive childhood. In the meantime the dead king's nephew, Philip d'Orléans, ruled France as regent, much to the dismay of the 'Old Court' faction led by Gannibal's sponsor, the duc du Maine.

The Old Court seethed with hidden plots to overthrow the regency. But it was not until the *Nègre du Czar* stepped into this world of disharmony and intrigue, on 26 April 1717, that we discover any obvious sign of Peter's keenness to exploit the chaos of French politics.

Twenty years after his Grand Embassy to Europe, the tsar again quit Russia for a year and a half to conduct a long, meandering tour of Germany, Denmark, Holland and Belgium. Aged twenty, Gannibal joined the ranks of young nobles and diplomats, scholars, soldiers and spies who left Petersburg, on 24 January 1716, heading to Danzig for the marriage of Peter's niece Catherine – the daughter of his half-brother Ivan – to duke Karl Leopold of Mecklenburg. Afterwards he spent a difficult month in the German spa town of Bad Pyrmont, discussing algebra with a gout-ridden Leibniz before travelling on to Copenhagen and Amsterdam. The tsar's caravan moved westwards slowly, making detours to Utrecht, the Hague and Rotterdam as it crossed a continent still riven by warfare. In the spring of 1717, Peter's 'jolly crew' landed at Boulogne and the African began to dream of seeing Paris.

On a fine day in late April, in the northern suburb of Saint Denis, business was quiet as usual. A few townsfolk stood conversing idly outside the *hôtel de ville* when a royal carriage suddenly swept past with its escort of red-coated cavalry. Perhaps some of the local merchants who glimpsed the splendid vehicle hurtling through Saint Denis's narrow arched streets recognised the coachman's livery as that of the tsar of Russia. They must have wondered at the black face staring out from the luxury of the carriage. Sitting beside his godfather, the African marvelled at the stone-paved streets and ornately carved façades. Under the Sun King, Paris had become 'the most beautiful and magnificent city in Europe', according to Prince Boris Kurakin, the diplomat who was also sitting in the tsar's carriage that day.[4] His description of Peter's arrival is a real eighteenth-century vignette.

Hearing the clatter of wheels as they approached the Observatoire, Gannibal turned expectantly to look out of the window at the hangings of rich tapestry that adorned the city's finest buildings. In 1717, with half a million citizens, Paris was the third largest city in Europe. Yet it occupied a much smaller area than London or Amsterdam. The great palaces and squares that lie at the heart of today's Paris – the Tuileries, the Luxembourg, the Place Vendôme, the Invalides – were then on the city's fringes. Inside was a strange teeming place that amazed Gannibal. He watched the noisy crowds spilling out of the coffee houses near St Germain des Près. He admired the fashionable ladies strolling in the Palais Royal. For a young man of wit and ambition this dazzling prospect seemed to offer a route to success. It also kindled a resolve to help the tsar with his latest plan.

Nobody knows when Peter first thought of negotiating a treaty with France. Louis XIV had always been a staunch ally of Sweden. Throughout his long reign the Sun King had opposed Russia in the Baltic and on the Black Sea. So his death meant an opportunity to redraw the map of Europe, coinciding as it did with the Hanoverian succession in Britain. At the start of the year, while revisiting old haunts in Amsterdam, the tsar learned that Britain, France and the Dutch Republic had formed a triple alliance. It threatened to isolate Russia. Therefore, hoping to persuade the next king of France to switch sides in the Great Northern War, to halt royal subsidies to Sweden and to pay the money to him instead, Peter embarked on the French leg of his European tour. But he had one major headache: who exactly would the next king of France be? The sickly orphan heir? His great-uncle Philip d'Orléans, or even Philip V of Spain, who was Louis's only surviving grandson? Peter wanted to hedge Russia's bets. 'To that end, the tsar, the great father of our country, saw fit to recommend me in person to the duc du Maine, prince of the blood, and grandmaster of the French artillery, the natural son of the illustrious French king Louis the Great, while he courted the Regent,' wrote Gannibal.[5] (A 'prince of the blood' was so called because he and the king shared a common ancestor.) Yet the young African questioned the wisdom of Peter's two-pronged approach to diplomacy. 'I am not yet convinced of the prudence of our mission,' he added, 'considering my years and the uncertain state in which France hangs between these warring princes of the blood.'

The next morning the regent came to welcome the tsar to the Louvre. A man of 'grand and imposing looks', according to one acquaintance, the 42-year-old prince made a theatrical entrance. Fashionably clad in a wide-skirted coat, unbuttoned to reveal a crimson waistcoat and cravat of Brussels lace, Philip d'Orléans wore a periwig of black curls that cascaded over his shoulders. He walked briskly through the royal apartments, searching for Peter, but to no avail. Sumptuously furnished in gold and silver, the walls draped in velvet and damask, ivory and tortoiseshell, these rooms had once belonged to the Sun King's mother, Anne of Austria. Much to the regent's consternation, however, the lavish stage set was empty. Strutting up and down, he could find no trace of the Muscovite guest. Nor could the reception committee made up of high-ranking officials and Orleanist hangers-on. The foreign minister, Abbé Guillaume Dubois, whom Saint-Simon memorably described as an 'ill-bred ferret', exchanged puzzled looks with the Scots gambler John Law, 'a kind of wizard perhaps as imaginary as Merlin', who was soon to bankrupt the country with his *monnaie de singe*, or 'funny money'.[6] The only sound echoing down those vast corridors was a murmur of French indignation.

Full of caprices and strange whims, Peter had already made a theatrical exit from the Louvre. Its palatial atmosphere overawed the jolly crew. Instead, the eccentric tsar opted for lodgings next to the Bastille, where he and Gannibal ordered two camp beds to be placed in a small dressing room. 'The Hotel de Lesdiguières was prepared for the Czar and his suite, under the idea that he might prefer a private house, with all his people around him, to the Louvre,' wrote Saint-Simon.

Here, in the shadow of the famous prison, Gannibal caught his first glimpse of Louis XV. Still wearing an infant's halter, as if to enhance the symbolism of a puppet regime, the 7-year-old king came to pay his respects to the tsar. Peter and his black godson stood waiting in the courtyard as the royal convoy drew up. It was just after midday on 29 April 1717. Eyewitnesses report that Peter rushed forward as the king stepped down from the carriage. To the astonishment of the French party, the outsize Russian ruler took the little boy in his arms, lifted him into the air until their faces were at the same level, and hugged and kissed him several times as he walked into the hallway where two armchairs had been placed. The young king sat down in the right-hand one, the tsar in the other. Prince Kurakin served as the interpreter. Hovering on the edge of the circle were Gannibal and the duc du Maine, who accompanied the king in his official role of superintendent over the boy's education.

Born with a deformed foot, the duc du Maine walked on crutches. His wife, Louise-Bénédicte de Bourbon-Condé, a legitimate great-granddaughter of Louis XIII, called him 'the lame bastard'. Indeed she gave him the nickname *gambillard*, an old French word for leg. Others called him Tamburlaine ('Timur the Lame') in mocking contrast to the all-conquering Mongol warlord. The Sun King's 'natural son' was a no-conqueror, a political zero.[7] His deformity led Maine to shun the public gaze and, being a recluse, he lacked magnetism and charm. If Dubois the *parvenu* was a ferret, then the duc du Maine was 'a little timid mole', according to Saint-Simon, 'very clever and cunning in reaching his goal through underground passages, but ineffective and blind if ever he ventured into the daylight'.

His wife had the intelligence and stature of a 10-year-old child. She was, like her husband, slightly deformed. Her paralysed right arm, much shorter than her left, gave rise to the cruel Orleanist jibe that her marriage was a union of the one-legged and the one-armed. Yet no one questioned her bedtime reading of Machiavelli's notes on conspiracy. At Sceaux, a château on the outskirts of Paris, where this snobbish votary of the cloak and dagger hoped to establish a court to rival Versailles, the duchess created her own order of chivalry, the Order of the Honeybee. Its motto, '*Piccola si, ma fa pur gravi le ferite*', was an allusion to her size: 'She may be small, but she still has a sting.'[8] One of its knights (or drones) was Gannibal. In a letter to Catherine I, written after his return to Russia, he recalled a ceremony at Sceaux conducted with the utmost gravity, at which he pledged his allegiance 'in person to the duc du Maine, prince of the blood, master of artillery, and natural heir of Louis the Great, and to his wife, the granddaughter of the Great Condé'.[9] On bended knee, as the duchess fastened to his shoulder the emblem of the Order, a little golden bee, the African swore 'by all the bees of Mount Hymettus' to help avenge the Maines against the regent.

Four years older than Philip d'Orléans, the duc du Maine was inferior to the regent in every other respect. Orléans was a debauched aristocrat, of course, but at least his vices were spectacular. Behind closed doors at the Palais Royal he held infamous all-night revelries at which his dissolute male friends and an eclectic mix of actresses and courtesans gorged, drank to excess and 'said vile things at the tops of their voices', according to rumour. Nevertheless he possessed an abundant if mercurial intellect, and an interest in philosophy, and science that won him an even more scandalous reputation as a free-thinker. He also possessed 'gentle and insinuating manners' that easily outshone the bilious duc du Maine.

The plotters welcomed Gannibal into the Sceaux circle. He was praised by Maine as a 'gentleman-scholar' who now 'is come to answer the complaint of Frenchmen'. The tone is one of instinctive patronage, and it is likely that Gannibal, on Peter's instructions, spent a great deal of time at Sceaux, making subterranean contacts, a Russian mole at the court of Saint-Simon's 'timid little mole'. Little remains of that Arcadia now. The stately gardens at Sceaux were designed by Le Nôtre, the genius of Versailles, and adorned with marble statues by Puget. The Maines employed scholars to argue the historical legiti-macy of royal bastards. But the results were often hard to read in the haze of allegory: a procession of cupids and sylphs, winding in and out of sylvan glades and purple prose. 'Examples drawn from the family of Nimrod were scarcely conclusive,' observed Madame de Staal-Delaunay, a disaffected member of the court at Sceaux.[10]

One of the duchess's ladies-in-waiting, Staal-Delaunay was a tall, angular, forceful-looking woman. By the time she met Gannibal at Sceaux, in late May, she was already thirty-three, twelve years older than the Moor. Her face, in a portrait by Mignard, cannot be called beautiful: rather long and horsey, and framed with frizzy hair, but it is strong, and bears some resemblance to the description of Countess D—, a woman 'no longer in the first bloom of her youth', with whom the Negro of Peter the Great falls in love in Pushkin's novel. Her letters mention that the African 'was worthy of praise on account of his cleverness', and that she was greatly taken with him, 'because he does all he can to please me'.[11]

The liaison remained secret, but inevitably there were rumours.

One piece of courtly tittle-tattle from Staal-Delaunay's memoirs resurfaces in the novel's opening scene. 'The countess received Ibrahim politely, but without any particular attention, which flattered him, since people usually regarded the young Negro as a freak and suffocated him with their curiosity and questions,' Pushkin wrote. 'Little by little she grew accustomed to the young Negro's appearance, and even began to find something rather pleasant about the curly head, so black amid the powdered wigs in her drawing-room.'[12]

Rose Staal-Delaunay was not a countess, nor even a member of the aristocracy. She was the daughter of an obscure French artist by the name of Cordier-Delaunay, and a friend of Antoine Watteau. The famous painter made a number of preliminary sketches for a portrait of Gannibal during a visit to Sceaux that summer. Unfortunately, Watteau never finished the portrait, or else it was lost when he fled to England in 1719 soon after the Maines were arrested on charges of treason. Staal-Delaunay blamed 'Watteau's secretiveness' for interrupting the *fête galante* at Sceaux. However, a tantalising page from his notebook, showing three chalk studies of a young African, is preserved in the Louvre museum.[13] In the wake of the arrests, Staal-Delaunay wrote to the marquis d'Argenson, the regent's *lieutenant de police*. This gimlet-eyed policeman was convinced that Gannibal had been plotting with the Maines, or perhaps that he constituted some other even more insidious threat. The undated letter from Staal-Delaunay ends:

> I mean to assure that, whether or not he is legally the tsar's godson, and notwithstanding the colour of his skin, this learned man is quite unlike those barbarous Russians whom we glimpsed of late, dead drunk and making such a great deal of noise. Nor is he a spy, or I would have imparted it to you, and therefore I beseech you to suppress any such malicious report.[14]

This was a lie, or a series of lies, but it arrived at a truthful moment of disquiet about Gannibal who, though 'absolute at Paris', according to Lady Mary Wortley Montagu, was soon to be exposed to public censure. Passing through the city in 1718 on her way back to England from Constantinople, Montagu compared Gannibal to that other inter-loper John Law, 'who treats their dukes and peers extremely *de haut en bas*, and is treated by them with the utmost submission and respect'.[15]

In the end Peter's diplomacy came to nothing. Neither the regent nor the Old Court responded to his overtures. 'The Muscovite tsar's six-week stay produced little more than a crop of dirty stories,' observed Nabokov, 'though why the grandees of the Regency, a filthy pack in a disgusting and talentless age, should have been so puzzled by Peter's habits is not quite clear.'[16]

'Disgusting and talentless' might seem a harsh verdict to deliver upon the age of Fontenelle, Voltaire and Montesquieu. Yet it reflects the view of Orléans's own mother, who characterised Paris as 'Sodom and Gomorrah', full of men who cheated on their wives and wives who sought out lovers. 'It is observable,' wrote one visitor, 'that the French allow their women all imaginable freedoms, and are seldom troubled by jealousy; nay, a Frenchman will almost suffer you to court his wife before his face, and is even angry if you do not admire her person.'[17] There were many rumours that Gannibal courted other men's wives as well as Madame de Staal-Delaunay. He was not immune to the charms of the Jacobite exile (and aptly named) Fanny Oglethorpe, according to the gossips, and may also have shared the favours of Claudine de Tencin, a renowned *salonnière* and former mistress of Dubois and the regent. 'The duc d'Orléans, combining many brilliant qualities with vices of every sort, unfortunately possessed not the slightest degree of hypocrisy. His orgies at the Palais Royal were no secret to Paris, and Gannibal found his example contagious,' wrote Pushkin. 'The regent more than once invited him to his wild evening parties. The Negro attended suppers enlivened by the youth of Arouet [who was yet to adopt the pen name of Voltaire], and the conversations of Montes-quieu and Fontenelle. He did not miss a single ball, fête or opening night at the theatre, and gave himself up to the general whirl with all the passion of his years and nature.'[18]

Some of these statements are untrue. Others are exclamatory or ironic. None can be squared with the opinions of Nabokov who says that he 'can find nothing in the French memoirs of the Régence that would corroborate such comments made by Pushkin'.[19] In fact, Gannibal did encounter the leading members of the Parisian intelligentsia. In his *Persian Letters*, written shortly after Gannibal arrived in Paris, Montesquieu describes one of those suppers at which Voltaire introduced him to the African *philosophe*:

> The other day, as I was on the Pont-Neuf with a friend of mine, he met a dark stranger he knew, who, he told me, was a mathematician; and so it certainly appeared, for he was deep in meditation, and my friend had to spend some time tugging at his sleeve and shaking him in order to bring him back to himself, so preoccupied was he with the properties of a curve which had been torturing him for perhaps a week or more. They greeted each other very politely and exchanged news about the world of learning. Their conversation brought them to the entrance of a coffee house and I went in with them.
>
> I noticed that everyone greeted our mathematician warmly, and that the waiters paid more attention to him than to the two musketeers sitting in a corner. As for him, it was clear that he was in a place that he liked, for his face relaxed a little, and he began to laugh as if he didn't know the first thing about mathematics.[20]

The meeting as described by Rica, the wandering hero of Montesquieu's *roman-à-clef*, gives a vivid picture of Gannibal as one of the musketeers of the French Enlightenment. The story corrects a negative opinion of Africans as savage and barbarian, but also remains tantalisingly unclear, somehow bleaching the colour of Gannibal's skin. *Tout cela est devenu blanc*, Montesquieu grumbled: everything has become white.

Other documentary evidence from this period of Gannibal's life is sparse. But among the African's definite acquaintances was the scientist and man of letters Bernard de Fontenelle, to whom Peter introduced him during a visit to the Académie des Sciences on 7 May 1717. That visit proved to be crucial for Gannibal's intellectual devel- opment because it put him in touch with a group of mathematicians, *philosophes* and natural scientists who operated within a narrow circle. Established in 1660 to promote scientific research, the Académie posed a serious challenge to the supremacy of the older Académie Française, which still claimed to be France's most prestigious cultural institution. As permanent secretary of the Académie des Sciences, Fontenelle held a very influential office. Not only did he keep abreast of international developments in science by corresponding with scholars in other European countries, including Leibniz (who may have recommended Gannibal to him as a student of military engi- neering), he also provided a useful link between dissident intellectuals and the sundry aristocrats who had sworn allegiance to the court of Sceaux.

A close friend of Montesquieu, who satirised the Maine plot in *Persian Letters*, and also well known to Voltaire, who mocked it in *Micromégas* as the 'conspiracy of grammarians', Fontenelle arranged a meeting, on 12 May, between Gannibal and the swashbuckling young duc de Richelieu.[21] The eponymous hero of Alexander Dumas's play *The Great Lover*, and indeed one of that black playwright's favourite characters since he also appears in many of his novels, Richelieu invited the African and his godfather to visit the tomb of his great- uncle, Cardinal Richelieu. Records show that, on 14 May, the tsar spent more than 130 *livres* on buying Gannibal a suit of new clothes for the occasion. Unexpectedly, the next day Voltaire showed up at the graveside, his first encounter with the '*le More*, the Negro, the natural son', as he later recalled in *Histoire de l'Empire de Russie sous Pierre le Grand*.

The son of a middle-class notary, and only two years older than Gannibal, the young Voltaire had recently become 'a sort of personage in the republic of letters', as Saint-Simon grudgingly conceded.[22] His epigrams were widely quoted, and it seemed that he was building himself patiently into the networks of Orleanist power, though he

had a wild side. In print he dared to mock the regent. His conversation was subversive. Yet his ideas fascinated Gannibal. Both men
were fast thinkers and witty talkers. Neither buttoned his lip. Both
were punished for loose talk, as Voltaire noted in his *Anecdotes*: 'Seeing
the tomb of Cardinal Richelieu, and his statue with its dignified
*ouvrage*, the tsar declared that there were some truly great individuals
in history, who stood apart. He climbed on top of the tomb, and
embraced the statue, saying: "Great minister, why are you not alive in
my lifetime! I would give you half my empire if you taught me how
to govern the other half."' Instantly – and he would later say unthink-
ingly – Gannibal, who was standing nearby, quipped: 'If you gave
him one half, you wouldn't hold on to the other for very long.' Some
experts argue that Voltaire himself was the heckler. Others deny he
was even present. Yet no version of this story occurs in any of the
sources he used to compile the *Anecdotes*, though it does appear in an
anonymous biography of the younger Richelieu, published in Paris
after Voltaire's death.[23]

One bystander who did apparently overhear Gannibal's remark,
however, was the marquis d'Argenson. The police chief hated
Voltaire. It is possible that he informed the regent of the writer's links
to Sceaux because a day later, on 15 May, in reply to a letter from
the secret policeman, Philip d'Orléans wrote: 'The intention of His
Royal Highness is that Monsieur Harrouet *fils* should be arrested and
taken to the Bastille.'[24]

The imprisonment of Voltaire was not the only setback for
Gannibal. Next door to the Bastille, at the Hotel de Lesdiguières,
the tsar was impatient to leave Paris, having abandoned hope of a
diplomatic breakthrough. (A treaty with Russia was unwelcome to
Dubois, who feared that such an arrangement would undermine the
Triple Alliance with Britain and Holland. 'If, in establishing the tsar,'
he warned the regent, 'you chase the English and the Dutch from the
Baltic Sea, you will be eternally odious to those two nations.')[25] On
8 June, the regent visited the hotel to bid Peter a sad goodbye. Later
the same day, Maine was present at a final meeting between the tsar

and Louis XV. They may have discussed Gannibal's future because immediately afterwards Peter ordered the payment of 15 ducats to his godson, the equivalent of half a year's salary. The tsar wanted Gannibal to return to Russia with him. But he relented when the African begged to stay in order to complete his 'intelligence' mission. 'In 1717, the tsar agreed out of the incomparable kindness of his heart to leave me in France to study military affairs,' Gannibal wrote in the preface to *Geometry and Fortification*.[26]

Also left behind in France were the diplomat Pyotr Tolstoy, who had rescued Gannibal from the clutches of the Ottoman Porte fourteen years earlier, and the Balkan adventurer Savva Raguzinsky, who became the new head of surveillance at the Russian legation. Both were under strict orders to keep an eye on Gannibal. The Topkapi trio were reunited: a different city, the same old web of intrigue. The tsar's parting words to Gannibal, on 10 June, were unexpectedly harsh. He warned his godson not to follow Voltaire's example. 'If you wind up in prison, don't hope for any clemency from me to get you out,' he said. 'But if you work hard and stay honest, then I will not abandon you.'[27] Unfortunately the warning came too late.

In the summer of 1717, the net was drawing in around the duc du Maine. Soon after Peter's departure, the regent moved unexpectedly against the Sceaux conspirators. In July, on the king's behalf, he issued a series of royal edicts that stripped Maine of his rank as a 'prince of the blood', thereby denying him the right to accede to the throne. A typically deft manoeuvre on the regent's part, since it gave legal authority to a *coup d'état*, the use of edicts was later criticised by the Bordeaux magistrate Montesquieu in *The Spirit of the Laws*. By law, if the *parlement* rejected an edict, the king could in person hold a *lit de justice* – at which his presence suspended any other authority.

Never did a king of France hold a more dramatic *lit de justice* than the one over which the now 8-year-old Louis XV presided on 26 August 1718. Talk of an uprising mounted until a deployment of troops in the capital – guards, gendarmes, light cavalry and musketeers – convinced the *parlementaires* that resistance was futile. In an atmosphere of high drama Orléans passed a decree stripping Maine of his last significant duty at court, that of supervising the king's education.

To add insult to political injury, the bastard duke was evicted from his royal apartment in the Tuileries. His expulsion sent the duchess into a fury. 'I have more heart than you,' she yelled at her husband, adding: 'I'll kill the regent. I'll hammer a nail into his brains,' before she finally vented her anger on the royal apartment itself. Not a single mirror was left intact. Every last chandelier was smashed to pieces. Marbles, wooden floors, paintings, sculptures – everything was broken. 'The horror of this flight,' wrote Staal-Delaunay, 'and still more the event which was the cause of it, made an impression on me such as I have never experienced on any other occasion.'

Gannibal was not the only member of the Sceaux cabal to advise the Maines that the legal battle with the regent was now lost. Voltaire had re-entered the orbit of conspiracy since his release from jail. In April 1718, Machaut, who had succeeded d'Argenson as police chief, noted the regent's wish that 'Monsieur Arouet *fils*, a prisoner in the Bastille, be set free and dispatched to the village of Châtenay, near Sceaux', where the duchess plotted her revenge.[28] Mindful of how her grandfather, the Great Condé, had made an ally of Spain during the civil wars of the mid-seventeenth century, she now fixed her hopes on installing Philip V as regent instead of Orléans. Her accomplice was the Spanish ambassador, Prince Cellamare, though Gannibal may have acted as a go-between. In any case, the French police watched his movements, and for a while the Bastille's shadow loomed over the African, as he reported in a series of dejected letters to the tsar.

Gannibal wrote seven letters to Peter or his secretary Makarov between 5 March and 24 December 1718. The recurring theme is an urgent need for money. 'I beg you not to abandon me,' he writes on 11 March, 'for the god of heaven's sake, sir, take pity on me.'[29] Yet the shift from a gruff, man-in-the-know tone to melodramatic self-abasement reflects the declining fortunes of the court at Sceaux.

The Cellamare affair had all the ingredients of a French farce, although its plot was more *opera buffa*, since the two main protagonists were Italians bidding to put a Spanish king on the French throne. The prime minister of Bourbon Spain, Giulio Alberoni, the exiled son of an Italian gardener, joined forces with the Maines in several failed attempts to poison Orléans. Gannibal watched the madness descend. Indeed, with his skill in 'secret writing', he may even have drafted several of the *Philippics* against Orléans (the Philip in question), some of which Cellamare handed to a young Spaniard, the Abbé Portecarrero, who was returning to Madrid. Unfortunately the poor novice was stopped at Poitiers, where Machaut's agents confiscated the papers and brought them back to the regent.[30]

Until that batch of secret documents fell into police hands, in December 1718, Orléans knew nothing of the plot. Its discovery was a godsend. The coded messages from Sceaux to Spain included a list of the names of sixty conspirators, many of whom fled the country. By now, however, with the Russian embassy under surveillance, and everyone spying on everyone else, the comic opera had reached its farcical limits. Accused of intrigues against the regent, the duc du Maine went to prison for a year. His wife and Cellamare were also arrested.

Gannibal, too, came under suspicion, but was bailed out of trouble by Raguzinsky, to whom he refers in a letter to the tsar dated 24 December 1718. He declines to elaborate but presents himself as a loyal servant of Russian interests – at no point does he use the word 'spying', or even the more respectable and ambiguous *svedeniye* ('intelligence') to describe his work – and rejects the charge of siding with the Maines. On the contrary, he claims actually to have rejected the chance of personal enrichment afforded by his contacts at Sceaux. 'I might have bettered my poor estate if only I had not respected the honour of the tsar,' he writes.

His excuses have the ring of self-justification, of papering over a failure. Nevertheless this letter, written just before Gannibal went into hiding (the next letter in the archive is dated 5 February 1722), casts light on his dark mood. Exile was now the only way to avoid imprisonment. Yet in the midst of his self-pity and complaining emerges a kind of political theme. It is there in Gannibal's strange formalisation of himself as a 'poor Negro boy and soldier', and also in a cryptic reference to the bail money put up by Raguzinsky. 'I know that a million souls have nothing but Your Majesty's kindness to thank for the gift of life,' he writes, using the Russian word 'souls', as in serfs or slaves:

> and that all of them are as blessed as I am to have been raised by your kindness, so I rejoice, my dear sovereign, even as I inform you that I am in deep trouble, and that things can only get worse, because Savva Raguzinsky, through his official contact, has only paid 200 roubles, which is not enough to stave off debt.[31]

That last sentence remains enigmatic, as does the truth behind it. What is not in doubt, however, is that Gannibal could not stay in Paris. Shortly after posting the letter, the *Nègre du Czar* packed his belongings and hit the road south, on foot, striding through the fields and forests, crisscrossing the Massif Central, and then by stagecoach through the Rhône Valley, and on to the Pyrenees.

# 13

# Man of Parts

In Jamaica, indeed, they talk of one Negro as a man of parts and learning; but it is likely he is admired for slender accomplishments, like a parrot who speaks a few words plainly.
—David Hume, *Essay on Human Understanding*

It is the middle of a Russian winter. In the oak-panelled reading room on the first floor of the Academy of Sciences in Saint Petersburg, the archivist lifts the two volumes of *Geometry and Fortification* to a narrow window of daylight overlooking the Neva and the fortress of Peter and Paul. '*Dobroye utro!*' she says, out of habit or politeness, but it doesn't feel like a very 'good morning'. Outside the temperature is minus twenty-five. Inside the heating system has packed up. The dozen scholars hunched over manuscripts in the freezing room seem almost comically overdressed in their hats and coats and scarves.

I sit at the wooden desk and finger the two heavy tomes, both three inches thick, a total of 700 pages bound in dark green leather. Rubber-stamped in big black letters on the front cover of each volume is the classmark: RAN PB 24/1, denoting a work of science. Underneath is written, in a neat clerical hand, 'never published'. As I open the first volume, which is entitled 'Practical Geometry' – the second is called 'Fortification' – I find myself pondering the end of another quest, a sequel of sorts to the daydreams of FUMMO immortalised in the Gannibal family crest. The author of *Geometry and Fortification*, which he wrote in 1724, was, in his own dry phrase, a 'poor exile' from Africa. The forgotten homeland cast a shadow of nostalgia.

It became, according to the literary theorist Mikhail Bakhtin, a 'chronotope', not a real place but an undiscovered country that allowed Gannibal to range through time and space, to see the past in the present. A similar nostalgia impelled Gogol to write *Dead Souls* in Rome, or so he thought, because he could see Russia only 'from a beautiful distance'.

Yet the poor exile, like the 'poor Negro soldier', is only an imagined version of himself, and like all such versions it would prove unsatisfactory. This is already implicit in the letters Gannibal wrote to Peter before he fled to Spain. It becomes explicit in the original documents bound in the two volumes of *Geometry and Fortification*, a textbook in which the brilliant visual rhetoric of siege maps resembles the kind of clandestine autobiography that Soviet scholars used to describe as the secret code written for an in-group or 'first circle'.

The book is hardly a masterpiece. It mostly consists of diagrams – 'points, pricks and lines' – and laborious interpretations thereof. But it is also the only sustained piece of writing by Gannibal to survive: a breaking of the silence. It is brusque, lucid and accurate. In a preface, the African commends his book to the Empress Catherine as 'precise'. It is, he goes on, 'the result of many years' work, a series of academic texts, sketches and technical drawings of siegecraft, including ravelins and ramparts, explosives and earthworks'.[1] It is, in other words, a mine of information not only about Gannibal himself, but also about mines.

The manuscript provides a rich seam for biography. Until recently, however, the archive was closed to scholars, and so few could take advantage. In the opening paragraph of his sixty-page essay, for example, Vladimir Nabokov confessed that he had 'keenly felt the want of original documents' while compiling his 'secret life' of Abram Gannibal. He made this observation from the unlikely vantage point of New York City Library, almost half a century after leaving Russia for exile, never to return. Wistfully, he spent the 1950s gathering material for his iconoclastic four-volume edition of *Eugene Onegin*, but regretting that the bulk of his research was second-hand.

His quarrel with the Soviet Union – 'a wary police state' – precluded access to important manuscripts such as *Geometry and Fortification*. So he rewrote Pushkin's novel in his own style – a scandalous rewriting as it turned out, and an object lesson in the value and neglect of primary sources.

Gannibal's secret life – his reclusiveness, his retreats – was neither dark nor shameful. Indeed, he thought of it as the very opposite, and was fully prepared to describe it, or a version of it, in the textbook's preface where we get occasional glimpses of the African's moody demeanour at the start of 1719, as he picks up his pen and attempts to make sense of the Sceaux imbroglio. (The earliest sketches date from his journey to the Pyrenees.) It is a constant theme of *Geometry and Fortification* that his real interest lay in military engineering. He trails the manuscript on its first page as 'a book of shapes and curves, in which I aim to explain the science of wars past, present and to come, such as geography and history, and the customs and politics of the various places I have visited, while illustrating my account with diagrams, maps and plans on all techniques and procedures and all the special measures used in constructing fortifications and other questions of geometry'.[2]

Nothing is explained in Gannibal's text, though some historians of mathematics wax lyrical about his knowledge of trigonometry and use of logarithmic tangents, or stereographic projections, across several hundred pages full of interesting shapes and spirals and curves. On page 130 of volume one, for instance, next to a drawing of a church tower ready for bombardment, you will find not only a Cartesian curve but also the cycloid studied by Galileo, who gave it his name. Twelve pages further on, you come across the tractrix or equitangential curve dissected by Huygens, Leibniz and Bernoulli, and something resembling the *versiera,* or versed sine curve, which, through a misunderstanding – *versicra* means 'she-devil' or 'witch' in Italian – became known in English as the Witch of Agnesi. Gannibal makes no reference to Maria Agnesi, thought to be the first woman in the west to achieve a reputation in mathematics, but that is only because her magnum opus, *Instituzioni analitiche ad uso della giuventù italiana* (*Analytical Institutions for the Use of Italian Youth*), to which scholars often compare *Geometry and Fortification* as a work of pedagogy, did not appear until 1748. Nevertheless Gannibal knew a precursor of the Agnesi curve which had been studied by Fermat as early as 1703. His manuscript, in other words, was largely an editorial job. The text was 'compiled' by Gannibal from 'information and notes I brought back from France, and translations into Russian from books by various celebrated authors and gifted engineers'.[3] It was as if the African, on his return, debriefed himself, taking the miscellaneous notes and information he had collected on his travels and knocking them into shape.

Such a method of composition explains why *Geometry and Fortification* often reads like a commonplace book, and perhaps why it was 'never published', in the brutal phrase of the unknown cataloguer. On 23 November 1726, Gannibal presented the two volumes to the Empress Catherine at a formal audience in the old Winter Palace. 'In the hope that it will help to educate the noble youth of Russia,' the African said, in a deft Agnesi-like touch, 'I, your very humble subject, place the result of my modest labours under the most august protection of Your Imperial Majesty, trusting that Your Majesty will follow in every direction the path laid out by your glorious husband, Peter the Great.'[4] That confident hope went unfulfilled, not least because Catherine died the following year, and Gannibal was once again sent into exile.

For decades *Geometry and Fortification* lay on a dusty shelf of the imperial library. But it did not go completely unnoticed. In 1753, when a young nobleman named Andrei Bolotov retired to his uncle's modest estate, he found evidence of Gannibal's 'very important and extremely useful' scientific work. 'One day, in the library,' Bolotov wrote in his memoirs, 'I found a number of mathematical texts, both printed and in manuscript form, of which by far the most excellent was a notebook devoted to geometry and fortification, map-making, surveying, and how to calculate the range of artillery, in which my uncle had copied all the notes and drawings from an original by Gannibal. This science was no art of the devil, as some may suppose it, but a part of trigonometry, which many wise men call the daughter of mathematics and geography.'⁵

Bolotov said of Gannibal that he 'could describe a country with his pen'. That pen also helped to redraw the boundary of knowledge in his adopted country by popularising the diabolical new sciences that he encountered in France. Not the least remarkable thing about the African's education, however, is the way it continued after the end of the idyll at Sceaux. Here, in January 1719, was an unexpected change of tempo: exile and the journey south to war – unexpected and no doubt unappealing to most *philosophes*, whose experience of travelling was confined to the daily shuttle between home and the Opéra or the Tuileries. Gannibal decided to enlist in the French army. No longer able to rely on the patronage of the duc du Maine, the former grand-master of the king's artillery, to gain admission to the new military academy at La Fère, outside Paris, the African hoped to win a place as a reward for valour on the battlefield. In the Spanish war zone of fleets and harbour fortresses, Gannibal would, he thought, apply his bookish knowledge of the soldier's art. Indeed, it was on the road south to Marseilles that he came up with the title for volume one of his *magnum opus*: 'Practical Geometry'.

At first, sitting in the arctic conditions of the reading room at the Russian Academy of Sciences, I was disappointed to find no jaunty note among the fragments of Gannibal's text relating to one of the strangest incarnations of a strange career: the mercenary soldier. The autobiographical element of *Geometry and Fortification* is mostly absent, held in check, pared away – it is a piece of crisp, factual reportage – but it seems that the circumstances of the report are not entirely divorced from the episode in Spain. And here, ironically, it was the disgraced court at Sceaux that came to Gannibal's rescue. The aftermath of the Cellamare affair yielded an opportunity for swift promotion through the ranks. Western Europe had been quick to show its indignation at Alberoni's adventures. On 8 January 1719, the French government employed the talented Fontenelle, 'who was incapable of writing badly', to justify its aggressive intentions towards Spain. On the following day a declaration of war appeared on walls throughout Paris as France joined with the other members of the Quadruple Alliance in launching an attack. The Duke of Berwick was sent with 40,000 men to the western Pyrenees to invade the Biscayan provinces. Among those soldiers who crossed the border from the French province of Navarre was the African godson of the Russian tsar. Recruited as a 'king's ordinary engineer', Gannibal was soon commissioned as an officer and assigned to 'special work' on fortification and siegecraft. After taking part in operations against various Spanish towns during the first half of 1719, he was promoted to the rank of lieutenant-engineer and given command of a unit of artillery.

Life was tough in the Basque country. The French troops were ill-equipped and underfed. Dysentery and other diseases were rife. Yet the armies of the Quadruple Alliance outnumbered the enemy. The coastal gateway of Fuenterrabia fell on 17 June 1719, and Berwick went on to attack the peninsula fortress of San Sebastian, east of Bilbao. In the second volume of *Geometry and Fortification* – under the heading 'about offensive fortification' – '*o fortifikatsii ofansif*', the last word being a strange non-Russian hybrid indicative perhaps of his travels – Gannibal recalls how he planted some heavy guns on the far bank of the river Urumea, to open up a front on the slopes of Mount Urgull, and then drove his trenches along the beach on the near bank.[6] The fortress capitulated on 19 August, but while the African was unleashing a final contraption to deliver buckshot into the Spanish camp, he was literally hoist with his own petard. The resulting head injury, though patched up, sent him into a delirium, and after two weeks he was honourably discharged back to France, still dreaming of pyramids and parallelepipeds, triangles and trapezoids.

The invalid returned to Paris to find the dark clouds hanging over his reputation had lifted. His old friends, such as Voltaire and Montesquieu, gave him a rapturous welcome, and his new-found fame as a war hero meant that once again the grand ladies of regency society lined up to invite the *Nègre du Czar* to their salons. More importantly, the African's status as a battle-scarred veteran of the Spanish war, in which he was seen to have volunteered on the French side, opened the doors to the prestigious new military academy he aspired to enter. The new School of Artillery at La Fère in Picardy, a hundred miles north of Paris, was founded by royal decree and opened by Louis XV in 1720. Gannibal was among the first intake of students, as he proudly informed his godfather in a letter to Makarov, dated 5 February 1722:

> I have the honour to report to His Majesty the Tsar that I have seen action as a lieutenant-engineer after serving as a volunteer in the French army for a year, but now I wish to stay in France for another year as a new military school was set up in 1720 for young engineers, and it is a school from which all foreigners are barred unless they have served in the French army, so in the circumstances I hope the Tsar will not object to my attendance because it has enabled me to obtain a higher level of education.[7]

Gannibal wrote this letter after receiving from Prince Dolgoruky, the Russian ambassador in Paris, a *ukaz* (or decree) signed by the tsar ordering his return. The African wanted to complete his studies under the guidance of a brilliant young professor at the École d'Artillérie.

Still only twenty-four years old, Bernard Forest de Belidor taught engineering, artillery, ballistics, and fortification at La Fère. Today his fame rests primarily on *Architecture hydraulique* (1737–53), a classic four-volume work about pumps and mechanics, harbours, mills and waterwheels. He encouraged Gannibal to analyse the role of science in warfare, to see fortification as a subject of theory. In a sense he was only reflecting the spirit of a new enlightened age. Just as the mysteries of mathematics and nature had been explained by the researches of Newton, Huygens and Boyle, the young African learned from Belidor to use his knowledge to experiment with a nation's defences.

He spent long hours poring over maps and military diagrams. Belidor also introduced to the curriculum a variety of non-scientific topics. Towards the end of 1722, he sent Gannibal to the artillery school at Metz, founded by Louis XIV's military engineer, Sébastien Le Preste, marquis de Vauban, where the African developed a taste for French literature by reading the works of Corneille, Molière and Racine, and even began a translation into Russian of the ancient Chinese classic, Sun Tzu's *Art of War*.

Such refinement in a black man unnerved his fellow pupils. Until the eighteenth century, the French view of blacks had been dominated by a long-standing equation of blackness and evil. Seeking to understand the differences between blacks and whites from a more 'scientific' perspective, Montesquieu highlighted environmental factors. He argued that the heat made Africans lazy and immoral. Others shared his negative opinion. In the coffee houses of Paris, however, a strange colour blindness prevailed. Among his friends, such as Voltaire and Richelieu, it was as if Gannibal's wit bleached the pigment of his skin.

Racism was the dark side of the Enlightenment. The *philosophes* hated outsiders. Just as Maria Agnesi was reviled as a mathematical witch, so Gannibal suffered as a black intellectual in Europe. Owing to his royal connections, and to his war record, the African was lionised as a personality in France. Yet even the freethinkers of the Enlightenment were unsettled by his former life as a slave.

He was not unique. With the establishment of colonies on Guadeloupe and Martinique in 1635, and of the West India Company in 1670, France entered into plantation slavery and a transatlantic slave trade in earnest. From that time onward, French plantation owners, military commanders and government officials frequently brought their slaves on trips to France as servants, status symbols and curiosities. The Negro slaves King Jesus I of Ethiopia presented to the French chemist Poncet were not the only ones sent to Paris as souvenirs from the dark continent. As French sugar plantations began to generate wealth, slave-trading ports such as Nantes and Bordeaux became boomtowns. African princes, both genuine and phoney, visited France. One of the most interesting impostors was Aniaba, who claimed to be heir to the throne of Assinie in Ivory Coast. He came to Paris in 1687 and received a royal welcome: Louis XIV became his godfather and the famous orator Bossuet presided at his baptism in Notre Dame in 1692. However, when the chief of Assinie died in 1700 and a French warship sent Aniaba back to claim his homeland, the indifferent reception given to him by the local people exposed Aniaba as a fraud. Nevertheless a curious echo of the impostor's name can be heard in Pushkin's aitchless preference for *Annibal* to denote his great-grandfather.

The French historian Henri Blet argues that his compatriots have 'never adopted a racial doctrine affirming the superiority of whites over blacks'. Yet the doctrine reared its ugly head in countless anthropological sections of the *Encyclopédie*. The worst offenders were Diderot and Voltaire, both of whom looked upon Gannibal as a brother, both of whom invoked the native villagers of Dahomey, in west Africa — bare-breasted and reportedly cannibalistic — as evidence of the Negro's savage nature. How could such hypocrisy go unremarked? Well, to begin with, the *philosophes*' knowledge of, and interest in, Africa was severely limited. Out of the 3,867 books in Voltaire's library, only four were about Africa. Most French intellectuals relied on early eighteenth-century travellers' tales for their information. In other words, the *philosophes* were happy to recycle African stereotypes even though Gannibal disproved them. Thus Voltaire said the intelligence of blacks was 'far inferior', that they were 'incapable of great attention', and had only 'a few more ideas than animals'. Yet in the same breath he could praise Gannibal's work on the Leibnizian calculus. In *The Spirit of Laws*, Montesquieu declared that 'slavery is against nature', only to add that 'in certain countries it is founded on natural reason'. Diderot felt the people of Ivory Coast were debauched, 'like the black race as a whole'. Yet, in the spring of 1774, he made a detour on his journey home from Saint Petersburg to visit the *Nègre du Czar*.[8] The Scottish magus David Hume shared the fear and disgust that lay behind the Frenchman's prejudice. In his essay on 'National Character' (1771), he remarked that 'there are Negro slaves dispersed all over Europe, of which none ever discovered any more symptoms of ingenuity than a monkey'.

The ingenuity of Gannibal was known to his compatriots. Nevertheless the tsar, who 'loved Gannibal like a son', according to Rotkirkh, wanted the African to earn his keep. In the autumn of 1721, after signing the treaty of Nystad, which at last brought an end to the Great Northern War, and ceded to Russia the eastern shores of the Baltic, Peter drew up plans to fortify the newly acquired Lake Ladoga and Kronstadt. He hired the German engineer Count Münnich to dig a canal from the lake to Petersburg, twenty-five miles to the west. In 1722, the tsar invited Gannibal to return to Russia as Münnich's deputy, but the African was reluctant to give up his place at the artillery school in Metz. He used his 'ingenuity', or scholarship, as a bargaining chip in a series of pleading letters to the tsar. 'I assure you, my sovereign, that all the Russians here know how hard I always labour at my science,' he wrote on 5 March. 'I have sought every opportunity to achieve the best results, and even volunteered for the French army in order to pursue my studies at a place where they do not accept foreigners as a rule, unless they have fought for France.'[9]

Yet science wasn't the only opportunity that Gannibal was seeking. He was also playing the stock market. Here the results were not so good. Unwisely, the African had bought shares in John Law's 'Mississippi Bubble' – or, more precisely, in his 'Company of the West', which held an exclusive right to develop France's territories in North America. (Ironically, Law's company also monopolised the French trade in African slaves.) The use of paper money led to a wild frenzy of speculation in Paris, but the vaunted profits failed to materialise and inevitably the stock market crashed, leaving Gannibal with spiralling debts. Bankrupt, and the nation's scapegoat, Law was obliged to flee France. Soon Gannibal faced the same option but he was adamant that he was not to blame for his misfortune. 'Do you remember, Your Majesty, how you warned me five years ago not to fall into bad habits or end up in prison,' he continued in his letter of 5 March:

> Instead you told me that if I worked hard at my studies, for the glory of Russia, you would never desert me. Well, I didn't let you down but we are all of us in debt here not because of any delinquency on our part, but simply because we are victims of the paper money, with such terrible consequences, as I am sure that Count Musin-Pushkin* has told you, that were it not for his kindness in feeding me lunch and supper every day, I would surely have died of hunger.[10]

Alexander Pushkin, however, put a rather different gloss on the circumstances of his ancestor's return to Russia. The question of bankruptcy doesn't arise in *The Negro of Peter the Great*, where the Moor is never starved of anything but sex. He portrays him as a pampered adept of the Palais Royal (where in fact Gannibal had not set foot since the downfall of the Maines) who finds himself improbably in the middle of a tug of love between two of Europe's most powerful rulers:

> One day the duke of Orléans came up to Ibrahim and handed him a letter, telling him to read it at his leisure. The letter was from Peter the Great. The tsar, realising the cause of Ibrahim's absence, had written to the regent to say he had no wish to force his will upon Ibrahim, that it was up to the African to decide whether to return to Russia. Nevertheless he would never abandon his godson. The letter touched Ibrahim's heart, and at that moment he made up his mind. The next day he informed the regent that he was determined to return to Russia as quickly as possible. 'Think about what you are doing,' Orléans

---

*Count Ivan Musin-Pushkin was Tsar Alexis's illegitimate son, hence Peter's half-brother, and a veteran of Poltava, also the governor of Smolensk and Astrakhan. The Musin-Pushkins were distantly related to the plain Pushkins.

said to him. 'Russia is not your homeland. I don't think that you will ever again see your native country, but your long residence in France has made you equally a stranger to the climate and way of life in semi-savage Russia. You were not born a subject of Peter. Believe me, take advantage of his kind permission. Stay in France, a country for which you have already spilled your blood, and be assured that your service and talent will not go unrewarded here.' Ibrahim thanked the regent for his kind words but said that his mind was made up. 'I am sorry to hear it,' Orléans replied.[11]

The scene in the novel ends with a disappointed regent taking his leave of Ibrahim and retiring to his study to compose a long and sentimental dispatch to the tsar. In reality that task was left to Gannibal, who dashed off a note to Peter's secretary, Alexei Makarov, setting out his terms:

> I am ready to obey His Majesty's wish that I return, only I beg you, sir, to remind the Imperial Sovereign, that I am no man of the sea. You yourself may remember how brave I have been at sea in the past, but right now I have lost the habit. I am scared of the deep and fear its great and awful dangers will be the death of me unless I am granted divine grace, because Prince Dolgoruky has informed me that we will make the whole journey by sea. If His Imperial Majesty does not provide us with the means to travel over land to Petersburg, I will be utterly ready and content to return on foot.[12]

It was a weak hand but the gambit worked. Peter had no time to argue with his wayward godson, whose letter reached him on the shores of the Caspian Sea. He was busy. He had plans. Even during the second half of the Great Northern War, the tsar had sent exploratory missions to the east – to the central Asian steppes in 1714 and to Khiva in 1717. Peace with Sweden left him free to resume a more active policy on his south-eastern frontier. In 1722, fearing the Ottoman Turks would take advantage of Persia's weakness and invade the Caspian, Peter led an army deep into Persian territory. It was not until the autumn that he learned of the debts Gannibal had accrued from his exposure to the failure of Law's system. In Astrakhan, on the northern shore of the Caspian, as he was returning from a victo- rious campaign, Peter finally received Gannibal's letter begging for help with his debts and asking permission to return overland. On 16 October he dispatched a *ukaz* to the state chancellor, Count Gavrila Golovkin:

> Abram the Moor has written from Paris that he is ready to come back to Russia, only he has to settle debts of around 200 gold *écus*, on top of which he will need another 300 *écus* for the journey. For that reason, please send to Paris to our ambassador Prince Dolgoruky the money necessary to pay his debts and travel expenses – use the attached invoice to withdraw the cash – and if Dolgoruky has already left, then send the money to Prince Kurakin and tell him to help Abram leave for Petersburg.[13]

In fact Dolgoruky left Paris the day after Peter wrote to Golovkin, having used embassy funds to settle up with Gannibal's creditors, but he took with him an extra travelling companion, as the official records show. 'On 17 October the scholar Abram the Moor departed from Paris, in Prince Dolgoruky's suite, his debts paid in full,' reads a document in the foreign ministry archives.[14]

On that bleak autumn morning, as they began the long journey overland to Russia, setting off down the old Flanders road through the low wooded hills and vineyards of the Ardennes, the atmosphere in the carriage was as cold as the weather outside. The first night they stopped in Rheims, in the heart of champagne country, but Gannibal was in no mood to drink any toasts. Instead he wrote to the tsar of 'being chased from here, like a dog, without money'. Soon the clouds lifted and his spirits revived. Having finished his studies, and run out of cash, he was glad to leave Paris where the crash of Law's system – and the hyperinflation of *monnaie de singe* – had now caused tens of thousands of bankruptcies. Life in Regency France was a murky business, but Gannibal had emerged from it still burning bright. He was a man of parts. The flame of the Enlightenment, with its flicker-ings of racism, left the African unsinged.

# 14

# Regime Change

He belonged to a species of opposite.
—Alexander Solzhenitsyn, *Gulag Archipelago*

On a snowy day in January 1723, in the village of Krasnoye Selo, fifteen miles west of Petersburg, a hooded sledge, or *kibitka*, drew up in front of an inn. Krasnoye Selo means 'beautiful village' but the inn itself was an ugly building. No plaster or stuccowork covered the exterior, with the result that its dark red bricks, always dingy, had grown yet dingier under the influence of bad weather. Yet the inn was of a type often found in the Russian countryside – the type where, for a rouble a day, as Gogol wrote in *Dead Souls*, the weary traveller could rest in a bed swarming with black beetles.

Out of the *kibitka* stepped a Russian nobleman of around fifty and a younger black man in periwig and kneebreeches, wearing the green tunic of the Preobrazhensky regiment over a pink silk waistcoat. This latest arrival caused hardly a stir in the village. Even in midwinter, Krasnoye Selo was a busy staging post on the road linking Petersburg to the west. The villagers were used to seeing exotic passers-by. Some were almost connoisseurs of the traffic. A couple of serfs, for example, who happened to be standing nearby, exchanged a few comments about the *kibitka* rather than its occupants. 'Look at that carriage,' said one of them. 'Do you think it will be going as far as Moscow?' 'I think it will,' replied his companion. 'But not as far as Kazan, eh?' 'No, not as far as Kazan.'

Running out with a napkin in one hand, and a bottle of vodka in the other, the innkeeper escorted Dolgoruky upstairs to the bedchamber, where a meal had been prepared. While the horses were being changed, Gannibal went inside to warm himself by the fire. The downstairs room was full of benches heaped with horse collars, rope, sheepskins and yellowing newspapers, but it was otherwise empty apart from a silent, motionless figure who occupied the window seat next to a samovar. Here is how Pushkin describes the scene:

> In the corner, sitting at a table, was a tall man also dressed in the green uniform of the Preobrazhensky. He had a clay pipe in his mouth, and was reading a newspaper printed in Hamburg, leaning with his elbows on the table. Hearing somebody come in, he looked up. 'Ah! There you are, Ibrahim! Welcome home, son!' he shouted out, clambering to his feet. Ibrahim, recognising Peter, rushed forward to him in delight, but stopped short out of respect. The tsar drew near and gave his godson a kiss on the forehead. 'I was informed of your arrival,' said Peter, 'so I decided to come and meet you. I've been waiting here since yesterday.' Ibrahim was speechless with gratitude. 'Let's go,' the tsar went on. 'Order your carriage to follow on behind. You must sit in my carriage and we'll ride to Petersburg together.'[1]

So goes the legend of Gannibal's return to Russia. But did this marvellous fiction actually happen? The whole thing has the lineaments of a fairy tale, a *skazka*: the return of the prodigal son. Inevitably, perhaps, it was the mythmaker Rotkirkh who invented this sentimental reunion. 'Receiving news of his approach, the tsar and his wife, the Empress Catherine, rode out to meet Gannibal at Krasnoye Selo, twenty-seven *versts* from Petersburg,' wrote the African's son-in-law.[2] Here was a detail that Pushkin could not resist. The legend of Krasnoye Selo even reverberates in *Beginning of an Autobiography*, where the poet sets out to demythologise the history of his ancestors: 'The tsar rode out to meet Gannibal and presented him with the icon of Peter and Paul, an honour he usually accorded only to his sons.' Yet Pushkin knew that such a meeting was impossible. In *History of*

*Peter I*, he cites an official record that the tsar was in Moscow from 18 December 1722 to 23 February 1723.[3] In other words, Peter was hundreds of miles away from the 'beautiful village' on the day in question.

It's not just a matter of chronology. Internal evidence also casts doubt on the story. What is curious is Dolgoruky's absence from the scene. In the *skazka* he is upstairs tucking into a hot meal, conveniently out of the picture. Peter knew that Gannibal was returning to Russia with the ambassador. Yet he shows no interest in the prince's whereabouts, and then leaves the poor man stranded at Krasnoye Selo, without transport, as he disappears to Petersburg with Gannibal and the *kibitka*. How did Dolgoruky get home? The lack of information seems at odds with the importance of his diplomatic mission to France. Surely the tsar would not have ignored a returning ambassador. One of the 'fledglings of Peter's nest', Dolgoruky was a powerful ally. His family's origins were thought to go back to the twelfth-century hero Yury Dolgoruky, the legendary founder of Moscow. Before serving in France, he had been ambassador to Denmark and Poland, and a key strategist in the Great Northern War. (In 1725, he was appointed Russian ambassador to Sweden.) Surely the tsar would have been impatient to receive his report from Paris.

There are in fact various court documents relating to Dolgoruky's return. Some deal with official protocol – bureaucratic and unremarkable, lists of names – but others give a more detailed picture of the homecoming. For example, a note in the army calendar dated '27 January 1723. *Moscow*' juxtaposes politics and the weather. 'This morning the secret adviser Prince Vasily Dolgoruky presented himself to His Majesty. Formerly the minister in Paris, he returned from there under orders. There was a violent snowstorm and it was wet.'[4] The note adds that also in attendance, besides Gannibal, were Menshikov and Golovkin, who had just returned from Berlin, and Andrei Osterman, the deputy head of the foreign ministry.

The ubiquitous Menshikov we have already met. He is always there, lurking in the background, a prince of darkness, unlike the brisk and colourless Golovkin. Osterman was a more sophisticated character. Having arrived in Russia from Germany in 1703, he worked for Peter as an interpreter and soon became a regular fixture in the tsar's backroom entourage. In his zeal, his minuteness and his total lack of scruples, Osterman was the ideal henchman. But he was a dangerous rival. 'You will not believe in what high favour lies our German friend, and how he plants suspicion in the tsar's mind,' wrote Dolgoruky of his cautious welcome in Moscow.

The 'high favour' was due in part to a treaty Osterman had just signed with Persia by which Russia gained the cities of Baku and Derbent on the Caspian Sea. The suspicion, too, was a sign of the times. The Soviet historian Eydelman once claimed that Peter interrogated Gannibal for half an hour on his return from Paris before satisfying himself that his godson remained loyal to Russia. Not everybody got the benefit of the doubt. Menshikov falsely accused Baron Pyotr Shafirov of various intrigues against the tsar. Shafirov was stripped of his titles and land, and condemned to death, though Peter later commuted the sentence to exile.[5] Others spent time in prison or in fear of arrest. Towards the end of Peter's reign, according to one expert, 'the whole country turned into a vast hierarchical GULAG'.[6]

As in France, uncertainty about the succession bred conspiracy. The rightful heir, according to primogeniture and Russian tradition, was the tsar's grandson, also called Peter, the 9-year-old son of poor murdered Alexei. An overwhelming majority of the aristocracy, the clergy and the nation at large regarded the boy as a natural successor. Yet the tsar chose to overlook his grandson's claim because he feared that acknowledging it would inevitably excite the hopes of people who had sympathised with Alexei – and the fears of others, such as Count Pyotr Tolstoy, who had conspired in the murder. Tolstoy was now one of four ministers, later called judges and even inquisitors, who ran what was called the Secret Chancellery, using sub-agents to investigate 'word and deed' crimes. Some blamed him for creating a 'well-regulated police state', with its reliance on informers, listeners and spies.[7]

Gannibal noticed, on his return, that the secretive atmosphere of the Russian court had increased since Alexei's death. Rival courtiers pressed the claims of rival candidates to the throne. Osterman favoured the tsar's daughters, Anna and Elizabeth, who were still only children. Golovkin backed Peter's nieces, the daughters of his brother Ivan, who had married foreign princes and gone abroad. Together with Menshikov and another fledgling, Pavel Yaguzhinsky – both 'new men', created by the tsar, with much to lose if the old nobility returned to power – Tolstoy supported Peter's wife Catherine, alias Marta Skowronska, though her 'foreign' origins in the Lithuanian peasantry sparked a protest from the old boyars.

Hoping to divide and rule these fractious courtiers, the tsar stayed above the fray. In the second chapter of *The Negro of Peter the Great*, where Gannibal is reunited with the other vipers in the nest, Pushkin captures the mood:

> Some of the people who belonged to the tsar's inner circle were hanging around the palace. Ibrahim recognised the all-powerful Prince Menshikov, who, on seeing the Moor in conversation with the Empress Catherine, looked proudly askance; Prince Dolgoruky, the tsar's secret adviser, the magus Bruce, described by people as a Russian 'Faust'; the young Raguzinsky, the former comrade of Ibrahim; and other courtiers who had come to the tsar to make their reports and to receive orders.[8]

The Russian Faust was actually a Scot called James Bruce (a distant relative and namesake of the African explorer), whose family had come to Russia during the English Civil War. In 1697, aged twenty-seven, he accompanied Peter on the Grand Embassy to London, where he studied under the astronomers John Flamsteed and Edmund Halley. On his return to Russia he became the country's 'first Newtonian', setting up a school of mathematics and an observatory in Moscow, while also practising as a soldier and a magician. He and Gannibal shared a passion for science, which they may have discussed on the battlefields of the

Great Northern War. Their careers overlapped in other ways, too. A commander of artillery at Poltava, Bruce served as Peter's supervisor of fortress-building until Münnich inherited that role. Indeed, he was the 'learned' engineer to whom the tsar apprenticed Gannibal. The African and the Scot became close friends.

Bruce and Peter shared a passion for alcohol. The two passions merged in a series of drunken conversations. Over vodka mugs, the tsar quizzed his godson about French strategy and architecture, politics, law, medicine and philosophy. Since his visit to the Parisian Académie des Sciences, in 1717, he had wanted to create a learned society in Peters-burg, 'like the ones in Paris, London, Berlin and other places'. Now it seemed the time was ripe. As the drink flowed, so did the rhetoric. Peter declared that his Academy of Sciences would 'put other civilised nations to shame'.[9] Bruce imagined a 'transmigration of knowledge' from ancient Greece via the Enlightenment to Russia. That image is captured in a well-known engraving in which the tsar presents scientific books to a maiden symbolising Russia.[10] Unfortunately, most Russians lacked the training and language skills to read such books.

In this respect, as in so many others, Gannibal was unusual. He had returned to Russia with an excellent command of French, as well as Dutch, German and Italian. Peter valued multilingualism and therefore named the African to the post of 'principal translator of foreign books at the Imperial Court'.[11] Many of the foreign books that Gannibal translated came from his own library. He had brought 300 volumes back from France. A lot of them were scientific or military textbooks, such as Euclid's *Elements* and Ozanam's *Récréations mathé-matiques et physiques*, the Port-Royal Logic and Geometry, Bitainvieu's *Universal Art of Fortification, The French Engineer* and Malthus's *Practice of War*. Others were subtly different in emphasis. Sun Tzu's *Ping-fa* (*The Art of War*), for example, *The Prince* by Machiavelli, and the anonymous *L'Espion dans les Cours des Princes Chrétiens*, suggest an unhealthy interest in politics and spying. The rest was utterly conventional in terms of the reading matter of an eighteenth-century gentleman: a handful of travel books, some history and a sprinkling of fashionable exotica, as well as the Bible and the Koran, Ovid's *Metamorphoses*, the works of Corneille and Racine and the scandalous letters of the French libertine Bussy Rabutin.

Foreign books were hardly unknown in Peter's Russia, but the primitive level of collecting is indicated by a decree of 1726 authorising the purchase of Gannibal's library. The state bought all his books for 200 roubles and gave them to the Academy of Sciences, which opened the same year.[12] So it could be argued that Gannibal performed the role allotted to Peter in the famous engraving. He brought hundreds of books to Russia, and not only published texts. To this day the academy's archive contains several of Gannibal's manuscript translations of French works on mathematics and fortification, as well as a nautical atlas of the Baltic and a hand-drawn map of the river Vyg in western Karelia, on the border with Finland, a territory obtained by Peter from Sweden in 1721.[13] The tsar seems to have acknowledged the African's key role in educating 'savage' Russia. In Peter's eyes he became a role model for other scholars: a point of reference, a point of light. In 1724, sending his naval expert Konon Zotov two books that he wanted translated from French, the tsar added the postscript: 'And if you find in these books certain words you don't understand, then ask Abram Petrov for help.'[14]

Peter lavished other honours and gifts upon his godson. Yet, in the hostile atmosphere of the Russian court, the more publicly Gannibal seemed to enjoy the tsar's favour the more enemies he made. His bitterest rival was Menshikov, then facing charges of embezzlement and corruption, which he only narrowly survived. Pushkin describes the 'haughty prince' welcoming Gannibal back from France with a shake of the hand. In fact, the African's return posed a threat to Menshikov. Peter sensed the rivalry and sometimes taunted the older man with his admiration for the young pretender. Thus, on 4 February 1724, the tsar wrote the following note to Menshikov:

> Most excellent prince, with regard to Abram the Moor who served in
> France with the rank of captain, and obtained a degree there, I would

like you to promote him to the rank of lieutenant in the Preobrazhensky regiment, with special duties as a bombardier in the Engineers
Corps, namely to select promising young men and boys for special
training in mathematics and fortification.[15]

Gannibal's courtly career was now at the height of its arc,
though his power derived less from formal rank than from his
intellectual authority and standing with the tsar. His influence over
Peter on questions of defence and fortress-building was absolute.
It earned him prestige. The Russian Faust nicknamed him the
'Russian Vauban', after Louis XIV's great military engineer,
because he cast a legacy in stone. On Kotlin Island, for instance,
near the head of the Gulf of Finland, he constructed the fort
of Kronstadt which guarded the approach to Petersburg. In the
1790s, Catherine II projected a new system of defence, supposing
that Gannibal's fortifications would soon crumble away. Over two
centuries later we are still waiting for them to fall down. Indeed
Kronstadt played a crucial role in the defence of Russia against
the Nazis, from 1941 to 1944, during the siege of Leningrad, as
the city was then called.

Gannibal's influence went beyond the military. He also took
charge of important projects of civil engineering. As expected,
the tsar sent Gannibal to work on the Lake Ladoga canal, where
Münnich had run into serious difficulties. The route was meant to
follow the southern coast of the lake, the biggest in Europe, from the
river Volkhov to the Neva. But storms and high waves on the lake
made the work treacherous. Gannibal spent a winter in Kronstadt
poring over sheets of plans until he found a solution: a network of
four sluice gates raising the canal two yards above the level of the lake,
and thus making it safe for boat traffic. His friends marvelled at the
prodigious energy he threw into the venture. 'He can toil terribly,'
wrote Bruce, no sloth himself. Others begged him to return to the life
of scholarship in Petersburg. Yet Gannibal revelled in the contrasts
and conjunctions of his different pursuits: the philosopher and man

of action, the soldier scientist, the plain-speaking courtier and the military engineer.

The unlearned Menshikov resented Gannibal's intellectual talents. He disliked being outsmarted by anybody – least of all by a black man. The Ladoga triumph only sharpened his competitive dislike. Work on the canal had begun disastrously in 1718 under a Menshikov protégé. That failure complicated his rage at Gannibal's success. The disappointed rival became neurotic and vicious. Moreover, the revenge plotted by this volatile schemer, a Russian Iago, was almost Shakespearean in detail. Hoping to 'blacken' Gannibal's name, he detonated the pun – *chyernit* – in a letter to Dolgoruky that condemned the African as 'a foreigner and a dangerous man'. The tsar, he wrote, 'should not be served by this kind of slave; for they are seldom found faithful, and at worst they are full of filth and unclean'. In the salons of Petersburg he circulated false rumours about the 'lascivious Moor'.

It was a strange line of attack for Menshikov for choose. He was, after all, a foreigner himself, a Lithuanian, and a former serf – i.e., another kind of slave. Yet such a quibble was hardly relevant to his plot. In any case, the danger he cited was less political than ethnic. It depended on the old racist stereotype – and fear – of African sexual incontinence: Menshikov accused Gannibal of unnamed sex crimes in Kronstadt and other islands of the Baltic archipelago.

He has left no record of the slander against Gannibal. He may have felt it was safer, more convenient, not to put anything in writing. These were edgy times, as the fate of Shafirov had made clear, and, in any case, he preferred to operate by means of a whispering campaign. As a result, the only contemporary document which mentions this ugly business is a letter from Gannibal to the wife of a court official, Asya Ivanovna, who was his mistress. (The liaison remained secret, but inevitably there were rumours.) No doubt she had picked up the latest gossip on the Petersburg grapevine, and had written to her lover demanding an explanation or rebuttal. His reply contains neither, yet is written with such brio, in the style of Bussy Rabutin, as to suggest that Gannibal was confident of silencing his accuser. He begins with a swipe at his rival's denigrating pun. 'My dear Asyochka,' writes the libertine of Lake Ladoga,

> how dare you, my little coquette, my monkey, my pretty clown, spread these wicked lies about your friend, Abram the Black, whom you seem to blame for all the sins of Kronstadt! And to think I spend every day on my knees praying to God and have nothing but the deepest respect for my duty here. You say you want to kiss me, and to lie with me, but you do me a great injustice if you believe I am capable of such wickedness. Let me tell you something, the weather here doesn't allow anything of the sort. For a week now it has rained every day, surely you can agree with me that, whenever it rains, it's hardly possible to commit such dalliances![16]

The Russian historian Shubinsky argued that the attack on Gannibal merely confirmed his absorption into the royal circle. In terms of a career his life was as tightly meshed as Othello's into the state machine. ('My services, which I have done the signory,/ Shall out-tongue his complaints,' boasts Shakespeare's soldier hero.)[17] The Negro of Peter the Great was an insider. But he also belonged to a world at large in which soldiers and courtiers were often hostile and afflicted human beings, anxious for power and sunk in the politics of their hostility. The art of survival, as practised by Gannibal, was revealed in the letter to Asya. He pretended to be an outsider in order to break, and yet not to break, with the life of the court. 'Tomorrow I leave for Riga to build a fortress there,' he writes. 'Please don't ask when I'm coming back. I don't even know myself, but I hope to see you soon, my little monkey.' Underneath the wordplay you sense anxiety, if not grievance. He got the message from Menshikov loud and clear, and was glad to escape the tawdry gossip of Petersburg, with its backbiting and envy, its falsehood and slander.

Gannibal boasted that his standing with the tsar would protect him from Menshikov's intrigues, and perhaps it did. Yet the protection

13. *The picture in the attic: a mysterious portrait of 'Gannibal' sparked almost two centuries of debate about his ethnic origins until a clean-up by art experts revealed the face of a white man.*

14. *This Negro of Peter the Great, as painted by French artist Jean-Baptiste Van Loo, was definitely black — unfortunately his was another case of mistaken identity: not Gannibal, once again, but a 'court Arab' named Piter Yelayev, here posing as an African slave prince, Oroonoko, after the novel by Aphra Behn.*

15. *One of the 'family legends' peddled by the social-climbing Pushkins had Peter the Great waiting at coaching inn outside St Petersburg for Gannibal's return from France. This fanciful scene, with Peter reading the newspaper and smoking a clay pipe – and Gannibal's look of surprise – found its way into* The Negro of Peter the Great, *even though, as Pushkin knew, the tsar was hundreds of miles away on the day in question.*

16. *The 'lost' fortress of Selenginsk, on the Siberian border with China. A wooden fort built by Gannibal to repel the army of the Manchu emperor burned to the ground in the century after his death, but its ditch and earthworks are still clearly visible in the middle of nowhere.*

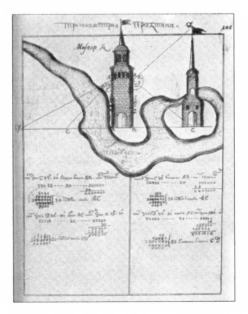

17. *A page from Gannibal's unpublished manuscript* Geometry and Fortification. *The heading at the top reads 'Practical Trigonometry', the practice in question being how to bombard an enemy's watchtower. The African's deft strokes of the pen seem to combine mathematical precision with an unusual talent for draughtsmanship.*

*18. The old citadel of Reval (now Tallinn) in Estonia, where Gannibal lived for a decade among the xenophobic Baltic Germans. In this nineteenth-century print, his house on Toompea Hill can be seen immediately to the right of the 'baroque' castle, which dates from the reign of Catherine the Great.*

*19. His other Baltic home in Pernau, where the Russian Othello suffered violent pangs of jealousy due to his wife's extramarital affairs and where he allegedly rigged up a torture chamber in the cellar, using leather whips, thumbscrews and iron clamps to make her confess her 'crimes'.*

20. *A lavish firework display to mark the birthday of Ivan VI in 1741. Gannibal specialised in pyrotechnics of this kind, not only to entertain the royal family but also to investigate the military potential of rocketry.*

*21. The modest single-storey wooden house at Mikhailovskoye, the country estate Elizabeth awarded to Gannibal in 1742. On either side stood even smaller buildings, on the left a bath-house, on the right a kitchen and servants' quarters. The two long low buildings at right angles to the kitchen housed the estate office and lodgings for the bailiff. In front of the house was a circular lawn where an exiled Pushkin paced up and down, in the summer of 1823, as he began to write* Eugene Onegin.

*22. Two miles away, at Petrovskoye, is the house where Gannibal moped after being sacked by Peter III, and where, according to his great-grandson, 'he thought in cool summers/Of his far-off Africa'. The living conditions were impossibly cramped: two-up, one-down. But this lack of grandeur was typical. Until the end of the eighteenth century, even the houses of wealthy Russians were barely distinguishable from peasant huts.*

23. The black ink drawing of Gannibal, sketched by Pushkin in the margins of the manuscript of The Negro of Peter the Great, *is obviously a caricature but its simian features — the woolly hair and 'goggle eyes' described by the Moor's friend in the novel, Korsakov, also pictured above — may hold a clue to Gannibal's origins. The 'ugly Negro mug', to quote Pushkin, reflects nineteenth-century Russian thinking about African physiognomy.*

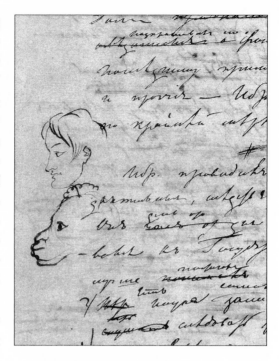

24. *Gannibal's wax seal on a letter of 1742: at the centre of his family crest stands an elephant, with a crown signifying perhaps the African land ruled by his father. Underneath, the enigmatic word FUMMO has puzzled literary experts for over two hundred years. Could it refer to the 'homeland' of the Kotoko tribe?*

25. Pushkin's self-portrait. 'Why is your marvellous pencil/Sketching my blackamoor profile?' he asked the English painter George Dawe. The poet was immensely proud of his African background, but he accepted unquestioningly racist notions of beauty.

26. The bronze inkstand with a statuette of a 'blackamoor' leaning on an anchor and standing in front of two bales of cotton – two inkwells – which Pushkin kept on his writing desk until the end of his life.

was only short-lived. Years of hard work had taken their toll on Peter's health. On 28 January 1725, aged fifty-two, he died from complications of a fever caught two months earlier while trying to rescue soldiers from a capsized boat in the icy waters of the Neva.

Rotkirkh weaves the death of the tsar seamlessly into legend by inserting the Negro of Peter the Great into the deathbed scene, even though he was hundreds of miles away in Latvia at the time. 'Not long before the tsar's death Gannibal was sent to Riga to lay the foundations for a new fortress,' writes the dutiful son-in-law, and then comes a sleight of biography:

> When he ran out of money to pay expenses, he wrote to Peter who ordered the sending of 2,000 Dutch ducats. And then, only moments after signing the order, the tsar's condition unexpectedly worsened, and he died. Therefore no greater tribute to his immortal memory can be paid than to say that even at death's door he did not forget his Gannibal.[18]

The African hurried back to comfort the Empress Catherine in a frozen Petersburg. He found a city in shock as well as in mourning. Over a quarter of a century Peter had transformed this Arctic wilderness into the capital of a new Russia. New buildings and customs had sprung up. Knowledge and the arts had flourished. Few could imagine life in Peter's paradise without the 'tsar-transformer' himself. Outside the Winter Palace it was deathly quiet. Only the irregular tolling of church bells and a funereal drumbeat from the parade ground broke the silence. Inside the palace the sound of wailing filled the empty rooms. 'I am a widow!' sobbed Catherine at her first interview with Gannibal. 'Yes,' he replied, 'and I am an orphan.'

The widow gave the orphan a role in arranging Peter's funeral, although she insisted the ceremony was 'to follow the customs of other European states'.[19] Thus, in a break with Muscovite tradition, where burial took place on the day after death, Gannibal supervised a month's lying-in-state for Peter at the Winter Palace. The delay was a symbol of the new Russia. Tens of thousands of red-eyed peasants and soldiers filed past the late tsar's body in the Hall of Mourning. Clad in velvet breeches and a shirt of silver brocade, with lace cuffs and a cravat, and wearing boots with spurs, a sword and the order of Saint Andrew, his giant figure lay on a sheet of cloth decorated with the words: 'RUSSIA – grieve and weep – your father PETER THE GREAT has left you'.[20] On 10 March, grief-stricken and in tears, Gannibal joined the funeral cortège across the ice on the Neva from the Winter Palace to the still unfinished cathedral of Saints Peter and Paul.

The death of the tsar-*batyushka* presented him with a tough challenge. He was so closely associated with his godfather that many Russians wondered if he could survive a change of regime. In Pushkin's novel, even the dying tsar wonders the same thing: 'Listen, Ibrahim: you are on your own in the world, without birth or family ties, a stranger to everybody but me. If I were to die today, what would happen to you tomorrow, my dear Moor?'[21] At first, in the wake of Peter's death, the omens looked good. The succession was quickly settled in favour of Catherine and she renewed her dead husband's patronage of the Moor. He was employed as a private tutor in mathematics and geometry to Alexei's 9-year-old son Peter, and the young hereditary prince soon fell under the African's spell. Here was the beginning of Gannibal's misfortune.

The real ruler of Russia during Catherine's brief reign was Menshikov whom the empress was unable to restrain now that he was out of her husband's shadow. Assuming the rank of 'generalissimo', he quickly wrested control over the levers of power and used them shamelessly to enlarge his personal wealth.[22] By the end of 1725, he had built up a sort of state within the state, owning 3,000 villages and seven towns spread over forty-two districts in Russia, the Baltic, Ukraine and Poland, not to mention 300,000 serfs. (Until then, the richest man in Russia, Prince Cherkasky, had only 33,000.) Lust for power made the upstart arrogant and brutal, while his corrupt rule provoked a general hatred. Soon there was talk of a plot against

Menshikov. In December 1725, for example, Münnich warned that 'in the present condition of the Russian state, the number of the prince's open and secret enemies has increased'.[23] The least secret, in Menshikov's eyes — and perhaps the most dangerous, given his influence over a likely future tsar — was Gannibal.

Skulking in the Winter Palace among his science books, the African waited grimly for the onslaught. It began with a flurry of reform. On 8 February 1726, a year after Catherine's accession, a new governing body, the Supreme Privy Council, was created 'to lighten the heavy burden of government for Her Majesty'. In theory, its six members — Menshikov, Apraxin, Golovkin, Osterman, Tolstoy and Prince Dmitry Golitsyn — shared the right to govern. In practice, the *generalissimo* held sway. Amid these shifting tides of political ascendancy Gannibal found himself at low ebb. Yet he remained defiant. 'I don't let myself get downhearted but it's an act of will,' he wrote to Asya Ivanovna. 'When you find yourself among unstable people, who bob up and down like a boat at sea, buffeted by the wind and waves, what else can you do but pray your own vessel's watertight and then cast anchor?'

Others took a less philosophical view. One of Catherine's ladies-in-waiting, for example, Princess Agrafena Volkonskaya, begged the empress to curb this abuse of power. Cold and aloof, a legendary beauty who struck fear into cabinet ministers, she soon emerged as the ringleader of the anti-Menshikov opposition. Her family, one of Russia's oldest, was numerous and politically active. Volkonskaya's husband was descended from a fourteenth-century prince, Mikhail Chernigovsky, who was rewarded for his part in Moscow's war of liberation against the Mongol hordes with a chunk of land on the Volkona river, to the south of Moscow, from which the dynasty derived its name. Her father, Pyotr Bestuzhev, had been a top civil servant until he fell out with Menshikov. Her brother Alexei, the Russian ambassador to Copenhagen, was a protégé of Tolstoy. For several generations the two families had intermarried, as they would continue to do in the next century. (The mother of Leo Tolstoy was another Princess Volkonskaya.) These dynastic connections lead us, as they led Gannibal, into the difficult and disturbing story of the Rabutin Plot.

It is hard to say exactly when the plot against Menshikov took shape – in a sense it never did – or why it bore the name of a low-ranking foreign diplomat. But one night at Volkonskaya's house, at a table strewn with the leftovers of a rich banquet, Gannibal met Count Rabutin, a nephew of the French aristocrat whose scandalous letters he had read in Paris. Now a diplomat in the Austrian service, Rabutin had been sent to Petersburg by the Emperor Charles VI, a maternal uncle of Gannibal's young pupil, to urge the boy's claims. Half-reclining on a sofa's arm, silent and distant, absorbed in her own thoughts, Volkonskaya listened to the wild talk of her guests – their heads filled with vodka, with dreams of turning back the clock to a golden age of Petrine rule, with an overheated devotion to the princess herself – and then uttered the words that turned years of resentment into a plan of action. 'I hope, for my sake,' she said to Gannibal, 'you will rather draw the tsar's grandson towards *Monsieur Rabutin* than let him fall into the hands of our enemy.' The African left the salon, in the early hours of the morning, with a new role as a go-between in the plot against Menshikov.

During Catherine's reign the boy prince Peter had been more or less ignored. Just before her death, however, it became clear to Menshikov that the grandson of Peter the Great could not be kept out of his inheritance much longer, if only because the majority of the nation and three-quarters of the nobility were on his side. The shifting focus left Gannibal in a predicament. Menshikov undoubtedly knew something of his dealings with the Volkonskaya circle. (Police spies had infiltrated the houses of the conspirators.) Belatedly he realised that Peter held the African in such high regard that the teacher could easily poison the young tsar's mind against his rival. Something had to be done, felt the *generalissimo*. The round-the-clock presence of Gannibal at the Winter Palace had become a serious risk. For his own safety Menshikov looked to interpose some distance between the Negro and Peter's grandson, and the instrument he used to accomplish this feat was the Supreme Privy Council.

Menshikov grabbed his chance in the winter of 1727, when Catherine fell ill with a series of chills and fevers. Her decline, so unexpected in a formerly robust woman still only middle-aged, was uncannily similar to that of her husband just two years earlier. On 21 January she took part in the ceremony of the Blessing of the Waters on the Neva ice, standing for hours in the frozen air, with a white plume in her hat and a marshal's baton in her hand, before retiring to bed for two months. The empress's health rallied with the spring thaw until a rainstorm backed up, forcing her to evacuate the Winter Palace in her nightdress, knee-deep in cold water. It was a shock to her system from which she never recovered.

On 12 April, Menshikov put in a rare appearance, alone and somewhat nervous, at Catherine's bedside. He approached the dying woman, paid customary homage to her radiance and beauty – though neither was much in evidence on this occasion – but then he warned of the political threat to which her long illness exposed the country. She had to be more cautious, he said, pay closer attention to the succes-sion – for her own sake, of course, but also for the well-being of her 11-year-old heir whose innocent and trusting nature was under siege from agents of a foreign government. Menshikov proposed that she write a new will in which she nominated the *generalissimo* as regent in case of her death and decreed the marriage of his 16-year-old daughter Maria to the future tsar. Actually we cannot be sure of the exact date of this conversation, which certainly took place before Dolgoruky, a new member of the Supreme Privy Council, warned Rabutin on the last day of April that Menshikov was urging the others to approve a codicil to the will recommending exile and even execution for the plotters of the Volkonskaya circle. (Dolgoruky had a sly motive for blowing the whistle on Menshikov's plan inasmuch as he was hoping to arrange the betrothal of his niece to the poor boy.)

Events were now moving ahead fast. On 6 May, only two years and three months after her accession, Catherine died and the youngster was proclaimed Tsar Peter II, though Menshikov immediately took control of the new sovereign and lodged him in his own palace on Petersburg's Vasilevsky Island. The following day Volkonskaya was arrested and sent to a village on the outskirts of Moscow. The other conspirators scattered. Warrants were issued, police checkpoints set up on the roads to Moscow and Reval, but still Gannibal remained at large. To begin with, Menshikov feared that, in terms of public evidence, the African seemed blameless. It was difficult to pin anything on him beyond friendship with a handful of the conspirators. But then a search of Volkonskaya's house allegedly found something incriminating, a long letter from Gannibal listing Menshikov's crimes. I say 'allegedly' because the letter doesn't survive and may even have been fabricated by an unknown clerk of the privy council. No doubt the *generalissimo* believed that the letter provided the necessary evidence to arrest Gannibal and to send him into exile hundreds of miles from Petersburg. Yet he had one more trick up his sleeve.

On the morning of 8 May, Rabutin wrote to Menshikov to protest at the treatment of Volkonskaya and her friends, adding in a postscript that the Austrian emperor, Charles VI – let alone his nephew, the young tsar of Russia – would oppose the sentencing to exile of the Negro of Peter the Great. That afternoon Rabutin was on the point of addressing a similar note to the privy council when he received an urgent summons to court. The Frenchman hurried to the Winter Palace where Menshikov gave him a detailed account of the meeting he had just had with his fellow councillors. 'Exile? Indeed you are quite mistaken, Count. The service of the Moor is indispensable to His Majesty, to the defence of Russia itself,' Menshikov concluded, with a sneer, as he handed Rabutin a sheet of paper, a copy of a document approved by the privy council less than half an hour earlier, the ink not yet dry:

May 8 1727. In the name of Peter II, the tsar of Russia, the supreme military college decrees that Abram Petrov, lieutenant-bombardier in the regiment of the Preobrazhensky Guards, shall be sent immediately to Kazan, and further orders him to carry out an inspection of the city's fortress, in order to determine the necessary steps to be taken for its reinforcement, if he does not conclude that an entire new citadel is required, and, in any case, he should draw up a plan and schedule, and once the inspection is completed, write to the Department of War with a full report on the duration of the reconstruction project.[24]

The decree was signed 'Alexander Menshikov': an ugly scrawl, blotched and partially crossed out, a testimony to the semi-literate prince and his difficulty with penmanship.

Here was a masterstroke. The African was cast into exile in all but name, or perhaps into something even worse, into a kind of official limbo, his punishment disguised as a timeless mission in the line of duty to a far-flung outpost. Five hundred miles east of Moscow, Kazan was the first stop on the way to a giant prison, the gateway to an area several times the size of France, the *Arkhipelag Gulag*, Solzhenitsyn's term for the vast labour camp where Russian despots from Ivan the Terrible to Stalin sent hundreds of thousands of people to incarceration and exile. Such was Gannibal's fate, though less masterful was the penstroke that sealed it, misspelling the word 'arap' in the official army list for the year: '*No. 1540, Petrov Arab Avraam, knight, transferred to Siberia*'.[25]

# 15

# The Arab of Siberia

On the road: white snow and a black man
—Mark Sergeyev, *Siberian Misadventures*

On the subject of his years in exile Gannibal has left a puzzling trail of self-contradiction. He told his son-in-law that Menshikov sent him to Asia on a 'top-secret assignment to the other side of the Amur river, to the border with China'.[1] The Amur's Chinese name, Hei-lung Chiang, means 'Black Dragon River', and predictably in Rotkirkh's narrative it encloses a land of fairy tale and romance. Pushkin tells us something different from the same source: 'He was sent to Siberia with orders to measure the Great Wall of China,' the poet writes.[2] How this *skazka* can be translated biographically is another matter. The ancient fortification may be visible from outer space, according to modern legend, but it could never have been seen, let alone measured, from the banks of the Amur over eight hundred miles away. Or perhaps it is all the same, given that Catherine the Great once described Russia's Orient as 'a fairy-tale land out of the *Arabian Nights*'.[3]

The arabianised knight spent a thousand and one days in Siberia if you discount a month of preamble in Kazan and half a year on the road. On 9 May the African said goodbye to Petersburg and began his long outward journey into the unknown. The ambiguity and incompleteness of the evidence make it impossible to do more than hazard a guess at his mood. By day, flying through the dust on post horses, he cast his gaze to the future and tried to imagine the obstacles that lay ahead of him. At night his thoughts returned to the past as he brooded over the document signed by Menshikov. Here we catch a glimpse of the indignation he felt at the looming prospect of exile. A copy of the decree by the privy council, perhaps the one that travelled to Siberia in his pocket, bears a note scribbled in the margin in Gannibal's handwriting. It reads simply: 'On the basis of this, I left Petersburg and went to Kazan, where I stayed for 25 days, yet I resolved to face each trial, whatever happened.'[4]

The tone of the sentence, that dismissive underscoring of the word 'this', implies that Gannibal was under no illusions about his fate. He understood the bogus nature of his assignment to Kazan, and even before he arrived in the city he was impatient with the task in hand. That impatience may explain why he took such a dangerous route to get there.

To begin with, Gannibal made rapid progress, hurtling through Novgorod, Tver and Sergiyev Posad – a sleepy town built around the walls of a monastery founded, in 1337, by Saint Sergius of Radonezh – and arriving in Boldino, in the province of Vladimir, on or about 15 May. One danger *en route* came as ever from Muscovite brigands. Law and order had scarcely improved in the quarter of a century since Johann Korb was shocked by the violence on Russia's roads. Yet the African risked bumping into government spies as well as murderous villains (not always two distinct groups) because the Vladimirka road took him directly past the village where Princess Volkonskaya was now living under surveillance.

The road, depicted in a famous nineteenth-century painting by Isaak Levitan, marked the beginning of the Siberian *trakt*, which Chekhov called 'the biggest and most absurd road in all the world' – and along which thousands of political prisoners dragged their chains.[5] Outside Boldino, it crossed a wooden bridge over the river Azanka and climbed towards the landowner's house where Volkon-skaya sulked. On the top of the hill, in an open space, where the line of the road vanished into the forests on the horizon, she stood that afternoon waiting for Gannibal to pass by.

The reunion was brief. 'I greeted him according to his rank, and according to the small means I had at my disposal,' wrote Volkon-skaya. 'We exchanged news of our friends. But in the silence of the landscape a feeling of sadness overwhelmed us, and so we parted.' Once again there are glimpses from the police side because Menshikov had spies in Boldino, watching Volkonskaya's every move. 'In the distance one could make out the figures of two people,' they reported on 16 May, adding a note of threat, 'the woman and a man, whom she treated very well, as if *persuading* him.' These words are a study in desolation. Yet the talk of persuasion may be a spy hedging his bets, just as Volkonskaya's sentimentality doesn't quite ring true. In any case, we cannot really choose between these two accounts. Each version is self-serving; each is partly true.

Soon Gannibal reached the land of the Tatars. His destination, the ancient city of Kazan, had been founded in the late-thirteenth century by the Mongols of the Golden Horde. Here, on the banks of the Volga, an Asiatic culture thrived for almost three hundred years. But from its capture by Ivan the Terrible in 1552 until the fall of the Soviet Union, as the Russian empire grew at a rate of 50,000 square miles a year, the city was slowly absorbed into the heart of European Russia. Fur trappers and Cossacks drove east across the Urals in search of minks and mines. The frontier advanced; it pushed Asia back across the steppe. The old Tatar fortress in Kazan was rebuilt as a Russian kremlin. Yet Gannibal saw at a glance that its white walls and towers were no military priority. His report to the department of war was doomed to go unread. The Supreme Privy Council had no concern with the defences of a city that had not been threatened for almost two hundred years. The African vented his frustration in a letter to Princess Volkonskaya: 'Then I received another decree, this time ordering me to head further east to Tobolsk in Siberia,' he wrote.

This second decree, signed by Menshikov and dated 28 May, seemed to confirm Gannibal's worst fears. 'Honoured sir, Abram Petrovich,' it began with mock formality, 'His Imperial Majesty has decreed that you should proceed immediately to Tobolsk and build a fortress there in accordance with the instructions of the governor, Prince Mikhail Dolgoruky.' In despair Gannibal wrote to the *generalissimo*, whom he addressed as the 'father and defender of orphans', begging him to reconsider the transfer. The plea fell on deaf ears, but the despair reverberates in a letter he sent to Volkonskaya:

> I must inform you that I have received another order from Petersburg and Prince M., a copy of which I have attached, and today I leave for Siberia, and Tobolsk: perhaps, as soon as I get there, I will receive a third order, sending me even further away. But I am resigned to going wherever, without the least distress, apart from that of knowing that I will be separated from my friends. At least I can hold my head up high, knowing that I am guilty of no crime. Perhaps this is the last time I will ever write to you, because they will soon send me to some deserted place where I shall die in solitude: so I entreat you to inform our friends in Petersburg and elsewhere that I have been banished to Siberia, to Tobolsk.

Gannibal yearned for these 'friends' to intervene on his behalf as they had done in the past. He recalled that in Paris, for example, having kept a paternal eye on him for several months, Dolgoruky and Tolstoy were able to rescue the African from bankruptcy. Times had changed, however. So, too, had the circumstances of his former protectors. Ironically Dolgoruky, now a privy councillor, was too busy plotting Menshikov's downfall, and his own family's rise, to help Gannibal. Eighty-two years old, and banished to a monastery on Solovetsky Island in the White Sea, Tolstoy had fallen predictably out of favour as a consequence of his role in Alexei's murder. Only Bestuzhev lodged a complaint with Menshikov. The rest were silent.

The orphan disappears from view. His name drops out of conversation. There are few references to him in the letters of the Volkonskaya circle. Once again, we are drawn back to the official record – to what it says, to what it doesn't say – to the dry concise summary, the scant details, of his years of wandering. But one can imagine the Negro of Peter the Great on the road to Tobolsk, hurrying through forest-blackened hills towards the huge glimmering emptiness of Siberia – a twelfth of the landmass of the world – the scenery wrapping itself around him like a fog.

Russian narratives of Gannibal's exile usually stress the orphan theme, as if his wandering was a kind of search for the lost father, but ignore the grey and prosaic reality of Siberian garrison towns. Beyond Tobolsk lay the outer regions of the Russian empire. Here the African posed a threat, as Menshikov understood. On 28 May, the *generalissimo* wrote to the military governor, Prince Mikhail Dolgoruky, ordering him to restrict Gannibal's freedom of movement. 'Because he is a foreigner and a dangerous man,' he warned,

> particularly if he is allowed to reach the border, it is vital that you keep him under high surveillance: as for the construction of the fortress, give him any instructions, a plan will be sent later.[6]

The letter casts doubt on Menshikov's reasons for sending Gannibal to Siberia. It seems clear that he was indifferent to the avowed task in hand – that of building a fortress in Tobolsk. Otherwise he wouldn't have used such a careless phrase as 'any instructions' to outline the work. Yet he remained wary of something, and his wariness focused on the border. That unspecified danger helps to explain the mirage of China in Gannibal's self-contradictory tales. It may also explain why Dolgoruky, at the behest of his cousin Vasily, the former ambassador in Paris, disobeyed Menshikov's orders and sent the 'dangerous man' straight to Outer Mongolia. ('Please get our friends to send money, as I am desperately short of cash,' the African wrote to Volkonskaya. 'Ask them to send it to Tobolsk and Prince Dolgoruky, who will forward it to the Chinese border.') Here the French connection becomes more intriguing. In the margin of his dispatch paper, Gannibal scribbled the following note: 'On the basis of this, I arrived at Tobolsk, and left there for the border with China to meet Savva Raguzinsky.'[7]

This was undoubtedly a high point for the exiled Gannibal. In a remote borderland, at the centre of mysterious events, he rediscov- ered the talismanic figure of Savva Raguzinsky. Now sixty years old, the Bosnian adventurer had a knack of turning up unexpectedly at moments of crisis in the African's life. The previous summer, on his way to Peking as Russian ambassador to negotiate for the disputed lands of Mongolia, Raguzinsky travelled along the shore of Lake Baikal from Irkutsk to Buryatiya, a wild unvisited place still agog with shamanism, the ancient faith of Siberia. Most of the inhabitants were Buddhists. Unlike the region's other non-Muslims, who even- tually converted to Christianity, the Buryats managed to keep their religion thanks in part to an eighteenth-century Buddhist revival led by missionaries from Tibet. At Goose Lake, where these priests (or lamas) built a temple known as a *datsan*, and stocked it with a library of sacred books, Raguzinsky witnessed the first steps on that revivalist path.

His caravan made slow progress through the wilderness of jagged ridges, following the long blade of the Selenga river until it reached the winter camp of Udinskoye, now the Buryat capital of Ulan-Ude, and a plateau beyond. Suddenly, in the distance, Raguzinsky could see the open fields of Mongolia. The sight – or, rather, the openness – disturbed him. He felt the mountains looked too shallow to form a frontier, let alone the divide between the two mighty empires. On 31 August 1726, in a state of alarm, he wrote to Petersburg that the Chinese border lacked defence and fortification. 'Take Selenginsk – I hesitate to call it a town or a village or even a settlement – because only 250 souls live there in a gathering of huts and two wooden settlements, really the most unsuitable place and without the least protection from dangerous raids.'[8] Raguzinsky urged the government to address the weakness urgently, in case a breakdown of diplomacy in Peking led to skirmishes on the border. 'During my reconnaissance I spotted a place on the right bank of the Selenga river, on the main highway from the sea of Baikal,' he wrote. 'To my mind, it represents the most perfect situation for building a fortress as I have ever seen. Not only is the site raised upon a hilltop, but it is also protected by the Selenga and by rocky cliffs.'

At first Menshikov opposed the plan on the grounds of unnecessary expense, but Dolgoruky used his family connections in Petersburg to lobby for the project until finally, a year later, the senate authorised Raguzinsky to go ahead. Talks were deadlocked in Peking so the ambassador returned to Russia along the ancient caravan track that linked the two countries. At the border, from the village of Kyakhta, he wrote to Dolgoruky on 3 August, summoning the Arab of Siberia.

The official record of his posting to the land of the Buryats is terse but significant. 'In the month of December 1727 there arrived here from Tobolsk the lieutenant-bombardier in the Preobrazhensky guard, Abram Petrov, the Arab known as Gannibal, in order to build a fortress at Selenginsk,' wrote an anonymous clerk in the Irkutsk register.[9] (Here is the first documentary use of the *nom de guerrre*.)

Selenginsk was where he lived for the next three years: a garrison against the Chinese, a base for reconnaissance of Mongolia, a gateway to the past: the silver dome of the wooden church brandished the Old Believer cross. To begin with, in this solitude of arid valleys, Gannibal's mood was upbeat. 'I went to Selenginsk, to build a fortress under the guidance of Savva Raguzinsky,' he recalled in a letter to the tsar in 1729, 'and I was glad to be with Raguzinsky again, also because you sent me to do technical work as I am a scientific person, and I was able to obtain instruments, maps, papers and all the other things I needed to carry out my work.' Yet life was dull after Petersburg and lacked variety, despite the constant reminder of Siberia's otherness – its ancestral spirits, its reverberating drums – and the unlikely presence of Old Believers fleeing the decadence of Europe. One priest lived with his family on the far riverbank opposite the garrison town, cursing Peter the Great in Manchu and Mongolian. Here was a civilisation as old as Africa. The harsh climate was anything but decadent. In December the snow reached waist high and the temperature dropped to minus fifty degrees. Winter lasted until May. Feeling the chill, Gannibal busied himself in the treeless tundra, making notes, drafting plans of the fortress. It was hard work, designing, building, organising the labour drafted from a nearby prison camp. 'Toiling like a donkey, uncertain of the future, dreaming of far-flung journeys, going nowhere,' he fretted to Raguz- insky at the end of the year. But then he added: 'Your lordship will shortly receive a large chart or map, which I have not yet finished, which I beg you to secrete and not to let out of your hands.'[10] It will show, he said, the plan of fortification at Selenginsk and other information based on his reconnaissance of the Mongolian plateau. Being, in his own words, a 'scientific person', Gannibal loved the shabby geometry of the permafrost: repeated freezing and thawing left stripes and circles and polygons in the black earth of the steppe. He marvelled at the Chinese architecture of the *datsan* on Goose Lake where he sketched the tilted eaves levitating in bright yellow, or listened nostalgically to the worship of a sacred elephant. The African was also drawn to the natural, mystical beauty of the land, the deep valleys and mountain ranges of Buryatiya. Yet he could never erase the memory of Peters- burg. Slowly, as the earthworks took shape, the ditches and bastions, the scarps and counterscarps, the ravelins and palisades, Gannibal began to pray for a return to that decadent world.

News came of Menshikov's disgrace. One of Volkonskaya's allies, Igor Pashkov, wrote from Petersburg to say that the Dolgoruky clan had finally succeeded in alienating Peter II from the *generalis- simo*. 'Our tormentor is exiled to Ranenburg [an estate in Ukraine], stripped of his rank, decorations and even the title of Prince,' wrote a breathless Pashkov. 'Thanks to the grace of God, we have witnessed a miracle, we now have nothing and nobody to fear, and indeed we are overcome with joy at the fall of this ogre, this Goliath, whom God has destroyed with a simple wave of his hand.'

Anticipating a swift recall to Petersburg, Gannibal packed his bags and returned to Tobolsk. He was impatient to begin the long journey out of Siberia. Yet the exit was premature. On 24 October, Pashkov wrote again with the news that Dolgoruky opposed the return of political exiles and was even stepping up the repression of

Peter the Great's favourites. Under pressure, Volkonskaya's servants denounced their mistress. The police confiscated her letters, including several from Gannibal. A secret meeting of the privy council accused the princess and her circle of seeking to establish a faction at court, of wanting to overthrow the government, and of 'having connived with the ambassador of the Court of Vienna, the now deceased Count Rabutin'. Volkonskaya was sent yet further into exile, to the remote convent of Tikhvin, near Novgorod. On her arrival she received a glum letter from Pashkov with other news of the clampdown. 'I am doing everything I can to secure Abram's return from exile,' he wrote. 'But nobody wants it to happen. All these blasted people treat him like a dog.'

How did Gannibal escape from Siberia? So much of the period's official record has vanished that there is inevitably an element of randomness and contradiction in what we know. Certainly the short-term outlook was bleak. The Dolgorukys were firmly in control of the government. Still only fourteen, Peter II was engaged to Vasily's niece Yekaterina. Before the marriage could take place, however, the tsar died of smallpox in January 1730, and his death crossed the plans of that ambitious family. The privy council, under the leadership of the old boyar Prince Dmitry Golitsyn, offered the throne to Anna, the dowager duchess of Courland and Peter's niece. Now, according to Pushkin, in a footnote to *Eugene Onegin*, Gannibal saw his opportunity:

> Getting bored with the absence of people and the harsh climate, he returned to Saint Petersburg of his own accord and appeared before his friend Münnich. Münnich was amazed and advised him to go into hiding straight away. Annibal retired to his country estate and lived there through the reign of Anna, while nominally serving in Siberia.[11]

I say 'according to Pushkin', because the story of his return is just another *skazka*. 'As Russian commentators have pointed out,' writes Nabokov, 'Pushkin's presentation of Abram's Siberian period is false.'[12] The *Onegin* note suggests why: the poet mixed up details from the reign of Peter II with the later history of the Empress Anna. It was a strange mistake for him to make because Pushkin had read widely on the subject. He knew, for instance, that Golitsyn hoped to limit the empress's power by forcing her to accept a set of conditions giving a decisive voice to the privy council. He also knew that the experiment with oligarchy soon failed because the nobility and the army opposed the reform. On 25 February, Anna tore up Golitsyn's conditions, abolished the privy council and re-established autocracy. Otherwise the opera-loving empress showed little interest in politics, devoting herself to 'exotic and irrational entertainments' at court in Saint Petersburg, while relying on her lover, Ernst Johann Biron, to run the government. Under Anna, this grandson of a German groom, who had served the duke of Courland, was now given that title in his own right. His equestrian background helped to win Anna's favour. The empress loved hunting. Indeed, she issued decrees banning the pursuit of certain animals and birds within a fifty-mile radius of her estates in order to reserve the game for herself. Her other forays into the statute book were equally trivial. She was upset by the sight of a funeral procession passing outside her window and so forbade the transport of corpses past her palace. The rest she left to Biron. Over the next decade he took advantage of the squabbling of Russia's noble families to sideline the old aristocracy while exploiting the country's resources for personal benefit and banishing his opponents to Siberia. No doubt Pushkin regarded Anna's lover as Menshikov Mark Two. Indeed, their likeness may have accounted for his erroneous claim in the *Onegin* note that Gannibal, 'a personal enemy of Biron, was dispatched, under a specious pretext, to Siberia'.[13]

Yet the earlier reference to Gannibal's friend Münnich also holds a key. Tall, gaunt and suave, potentially sinister if he were not so charming, Münnich was the eighteenth-century military adventurer *par excellence*. Born in northern Germany in 1683, and a veteran of the War of Spanish Succession, he had come to Russia in his late thirties ostensibly to work on the Lake Ladoga canal, and then had risen steadily in the military hierarchy during the restless years after Peter the Great's death. In 1727, for instance, he was appointed head of Russia's fortifications and artillery. Three years later, as field marshal, he seized control of the army. Such a promotion gave him the opportunity to rescue Gannibal – and he seized that too. In January 1730, 'by a decree of the former Supreme Privy Council', as Münnich noted in a letter to the empress, the African 'was posted to the garrison at Tobolsk, with the rank of major'.[14]

From Selenginsk to Petersburg was a distance of 4,000 miles. It was a long way back. Nevertheless Gannibal had at least begun the journey. Now it was just a matter of time. On 12 July Münnich wrote to Yaguzhinsky, the prosecutor-general, and said *en passant* that he 'trusts' Gannibal 'will now shortly return'. Was this subtle pressure or a response to hearing advance news? Either way, on 25 September, Yaguzhinsky told the senate that the Empress Anna Ivanovna had decreed that 'lieutenant-bombardier Abram Petrov, who is in charge of the Tobolsk garrison, should be dispatched to the headquarters of Count von Münnich, and in turn by him to Pernau [in Estonia], to carry out engineering and fortification works at his level of expertise'.[15] The homecoming was symmetrical at least. Exiled as a scientist by Menshikov, the African returned to Petersburg in the same guise.

# 16

# Fortress Mentality

Look! How this fragile crystal lives!
—A. A. Alexeyev, *Baikal*

The purpose of my journey was to find the lost fortress of Selen-ginsk. It began on the Trans-Siberian Express, in a snowstorm, with two maps lying crumpled on my lap. One was the 1:500,000-scale land survey published by the Russian Bureau of Cartography. It showed our position at a longitude of 107 degrees east and 51 degrees north, on the border of Outer Mongolia. The other was a photo-graphic copy of Gannibal's chart, according to which the train was already crawling through a vast and imaginary China.

On first examining Gannibal's chart at the Russian Academy of Sciences — it is drawn in green ink on a sheet of paper folded into the second volume of *Geometry and Fortification* — I assumed the task of locating Selenginsk would not be too difficult. The name of the place is written in a neat, semi-italic script between the red lines of longitude and latitude, and the same name appears on the Russian land survey published in 1998.

It was the same name but a different place, as I learned on the train from Irkutsk. The city, only forty miles from the shores of Lake Baikal, was known in its nineteenth-century heyday as the Paris of Siberia, thanks to a colony of Decembrist exiles who built the original blue and green wooden houses off what is now Karl Marx Street. 'I saw the unhappy Princess Volkonskaya [in Moscow] on her way to Siberia to join her husband Sergei,' wrote her friend Pushkin in 1827, a hundred years after Gannibal met *his* friend – same name, different woman –on that Vladimirka road.[1] In mid-February, however, with ice under the tundra, and its oppressively monumental Soviet archi-tecture, Irkutsk seemed dark and cold and uninviting, less a fashion-able outpost of Decembrism than the one-horse town Gannibal had known a hundred years earlier.

That is one more horse than you'll find in Selenginsk today, because the town no longer exists. In search of this phantom nowhere, on the Trans-Siberian railway, I crossed the Angara river and rounded the southern tip of Baikal. Now I was on Gannibal's trail, sharing the wintry discomforts of his journey, seeing much of what he saw as he looped the frozen lake, and perhaps feeling a little of what he felt under the blank gaze of snow clouds. Each spring the ice melts and the 'sea of Baikal' once again becomes an aquatic marvel, plunging to a depth of over a mile, not only the deepest but also the oldest lake in the world by a sizeable margin: clay samples taken in 1990 show that Baikal is at least thirty million years old – few of its rivals go back more than 30,000 years – and so vast, with a shoreline of 1,200 miles, and a volume equal to the five Great Lakes of North America put together, that it contains nearly a fifth of all the fresh water on the planet.

Being a scientist, Gannibal paid attention to this aquatic marvel and its seasonal changes, which he reproduced in a sketch of the lake's contours. The African was a keen naturalist, too. In his notebook he drew up lists of the hundreds of unique animal and plant species that live on Baikal. Some of them could be dated to prehistoric times, a throwback to the ancient seas that covered Siberia. For instance, one page of his notebook divides fifty species of fish, such as the grayling, whitefish, sturgeon, omul salmon and various kinds of goby, into a league table of uniqueness – a fish called *golomyanka* came first – but here uniqueness is common. The lake's nerpa seals are found nowhere else. Rare bears, elk, lynx and sables abound in Baikal's forests.

I was still poring over the map when the train came to a halt in Selenginsk, 200 miles east of Irkutsk. In the absence of any more reliable data I got out and headed for the oldest building in the town. The Troitskoye monastery, built in 1847, stood behind high walls on an empty street glistening in the snow. A tall monk, in his mid-thirties, stepped out of the gateway. He was holding an icon of the Virgin and shivering with cold. 'What do you want?' he said from behind a huge black beard.

'I heard there was a fortress here.'

'A fortress!' he said, repeating the word *krepost* – it can also mean 'strength'. He looked uncomprehending. 'No fortress here.'

'It may be in ruins,' I went on. 'It was built three hundred years ago.'

Out of the doorway came another voice. 'Father Kyril is right. Nothing existed here then. No fortress, no people even. Only thick mists and snow.'

The speaker was a middle-aged Buryat in a fur hat. He emerged from the shadows already talking fast. On the question of local history Kyril seemed to defer to the ethnic Mongol who had lived here since childhood. His name was Boris and his father had moved to Selenginsk forty years ago to work at the new pulp mill. Lured by the promise of higher wages, his family resettled in the *kombinat*, a Soviet word meaning 'industrial complex'. It was back in the early days of the Cold War. The Troitskoye monastery stood in open fields. Everything changed when the Soviet leadership decided to build two mills here and at Baikalsk on the grounds that heating the lake's mineral-free water, then spraying it over the pulp of Siberian pines, would produce a 'super' cellulose needed to make heavy-duty tyres for military aeroplanes. The development was kept an official secret for four years. Selenginsk was closed to outsiders. The Kremlin imposed a nationwide ban on printing information about the lake's ecosystem. However, towards the end of the Khrushchev era, news did leak out, prompting the Siberian branch of the Academy of Sciences to warn that toxic waste from the mills would inevitably contaminate the waters of Baikal. 'The Selenginsk pulp mill does not have a specific project design yet, but strangely enough, it is already being built,' the scientists wrote in a letter of protest to Moscow in 1963. Even now, long after the end of the Soviet utopia, with the factory making ordinary paper instead of military components, the dumping of chlorines still pollutes 200 square miles of the lake.

We stood on the riverbank, next to the mill, and gazed at the bilious smoke pouring out of a tall chimney into the grey indeterminate air.

'So what do you think of our brave new world?' asked Boris.

It was a Russian question, and the sarcasm had to be dismissed. But then he added, with a defiant look of Ghengis Khan, whose mother came from Buryatiya, 'No fortress here, my friend. Try old Selenginsk, a hundred miles upriver.'

'You mean, there's another one?'

'Not any more. Used to be – a wooden fort – burned to the ground years ago. The *kombinat* took its name.'

The original meaning of the word 'Selenginsk', like that of 'Exeter' or 'Cambridge', for example, refers to the crossing of a river. The river in question is the Selenga, one of more than 330 that flow into Baikal. Only one flows out of the lake, and that is the Angara, a major tributary of the Yenisey river, which it joins near Yeniseysk and then runs another 2000 miles through northern Siberia into the icy Kara Sea. The naming of Selenginsk was pseudo-historical, an act of Soviet possession. It claimed the past for a new world but also muddied the waters. Raguzinsky believed those waters, rising in western Mongolia, were the ultimate source of the Yenisey river. Nevertheless his first experience of Buryatiya was of being hopelessly lost. 'We might have wandered for a year in that labyrinth of rivers, had we not found the Selenga,' he wrote in July 1726, expressing the disorientations of Siberian travel. His confusion is easy to understand in a profoundly confusing landscape. It was my first experience, too – in spite, or perhaps because, of having Gannibal's chart – as we made our way south to the border.

The flags were out in Ulan-Ude for Buddhist new year, and a banner slung from the rooftops on Goose Lake, the old holy place, read enigmatically: 'Welcome to Tibet'. Twenty miles on, the snow was thickening as we reached Novoselenginsk. 'New Selenginsk', as the name implied, was a deserted frontier town on a shelf of rough farmland that fell oddly into two halves, with the river in between. The old settlement, where Gannibal lived for two years, had disap peared without trace. Its absence was unsettling. I had spent months puzzling over maps of Selenginsk, but now I was actually here I saw nothing I had expected. No scarp or counterscarp, no sign of a main fortress wall.

Novoselenginsk was just an ordinary Russian town with its handful of shops, a ruined church, a bankrupt state farm. It had nothing special, except for a name, and even that was disguised by the modern prefix. The new had buried the old. Television and wood smoke seeped out of doorways. In front of the schoolhouse half a dozen teenagers played football, using snowmen for goalposts. When I asked after the fortress, people shook their heads or pointed to the site of a former Christian mission. In 1818, Tsar Alexander I gave Edward Stallybrass and two other priests from the London Missionary Society a plot on the east bank of the Selenga. Stallybrass was an energetic, dark bearded young Englishman who came to Buryatiya hoping to save souls. The foreigners stayed in Selenginsk for twenty two years, but even though they lived like Russians, eating pickled cabbage and black bread as they translated the Bible into Mongolian, the mission was a disappointing failure. The Buryats clung to Buddhism. In 1839, Stallybrass's wife Charlotte died from a mysterious illness, and then finally, a year later, the work of the missionary society in Russia was suppressed by a decree of the Orthodox synod. Stallybrass returned to England with 'a broken mind and a sick body'.[2]

The name of Charlotte Stallybrass is unknown in Selenginsk today. But the dead wife of another missionary enjoys a kind of immortality. It has been suggested that Martha Cowie was responding to a religious cult of self sacrifice when she gave up everything at home a dozen years earlier and followed her husband to the last outpost of Russian civilisation in Asia. She did not speak Russian, let alone Mongolian, and took three months to travel the 5,000 miles from London to the bleak, ramshackle settlement of wooden huts on the Chinese border. Crossing the snow-bound steppe in an open carriage, she immediately took against the unfamiliar surroundings, yet embraced her fate with dignity: a Scottish counterpart to Volkon- skaya, whom she may have met in 1827, when the princess visited her cousin Alexander Bestuzhev, one of Pushkin's closest friends, in exile at Selenginsk. Martha's premature death occurred the same year. Her grief-stricken husband, Robert Yuille, wrote that she died of cold after 'a hazardous adventure on the icy mountain paths beyond the fort'.[3]

Here was a clue. Not just the sad tale of Martha Cowie's demise, but the twenty-foot obelisk in rough white stone erected by Yuille as a gravestone. The tomb now empty of her bones still stands in Selenginsk, and I found it there one afternoon in a gully by the river, next to a breached cattle pen. Its Latin inscription – *Memoriae Marthae Cowie, Fidelis Uxor, Nata in Scotia in Urbe Glasguae* – reached across vast distances of geography and time.

The intertwined stories of Cowie and Volkonskaya, Bestuzhev and Gannibal, make up a forgotten chapter of the strangely actualised myth and, as I retraced their steps, the obelisk seemed to point the way. Half a mile from the tombstone a narrow path led down to the Selenga, where a herdsman chased the fugitive cows, his donkey cart gliding over the snow. Beyond the river a wide open ice field stood empty like a painted land, with the immense sombre face of Mongolia looking down. Dusk fell with its celebrated abruptness as we crossed the frozen river, leaving Novoselenginsk behind and entering a space that seemed to belong to an older, half-mythic Siberia.

We were wading fast through shin-deep snow – and then it happened. Rounding a bend, we got our first view of huge earth- works dropped into the ground behind a ditch. Sloping ramparts protected the rest of the hillside from Chinese attack, while a sunken level path completed the layout of the fortress. It was a simple design, without masonry, but with the characteristic star shape I had seen in *Geometry and Fortification*. In Selenginsk there was no separation – it had become apparent during the journey – between Gannibal's interest in military engineering and his fascination with the land. His fascination outlived the siege mentality. The Chinese never did attack. However, in 1843 destruction came from within. Fire destroyed the log huts, razing Selenginsk to the ground. The only memorial is the white shell of an onion-domed church. Yet the ground had its revenge. The outline of Gannibal's fortress gleams indestructibly out of the snowdrifts. Ice preserves the fabric of walls that crouch lower and lower into massive bunks of earth.

Reaching the fortress at Selenginsk provided an ironic climax to my journey. Amid the signs of the past the only thing missing was an indication of Gannibal's presence. The old town was deserted, and I hesitate to think of Novoselenginsk as Gannibal's home in Siberia. It was just a place where he worked, and where he lived while he did that work. A sense of imprisonment and hopelessness sears his letters back to Petersburg. For him, Selenginsk always was the ghost town that it later became.

# 17

# The Othello Music

The Negro wasn't jealous; he was trusting
—Alexander Pushkin, *Table Talk*

The return of Gannibal was front page news – or would have been had newspapers, in the modern sense, existed in Russia in 1730.* The exact date of his return is unrecorded, although it can be estimated quite precisely. The fragments of evidence point to the last few weeks of the year. Unfortunately there is a limit to what you can reconstruct by fussing over such details. Of his joyful reunion with friends and lovers in Petersburg, of how he looked after the years in exile, of the changes he saw on the banks of the Neva – the late tsar had briefly transferred the capital of Russia back to Moscow – of these no records remain.

One significant change was the influx of foreigners, like Biron and Münnich, who now dominated Russia in the wake of Peter the Great. To some extent, at least, the Russians had only themselves to blame for this unnatural state of things. Hatreds and mutual jealousies had led to infighting among the most powerful aristocratic families. Between 1725 and 1730, Menshikov had ruined Tolstoy, while the Dolgorukys and Golitsyns had ruined Menshikov, leaving Yaguzhinsky more or less single-handedly to destroy the Dolgorukys

---

*The first Russian broadsheet, *Vedomosti*, appeared on 16 December 1702, carrying 'news about military and other affairs', but was really a celebration of war and authority instead of a newspaper.

and the Golitsyns. The only survivor under Anna of Peter's 'fledglings', Yaguzhinsky was later sent into honourable exile as the Russian ambassador to Berlin.

That Gannibal should see an opportunity in this cutthroat atmo-sphere is hardly surprising, given Münnich's depiction of him as a 'knight of Africke' straight from the pages of *Orlando Furioso*. Like Rogero, the *inamorato* of Ariosto's heroine, and a heroic Pagan, the Moor bridged a gap. Neither an insider nor an outsider, he could appeal to both groups. That was a clever trick, in Anna's Russia, for a career-minded soldier to pull off. The eighteenth century was the age *par excellence* of the cosmopolitan officer, but in Russia the dependence on aliens went far beyond the European norm. The nineteenth-century military expert Christoph Hermann von Manstein claimed that the Russians needed plenty of foreign officers, 'because the soldiers repose more confidence in strangers than in officers of their own nation'. At the same time, Münnich wished to redress the imbalance by promoting native Russians – a category in which he placed Gannibal – within the Engineering Corps. 'The majority of its officers were foreigners,' wrote Manstein, 'because Russians had no inclination or aptitude for engineering.'[1] His strangeness, in other words, had made Gannibal a 'personality', from the Seine to the Selenga, but it was his Russian-ness, in 1731, that earned him the rank of captain.

The opposition between the two views of Gannibal as a gifted stranger and a home-grown talent was nowhere more dramatically evident than in Pernau on the Baltic coast. Nor did the personality of the 'personality' escape criticism. 'Cruel and ambitious' was Nabokov's verdict. Others have felt the same. 'His main flaw was a violent character,' wrote Prince Pyotr Dolgoruky, though he was hardly a neutral observer, given his own family's long-running feud with Gannibal. 'He often lost his temper because he had a wild jealousy.'[2] Even Pushkin, who disapproved of racial stereotypes, caused a stir by identifying the green-eyed monster with his ancestor's 'African character'.[3] His unfinished novel makes veiled allusion to the brutal world of favouritism and political intrigue that Nabokov so detested. Yet his poetic and idealised view of the 'noble Moor' also resembles the work of a very different author who wrote a harrowing drama about the fall of a black personality.

The author was Shakespeare, and the drama was, of course, *Othello*, which he wrote between 1602 and 1604, soon after *Hamlet* and not long before *King Lear*. It is the only domestic tragedy by Shakespeare, who found the plot in Giraldi Cinthio's sordid collection of tales *Hecatommithi* (1565). In the middle of the play comes a totally unexpected window onto the Negro of Peter the Great and his career as a black commander of a white army. The line is spoken by the duke of Venice as he dispatches Othello to defend Cyprus against the Turks. It is a single sentence of businesslike prose:

> Othello, the fortitude of the place is best known to you, and though we have a substitute of most allowed sufficiency, yet opinion, a more sovereign mistress of effects, throws a more safer voice on you.[4]

It sounds like a riddle or perhaps an old wartime newsreel – *the fortitude of the place!* – the clue to the riddle being Othello's delayed response: 'This fortification, gentlemen, shall we see't?'[5] In this unnoticed line Shakespeare seems to predict, in a kind of vivid shorthand, exactly the wording of Münnich's letter of 1730 to the Empress Anna, requesting Gannibal's 'safe' pair of hands at the Baltic fort of Pernau.[6] Shakespeare made a professional soldier out of Cinthio's passionate and bloody lover. But he also – and this explains the duke's urgency – made him a military engineer. Was black Othello, like the 'arithmetician' Cassio whom he made his deputy, an expert in geometry and fortification too?[7]

Gannibal did not only share his blackness with Othello. The two of them had much else in common. Both claimed royal origins. Both were enslaved by the Turks, converted to Islam, and then baptised as Christians after gaining freedom on the shores of the Black Sea. Both rose through the military hierarchy of a white imperialist power to become its general-in-chief, helped by a romantic bravura of manner, and to fight a long-running war against the Ottoman Empire. Indeed, Othello, like Gannibal, was a Janissary in reverse: not a Christian turned Muslim fighting against Christians, but the other way round.

To understand what happened to Gannibal in Pernau in the years 1730–33 we must first examine Shakespeare's riddle. How did he come to face what the critic G. Wilson Knight called 'the Othello music'?[8]

Lack of self-knowledge is a theme in Shakespeare's play. Othello was vulnerable to jealousy as an outsider who had married Desdemona apparently without any previous experience of love. In some respects Gannibal, too, was a late developer, though his sexuality remains, like everything about him, elusive. His private life is wrapped in biographical obscurity. Nevertheless we get occasional hints, such as the mock letter of reproof to Asya Ivanovna for talking 'smuttily', that Abram the Black understood at least something of the manners and morals of sophisticated ladies. He was in love with the idea of women, and his mood in the winter of 1730 showed signs of romantic impatience, of unrequitedness, of snatched and unsatisfactory consummations.

On his arrival in Pernau, for example, Gannibal was feted like Othello docking at Cyprus. The old town on the Gulf of Riga was crying out for a hero. Once a powerful member of the Hanseatic League, Pernau had declined since the medieval heyday of the Teutonic knights. In the sixteenth and seventeenth centuries it fell under the control of Poland and then Sweden, and thus it remained until 1710, when Peter the Great captured the town. On that occasion a 14-year-old Gannibal rode roughshod over Pernau's antiquated defences as the all-conquering Russian army entered the town. Now, twenty years later, his job was to bolster those defences against a Polish counterattack.

He set about reconstructing the knights' fort and building a line of defence at the mouth of the Pernau river. In the process he cut a rather dashing figure. The townsfolk marvelled at the work rate of the black engineer. Not only was the 'noble Moor' at the peak of his profession. His exotic background and sense of duty lent him a certain glamour in the eyes of the female population. 'The thought that nature had not created him for the joys of sex rid him of conceit and pretension, and this gave a rare charm to his behaviour with women,' writes Pushkin in *The Negro of Peter the Great*.[9] Yet it can seem hard to reconstruct Gannibal in this way because he was himself so unconstructed, so much in flux. No doubt he attracted women because he was talented, energetic and strong-willed. He was also cruel and despotic and arbitrary – and his first marriage yields ample evidence of what Pushkin regarded as a strange compound of innocence and brutality.

Shortly after his return from exile Gannibal made the acquaintance of a Greek naval captain serving in the Russian fleet. In addition to having two daughters of marriageable age, Andrei Dioper had a wholly erroneous impression of Gannibal's royal connections. As a result, he couldn't help sizing up the African as a possible son-in-law. At the winter ball held in the Admiralty he introduced Gannibal to his family. The dashing suitor in his Preobrazhensky uniform immediately asked Dioper's younger daughter, the dark-haired Yevdokiya, to dance a minuet. She was taciturn and shy, and blushed as the African saluted her ceremonially in his elegant attire. Soon the couple were bowing and mincing daintily across the room, with little steps and glides, to the right and to the left, approaching and retreating hand in hand. Gannibal was overcome by his partner's beauty, the sweetness of her features, her pale complexion, the ringlets framing her temples, the luxuriant snow white décolletage, her improbably narrow waist. The other women seemed to fade in the aura of her charm. By the time the minuet ended, and the dancers ended up at the very spot where they had begun, Gannibal had fallen in love with the 'most gracious creature' Yevdokiya.[10]

Unfortunately, the object of his infatuation was already engaged to a young naval officer by the name of Alexander Kaisarov. Neither she nor her lover had informed Dioper of the secret attachment but they were planning to elope. Her response to Gannibal's lovemaking was therefore rather curt. 'The old Negro [he was only thirty-five] hoped to captivate her with stories of his wanderings and battles,' observed Pushkin, quoting Shakespeare.[11] Yet to no avail. Unlike Desdemona, Yevdokiya was 'devoid of poetry' and also perhaps frightened of the black man's appearance. ('Your appearance! What nonsense! A fellow like you? A young girl must obey her parents,' the tsar tells Ibrahim in Pushkin's novel.)[12]

The traditional Russian marriage was a patriarchal one. Romance and sentiment were often disregarded. True love was seen as a foreign luxury. When her father told Yevdokiya that Gannibal had proposed, she flew into a rage and shouted, 'The Black is not of our race.'[13] Her protests fell on deaf ears. In the end, having no choice, she submitted to the inconvenient marriage.

The story of Gannibal's post-nuptial crisis reverberates in Pushkin's novel. Even before the ceremony Pushkin sounds an ominous note. 'Get this crazy notion out of your head. Don't marry!' his friend Korsakov tells Ibrahim:

> 'Don't marry. If you want my opinion, your betrothed can't stand the sight of you. Besides it's useless to hope for female fidelity. Envy the husband who doesn't give a damn. But not you! With your brooding and suspicious nature, with your flat nose, your thick lips and your rough woolly head — it'd be crazy for you to hurl yourself into the perils of marriage!'[14]

Here Pushkin echoes the racist language in *Othello* as if to underline the vulnerable otherness of the Moor. In Petersburg, as in Venice, the courtship happened very fast. Othello sailed to defend Cyprus. Urgent duties awaited Gannibal in Pernau. Yet a simple twist inverts the Russian plot. Othello was 'not jealous but trusting', according to Pushkin.[15] The poet also wrote of the nuptials in an uncompleted poem that exists only in a rough draft. 'When the Tsar's Negro Took a Notion to Get Married' is one of Pushkin's earliest experiments at imitating Russian folk tales. It ends, ominously:

The Negro has chosen a lady for himself:
The black raven a white swan.
But he is a black blackamoor,
And she is a white darling.[16]

Yet Gannibal did not suspect his wife. Even on 17 January 1731, the day of his wedding, the bridegroom had no inkling of Yevdokiya's secret affair. Having married in haste, he would repent at leisure.

Soon after the wedding the Gannibals departed for the Baltic coast while Kaisarov fled broken-hearted to Astrakhan on the Caspian Sea. No doubt the African would have preferred to stay in Petersburg. After the years in exile he felt the lure of the metropolis. Life in Estonia was a far cry from the Neva's cosmopolitan milieu. 'I am married – and happy,' Gannibal wrote in March 1731, but he couldn't help noticing that Pernau's diminished role seemed to foster a small-town mentality among its residents. The African was met with hostility at the town's famous military academy, where he began to teach mathematics, fortification and technical drawing to young cadets. The newly-weds had an uneventful social life. As a result, they both found the atmosphere dull and claustrophobic. In a letter to Münnich, Gannibal evokes this sombre chapter of his first marriage – the shabby, depressing town house near the port, the little garden out back, the sour smell of damp over everything.[17] He omits to mention the baleful presence of Yevdokiya, who quickly revealed herself to be not only deceitful but also snobbish and affected. Marriage, it seems, had no impact on her behaviour. There were domestic problems. Her airs and graces offended the servants. But her real offence was against propriety in a small town. In April 1731, within two months of her arrival, she made the fateful decision to alleviate the Baltic boredom by taking one of her husband's pupils as a lover.

The details of the affair were commonplace or perhaps archetypal. Yet one should resist the urge to assimilate Madame Gannibal to Madame Bovary. Yevdokiya met the cadet Yakov Shishkov, known as the 'Don Juan of Pernau', at a supper party given rather wonderfully at the house of a 'Madame Moor', who is described somewhat economically as a *meshchanka*, or 'bourgeoise'.[18] Shishkov was a rake who no longer feared the world's censure. Over a game of cards, he showered the married woman with 'illicit gestures of admiration', according to one source, the shadowy clerk Timofeyev, who later acted as their go-between.[19] The dangerous liaison set tongues wagging. Even before the affair with Shishkov, the townsfolk of Pernau were agog with the melodrama of the black engineer and his unhappy wife. Now the gossips went into overdrive. Could Gannibal have been unaware of what was so obvious to the whole town that it soon became the subject of jocular remarks? Or did he really not suspect Yevdokiya's infidelity until she gave birth in October 1731 to a white baby? Pushkin drops a hint in his novel, where he tells the story in reverse and also transfers the action to Paris, where the Countess Lénore de D— bears Ibrahim a mixed race child:

> She was in labour for a long time. Her every groan tore at his soul; each interval of silence heightened his anguish. Suddenly he heard the tiny cry of a child and, unable to hide his joy, he rushed into the Countess's room. A black baby lay on the bed at her feet.[20]

Scandal is averted in the novel by a quick-thinking doctor who replaces the black baby with a changeling. The count later returns home to welcome a safe delivery and to raise the white infant as his own. 'The butt of all jokes was the poor husband who alone in Paris neither knew nor suspected anything,' adds Pushkin.

No such deception occurred in real life, though Gannibal did adopt his wife's child, whom he named Yevdokiya after its mother. Meanwhile the local wags in Pernau, helped by Gannibal's enemies at court, gleefully spread word that the African had been cuckolded. Even among the officers of the garrison, the birth of a white daughter to the 'Tsar's Moor' caused a sensation disagreeable to Gannibal. On 11 October, he wrote to Münnich begging to be released from his duties in Pernau so that he could escape the gossip. 'I have undergone many injustices and gross lies,' he complained, 'and therefore it will be harder for me to recover in Estonia than elsewhere.'[21] Münnich forwarded the request to Petersburg. However, the military authorities declined to accept Gannibal's resignation on the grounds that his presence in the Baltic was vital to national security.

The upshot of the baby scandal was a new round of marital strife. Relations between Gannibal and Yevdokiya deteriorated rapidly after a bizarre turn of events. In February 1732, the African received a tip-off from another young cadet that his wife and Shishkov intended to poison him. The young engineer, Gabriel Kuzminsky, had apparently been drawn into the plot only to withdraw at the eleventh hour. 'Abram Petrov is ill,' Kuzminsky reported Shishkov as saying to Madame Moor, 'and if his wife is smart she'll go to the apothecary and buy something and give it to Petrov so that he won't live very long.'[22] On 28 February, Gannibal lodged a formal complaint with the military authorities, accusing his wife of adultery and attempted murder, and suing her for a divorce.

Was Gannibal really ill? His letter of resignation to Münnich did cite a lingering discomfort from the head wound he had received twelve years earlier in Spain as another reason to withdraw from public life. Pushkin suggests that the damage to the brain may have driven his ancestor mad. But it is just as likely that he was deranged by the disclosure of a threat to his life.

Under police interrogation Yevdokiya confessed her guilt on both counts – adultery and poisoning – and was sentenced to imprisonment in the Gospitalny Dvor, a hospital for the criminally insane.[23] Several years later, however, she withdrew her confession and proclaimed her innocence of all charges. She argued that she had pleaded guilty in the first place only because Gannibal beat her cruelly to within an inch of her life.

The nineteenth-century historian Stepan Opatovich claimed to have read in secret police documents that the African rigged up a private torture chamber in the cellar of his house in Pernau, complete with pulleys, iron clamps, thumbscrews, leather whips and so forth, and that he repeatedly hanged Yevdokiya from the wrists until she confessed to her crimes. Such evidence might portray Gannibal in a harsh and altogether sinister light – not so much Russia's Othello as a Baltic Bluebeard. Unfortunately these documents have vanished without trace.

Some recent critics have questioned Opatovich's claims. Others have gone so far as to deconstruct a racist subtext in his interpretation of Gannibal's 'African temperament'. Without doubt, many nine-teenth-century Russian writers, such as Anuchin and Annenkov, jumped to false conclusions about the undeniable streak of cruelty in the Moor's character. Yet Nabokov was surely right to argue that, in his mistreatment of Yevdokiya, Gannibal acted no differently than many a 'coarse, wife-flogging Russian' of his day. From reading family chronicles, and stories of serfdom in Russia, it becomes clear that such cruelty was part of the fabric of the time. Divorce was rare – about twenty a year for the whole of Russia in the 1750s, rising to no more than a few hundred by the end of the nineteenth century – because the Russian church retained control of marriage. Both state and church conceived the husband as an autocrat. His absolute power over his wife and family were seen as a part of the divine and natural order. As late as 1836 Russia's legal code stated that 'a woman must obey her husband, reside with him in love, respect and unlimited obedience, and offer him every pleasantness and affection as the ruler of the household'.[24] Wife-beating was common and, legally, an abused wife could not leave a tyrannical husband.

Yevdokiya remained in jail for five years. But then, in 1746, she petitioned the Holy Synod for a legal separation on the grounds that her 'unloving' husband had remarried illegally ten years earlier, using a forged certificate. She begged for an annulment that would enable her to lead 'a peaceful, secure life until the end of my days'. At first the church said that it did not recognise Gannibal's marriage to Christina-Regina von Schöberg, a Swedish-German woman by whom he now had five children. The synod ordered the African to clarify his matri-monial situation. He took three years to respond – or perhaps he was just brooding. It's hard to say. Certainly the letter he sent in September 1749, and its accompanying request that Yevdokiya be sent to the remote Tikhvin convent, where his friend Princess Volkonskaya had died in the meantime, betrays not only signs of pure derangement but also the cruel strain of the Othello music:

> I demand that the Church, on the grounds of my long and irre-proachable service, and of my second marriage, defends my rights and detains my former wife Yevdokiya at the convent – for the simple rea-son that she committed adultery – and that the Church also keeps her at a safe distance from me, and never allows this sinner to call herself my wife ever again, because if she is allowed out at liberty, I fear that she will drag my name into dishonour because of her dirty affairs.[25]

The divorce finally came through in 1753, at which time Yevdokiya was sent to the convent, where she too died soon afterwards. Gannibal never showed any remorse but he wept at the news of her death. Did he already have an inkling, perhaps, that his own life was about to slip its moorings?

# 18

# Unmoored

The Emperor of Russia was my father
—Shakespeare, *The Winter's Tale*

On 21 May 1733, in the aftermath of his marriage scandal, Gannibal left Pernau – and the army – and disappeared from view. His bolthole was the small estate of Kyrkyula, twenty miles south-west of Reval. He had bought the property a year earlier, in the name of 'Cap[tain] Hannibal', as if hoping to forge a new identity in the country.[1] The pseudonym was a kind of disguise and slowly it was absorbed into the official record of his life. Both Münnich and the Empress Anna signed a decree confirming the African's retirement from the military and his pension of 100 roubles a year. This decree marks the first official use of the name here misspelled as 'Abram Ganibal', with a Latin *i* instead of the Cyrillic и.

The house at Kyrkyula, with its fifty acres and dozen serfs, was a typical mid-eighteenth-century nest of the gentry: small and built of pine, with a picket fence. The lack of grandeur was also typical. Before the great age of estate building, which began in 1762 when Peter III excused the nobility from state service, even the houses of wealthy Russians were barely distinguishable from peasant huts. An inventory of the estate of Prince Dmitry Golitsyn, made in 1737, showed that the manor house consisted of two rooms only. The set-up at Kyrkyula was equally modest. Since 1723, the house had belonged to Gannibal's friend Admiral Ivan Mikhailovich Golovin, who had been given it — along with a mock-title, 'our second Noah' — by Peter the Great as a reward for years of shipbuilding.[2]

The forlorn atmosphere of the house suited Gannibal. Here, steeped in memories of the Petrine era, he lived the quiet and reclusive life of a Russian country gentleman. He became the 'unpretentious sage' of Pushkin family legend.[3] An exaggeration perhaps, though by no means a figure of speech. Gannibal was thirty-seven years old when he moved to Kyrkyula: in the strange curriculum of his life, he was already an old man.

He also became a keen gardener. The 'manor' stood on rough land above a boggy stretch of the river Vääna. The area was cleared and planted with lilac bushes and fruit trees: it is marked on Ganni-bal's plot as *vishnyovy sad*, or 'cherry orchard', though, as in Chekhov's play, the trees were doomed to be cut down. The orchard is now a reservoir. Beyond it — below the curve of the hill — is a line of tall, wind-blasted Siberian pines. A couple of them were felled recently in a storm. Having done an informal ring-count on the stumps, I would say they are just over 250 years old, and therefore a direct link to Gannibal.

In winter, sitting at his desk among the rough drafts of math-ematical papers, charts and diagrams of unbuilt forts, he began to write down the story of his life — the boyhood in Africa, the years of slavery, his escape to Russia, the journey to France — as if with surprise, as if seeing it whole for the first time.

He wrote in French but inserted Russian phrases to underline key points. Sometimes a word of German crept into the text because it was a language spoken in the house and he felt safe within its syntax, its form. His wife Christina (whom he had probably married in 1736) was, according to Rotkirkh, the daughter of 'a local captain [in Reval], Matvey von Schöberg', a former Swedish officer who had switched allegiance to Russia after being captured. But, significantly, her mother was a Baltic German whose maiden name, von Albedil, denotes one of the oldest families in Livonia.

The African had reason to be grateful for his wife's connections because, as we have seen, he had private worries in the 1730s. Some of these worries found their way into the writing of his memoir, albeit indirectly, since the autobiography, like the garden, was full of hedgings. Retrospectively, on the page, his anger found its bitter voice and the public humiliation of his divorce was overshadowed by a wider antipathy to the *Bironovshchina*, or 'rule of Biron', to give the German ascendancy its proper name. Nor was Gannibal the only Russian – if indeed he was a Russian – to deplore this power behind the throne. While the Empress Anna concerned herself primarily with extravagant amusements at court in Petersburg, her favourite Biron held sway throughout the empire. His dictatorship was invisible since he held no official post until, in 1737, he was elected duke of Courland – a 'famous farce' to which his namesake Lord Byron alludes in *Don Juan* – but it was also severe.[4] If Gannibal was, as Pushkin claimed, Biron's 'personal enemy', then he 'had no choice but to spend the whole of Anna's reign hiding away on his estate'.[5] His in-laws were a kind of refuge as he sought shelter from the Bironic storm under a German branch of the family tree.

Being francophone made life uncomfortable. Gannibal had to watch his tongue. It didn't seem to matter that he was now regarded as yesterday's man. He was a living reminder of the days of Peter the Great and therefore posed a threat, or at any rate he thought he did. Such a threat failed to convince Pushkin, however. On the contrary, he describes Gannibal in a poem of 1824 as 'the forgotten one', and the poet marvelled that even in the wilds of the Estonian countryside his ancestor should have lived in 'constant fear' of Biron and the other Teutonic tyrants.[6] He feared the knock on the door in the middle of the night. That fear clouded his nostalgia and forced him to question at least one aspect of the Petrine legacy. The African was not the only one. 'Many things in our past history can be explained by the fact that a Russian, Peter the Great, sought to make us Germans,' wrote Pushkin's friend Vyazemsky. Certainly a few Muscovite boyars held the tsar-*batyushka* to blame for the stranglehold of foreigners at court. When Livonia and Estonia were conquered and absorbed into the Russian empire in 1710, Peter guaranteed the Baltic Germans a number of privileges as a bribe to switch sides. He wanted to use their administrative experience to put his reforms into effect. So they were allowed to continue worshipping in the Lutheran faith, to use the German language for official business and to live under German law, while occupying a disproportionate number of senior posts in the Russian government and military intelligence.[7] The consequences of Peter's recruitment drive were profound. Even in the mid-nineteenth century the Third Department, or secret police, was known as the 'German department'.

One of these foreign adventurers, Burkhard Münnich, had seized control of the army while his old friend Gannibal sulked on the sidelines. After a string of victories over the French in the War of the Polish Succession, this arch-German launched a new crusade against the Turks. On the eve of the campaign of 1736, he outlined to Biron a four-year programme of conquest, saying: 'We shall raise the standards of Her Imperial Highness. Where? Why, over Constantinople!'[8] It didn't quite work out like that. Münnich conquered Ochakov and Azov on the Black Sea. He routed the Turks at Stavuchany, near Khotin in Bessarabia, and advanced into the Balkans, only to have to abandon the spoils of war because his Austrian allies unexpectedly signed an Ottoman peace deal at Belgrade.

In his memoirs Gannibal wrote of his early admiration for Münnich, that 'he was a strategist, which I was not, that he was a man of intuition, which I was not; and that, as such, he saw many things long before me, which I could only grasp when they were pointed out to me'.[9] This kept the African from judging him. Nevertheless he began to feel that the outcome of the Russo-Turkish war had scarcely justified its tremendous cost in human life and money. The outbreak of peace brought him out of retirement. When Anna died in 1740, leaving the Russian throne to her infant grandnephew Ivan VI and naming Biron as regent, Münnich feared that Biron's widespread unpopularity would cause the entire ruling German clique to lose power. Three weeks into the new regime, he ordered his soldiers to arrest Biron in the middle of the night – after a knock on the door – and sent him to Siberia.

Life's mutability was the underlying theme of Gannibal's memoir. Now the fall of Biron prompted another change. The infant tsar was still only a few months old, so Münnich installed the baby's mother Anna Leopoldovna as regent, assuming the role of prime minister himself. His first act in office was to cast a wary eye at Sweden, where a change of government after twenty years – and a new alliance with France – had once again raised the spectre of war. In the circum-stances, with an urgent need to reinforce the Baltic forts, it was hardly surprising that Münnich should have recalled the sage of Kyrkyula to active duty. Yet the summons was unexpected. In January 1741, one of the first decrees signed by Anna Leopoldovna conferred the rank of lieutenant-colonel on 'Abram Petrovich Gannibal, who has served Russia irreproachably for many years'.[10] His promotion brought its own reward in the form of an estate at Rakhula, three times larger than Kyrkyula, and a dozen miles nearer Reval, but it also imposed on Gannibal a heavy burden of responsibility as commander of that city's garrison.

Gannibal wrote that he accepted the posting to Reval 'without hesitation'.[11] In fact, he had no choice but to come out of retirement. The life of a country gent was expensive. His 100-rouble-a-year pension could not support a growing family, and Christina was to give birth to eleven children over the next two decades. A son Ivan, who grew up to have a distinguished military career in the reign of Catherine the Great, was born in 1735, and a daughter, Yelizaveta, two years later. At the time of the move to Reval, Christina was pregnant with another daughter, Anna. A fourth child, Pyotr, whom Pushkin knew at Mikhailovskoye, was born the following year and a fifth, Osip, the poet's grandfather, in 1744. The youngest children to survive were Isaak, born in 1747, and Sofiya, twelve years Isaak's junior and the future wife of Gannibal's biographer, Adam Rotkirkh.

Some things were immutable, however. Take, for example, Gannibal's affinity with scandal and intrigue, both of which he found in Reval. At first he welcomed the return to a city he had visited at the time of its conquest. His wife's family still lived in the old town, and the couple had met in Reval, so he felt at home among its winding streets and wooden houses. The omens were favourable, too. The Gannibals moved into an apartment on Pikk tänav (Long Street) overlooking the headquarters of the Brotherhood of Blackheads, a merchants' guild dating back to the fourteenth century. The Blackheads were unmarried merchants who took their name from an African soldier who was martyred in the third century for refusing to wage war on his fellow Christians. A carved head of Saint Maurice, as he was known, still decorates the building's façade.[12]

Brotherly love did not extend very far in eighteenthcentury Reval. Scarcely had Gannibal set to work inspecting the city's defences than he began to feel ill at ease among its Nordic inhabitants due to the colour of his skin, rough manners and inability, as he put it, to 'endear myself to my superior', Baron Waldemar von Löwendahl. The racist and choleric Löwendahl had nominated a Swedish officer by the name of Major Peter Holmer for the post of garrison commander. He thus resented the Moor's appointment. The first meeting between these two blustery, hottempered men degenerated into a shouting match. Löwendahl 'scolded me as if he were addressing one of his serfs', wrote Gannibal. But this was only the beginning of his misfortune. The citizens of Reval were ultraconservative. The idea of mixed marriages, let alone mixedrace children, offended some bigots. In their eyes the black soldier and his blonde Scandinavian wife made an outrageous couple. Once again there was scope here for those who were hostile to Gannibal. Old gossip was dug up, mostly about Yevdokiya. New rumours drifted back to Petersburg. Indeed, so desperate was Löwendahl to oust Gannibal that he encouraged Reval's military commander, General Adrian de Brigny, to spread lies about 'the Negro's misconduct'. In dealing with the smear campaign, Gannibal flaunted his own political connections. Never one to shy away from confrontation, he wrote a letter of protest to the imperial cabinet in Petersburg, listing twenty-two complaints against Löwendahl, who

> has made no secret of the enmity and dislike that he bears me. It has
> been clear from the very beginning that he objects to my involvement
> in the mission at Reval, not least because he has subjected me to a
> constant stream of abuse and intrigues, hoping to besmirch my repu-
> tation and to present a false impression of my conduct likely to result
> in disciplinary charges. In short, he has treated me like a slave, and
> has done everything in his power to bring about the termination of
> my duties here at Reval. I have suffered insults and offences not only
> from him but also from de Brigny who tried by every possible means
> to bring about my ruin.[13]

Then, in different ink, he added: '[A]mong the various disgraceful offences against me was de Brigny's threat to evict me from my apartment – at a time when my wife was only hours from giving birth – and to throw all my belongings into the street.'

The African's breach of protocol infuriated Löwendahl. He sent a message to the Winter Palace with his own version of events. The remonstrance fell on deaf ears. In part this was because, as everybody knew, the context of the dispute was the pro-Swedish tendency of the Baltic Germans. Having inspected Reval's defences, Gannibal drafted a bold plan to repel a Swedish attack by upgrading the artillery at Reval's coastal forts. Such an improvement was likely to deter an invader. Münnich thought so, and so might anyone think, contemplating the maps and diagrams of the Baltic Sea that lay open on the African's desk as he sat writing his memoirs. Instead of sacking Gannibal, as Löwendahl demanded, Münnich replaced de Brigny with a Russian officer, Mikhail Filosofov, who held the 'black Vauban' in high regard.

Surviving the plot was an unexpected triumph for the African. He felt that he had acted in some ways as the conscience of Russia. But much odder and more telling was the way in which, over time, the truth and falsehood of the Teutonic conspiracy became reversed in his mind. Without doubt he owed his survival to Münnich. Yet the treachery of Löwendahl, Holmer and de Brigny made him question the legitimacy of rule by foreigners. His ultimate betrayal of his friend Münnich was something the intuitive prime minister did not foresee.

Even after the fall of Biron the dominance of Germans in political life continued to incense the Russian nobility. Soon the malcontents united behind Peter the Great's daughter Elizabeth. She was popular because of her Russian outlook, which she emphasised, and because she shared the aura of her father. Under the influence of Princess Volkonskaya's brother, Alexei Bestuzhev, and other courtiers who hoped to reverse Russia's anti-French foreign policy – a movement to which Gannibal lent discreet support – Elizabeth agreed to return the Baltic territories to France's ally Sweden in exchange for help in seizing the Russian throne. In July 1741 the Swedes declared war on Russia, announcing that they would only withdraw when Elizabeth became the Russian empress. Despite losing a major battle at Vilman-strand, they advanced toward Petersburg during the late summer. The threat to the Russian capital enabled Peter's daughter to stage a successful *coup d'état* in the early hours of 25 November, whereupon the Swedes retreated into Finland.

The staging itself was a theatrical affair. At two o'clock in the morning, buckling on a cuirass and arming herself with a pike, the 32-year-old princess went to the barracks of the Preobrazhensky guards in Saint Petersburg and won them over with a spirited harangue. Rallying her supporters, she sledged over the snow to the Winter Palace, arresting both real and imagined adversaries on her way. Aroused from slumber, the regent Anna Leopoldovna submitted quietly and was conveyed to Elizabeth's sledge. The baby tsar followed behind in a second sledge. Münnich was also deposed and sent to Pelym in Siberia, to reside in the very house which he had himself designed for the reception of Biron, whom by a singular twist of fate he chanced to encounter in the midst of the frozen wilderness, dashing hopefully back to all that his rival was now leaving behind.

The accession of the Empress Elizabeth called forth a wave of national rejoicing. Contemporary accounts suggest that, in Moscow, the festivity eclipsed the 'holy nights' of Christmas, while the streets of Petersburg came alive with dance, music, parades and fireworks. Orthodox priests led the celebration. They had always distrusted the Lutheran heresy. Now they felt vindicated. 'The Holy Ghost has restored the great Peter's spirit to us in the form of his daughter,' proclaimed the archimandrite Kirill. 'He has helped her to wrest her father's sceptre out of foreign hands, and to free nobles and people from the iniquity which they have suffered at the hands of their German masters.'[14] Here was another truth or falsehood, and a strange reformulation of history. The coup leaders incorporated Peter into a notion of Russian-ness, one that he had deliberately undermined by importing those very Germans in the first place.

The fall of Münnich came as a shock to the Baltic Germans of Reval. Of course they felt deceived by Sweden's intrigue. It didn't help that Gannibal was so vociferous a cheerleader for the new regime. On the day of Elizabeth's coronation he organised a magnificent fireworks display in the night sky over the garrison. It was a spectacular occasion, dazzling and deafening in equal measure. Some of the rockets were so powerful that their exhaust flames bored deep holes in the ground even before lift-off. Connoisseurs declared that never had such an entertainment been seen outside Moscow and Petersburg. 'Many great fireworks burned very harmoniously and properly and gave out many different coloured lights and the rockets were very good and flew high,' Gannibal wrote proudly to Elizabeth, as if to remind the sovereign that his experiments with gunpowder had a serious purpose.[15] For him, the art of pyrotechnics was closely linked to a love of shells and explosions. It was also linked to his earliest memory of Reval. 'It would be better to spend millions on fireworks [than on howitzers], on something wondrous and memorable in which the people can take great pleasure,' Peter the Great had written after capturing the city in 1710.[16] As a young man, Gannibal derived much the same pleasure from these ceremonial displays. But as he grew up, he began to use

fireworks to investigate the military potential of rocketry. In the eighteenth century, the making and display of fireworks was the province
of a small number of highly skilled artisans. Pyrotechnic knowledge
was often non-textual; it was learnt by experience. Gannibal was
unusual. He wrote everything down in an unpublished manuscript
book entitled 'Artificial Fireworks'. He did this because he wanted
to show that the technical advantages of rockets, such as their lack
of recoil, would prove cheaper and more efficient for Russian forces
than traditional ordnance – and also because he needed a sponsor. His
letter to Elizabeth ended with a plea in the form of quotation from the
Bible: 'Remember me when you come into your Kingdom.'[17]

The new empress did remember Gannibal, though Rotkirkh
certainly exaggerates in describing an almost sibling-like relationship
between Elizabeth and the Moor. 'He was known to her,' the biographer writes, 'and out of fondness she recalled this playmate of her
childhood and his service to her parents.'[18] The same theme recurs in
Pushkin's novel, where the tsar re-introduces them after Gannibal's
return from Paris:

> 'Lisa,' he said to the young woman. 'Do you remember the little
> Negro, who used to steal apples from my orchard at Oranienbaum
> for you?'[19]

Elsewhere, however, Pushkin paints a very different picture of
Gannibal as 'Peter's adopted child,/The beloved slave of tsars and
tsarinas,/the forgotten one', hiding in the country at Mikhailovskoye,
where, as we saw, having forgotten the solemn promises of Elizabeth,

> In the shade of lime-tree arbours,
> He thought in cool summers
> Of his far-off Africa.[20]

Pushkin wrote these lines 'To Yazikov', a fellow poet, in September
1824 at Mikhailovskoye. The previous year he had written the

mysterious stanza of *Eugene Onegin* in which Gannibal apparently yearns to go back to Logone and, 'under the sky of my Africa,/To sigh for gloomy Russia'. The difference is poignant. In the earlier poem, Gannibal imagines being in 'my Africa' yet remembering Russia. In the later poem, Pushkin describes his great-grandfather stuck in Russia but remembering 'his Africa' from the neglect and isolation of Mikhailovskoye.

Such an outcome would have been unthinkable had Elizabeth not kept at least one of her 'splendid promises' – Mikhailovskoye itself – and promptly, too. Upon ascending the throne, she promoted Gannibal to the rank of major-general from lieutenant-colonel, and appointed him military commander of Reval. The decree signed by Elizabeth declared:

> On 12 January in this year of 1742, by the decree of Her Imperial Majesty, it is her wish that Major-General Abram Gannibal, son of Peter, and the *ober-commandant* of Reval, should have bestowed upon him, as a reward for his long-standing and faithful service, the estate of Mikhailovskoye, near the town of Voronich, in the province of Pskov, which the Crown inherited on the death [in 1733] of Catherine Ivanovna [the sister of the later Empress Anna], and which comprises 569 souls living, according to palace records. All of these shall pass to [Gannibal], in addition to the surrounding land.[21]

That land, comprising 6,000 acres of wood, park and farmland, made Gannibal a wealthy man. At the same time his living quarters in Reval improved as a result of promotion. The family said goodbye to the Brotherhood of Blackheads and moved into an imposing mansion inside the walls of the city's medieval fortress.

Number One, Toompea Hill, is an elegant two-storey house dating back to the fifteenth century. Its tall façade rendered with a dressing of Finnish stone, now painted a rich honey colour, shades a walled garden. Here, in a genteel environment crammed with objects for stimulating the intellect and the imagination as he amassed his own eclectic mix of items – scientific instruments, globes, maps, fireworks and foreign wines – Gannibal lived for over a decade. These years were the most successful of his life in military terms and – until the end – the happiest. Perhaps a certain air of defeat hangs over them: a diminution of his strength and will. There were no more big journeys planned, no more thoughts of becoming a famous scientist or a mathematician as opposed to a powerful courtier. The source of his power can be glimpsed in the subtext, literally, of Elizabeth's decree. At the foot of the document, now in the archive of the Russian Academy of Sciences – the ink greyish but still clear – Alexei Bestuzhev endorses the tsarina's gift of Mikhailovskoye with his own signature in a dark scratchy hand.

It is all a question of context. This is not the first time Bestuzhev's name has been associated with Gannibal. Fifteen years earlier, while serving as Russian minister in Copenhagen, Volkonskaya's brother had been implicated in the plot against Menshikov. His subsequent career followed a similar arc to Gannibal's. 'He was clever,' wrote Manstein, 'but treacherous.'[22] His reputation as one of Peter's 'fledglings' prevented Bestuzhev's advancement until 1740, and he was even briefly imprisoned by Münnich, but the diplomat's fortunes improved a year later when Elizabeth appointed him chancellor, or foreign minister. The Bestuzhev clique was soon wresting control of the levers of power. Alexei's brother Mikhail became the empress's chief-of-staff while Gannibal's old friend Ivan Cherkasov enjoyed a rapid promotion to the influential office of Cabinet Secretary.

The reshuffle was good news for Gannibal, too. The Volkonskaya circle was back in power. Now, for the first time since Peter the Great's death, the African enjoyed the protection of the sovereign, and with that protection came opportunity. He could petition the senate to join the nobility. Bestuzhev also put him in charge of disentangling Elizabeth from her commitments to Sweden. Shortly after her accession the empress reneged on a pledge to return Estonia, Livonia, Ingria, and part of Karelia. Instead, Russian troops conquered Helsingfors and Åbo (now Turku), where they forced the Swedes to sign a peace treaty in 1743, ceding a strip of southern Finland. As head of a delegation in charge of mapping the new border, Gannibal visited every town and village in the 20,000 square miles of territory annexed by Russia. In the absence of Löwendahl, who quit Russia for France the same year, the African ruled Estonia more or less single-handedly for seven months, dispatching orders sealed with a family crest that bore the mysterious word 'FUMMO'.[23]

That a black slave should have risen to such a position in Russian society is extraordinary. Yet his unique achievement often leaves Gannibal resembling an isolated, somewhat flattened figure, visible from one side only: the 'beloved slave of tsars and tsarinas', in Pushkin's phrase, the dashing hero of *The Negro of Peter the Great* who navigates the eighteenth century in a blur of beauty spots and tricorne hats. The inclusion of the discrepant episode of slavery was not so much a digression, therefore, as a heroic simile, carefully placed to magnify the fairy-tale experience of the text.

In fact the question of slavery haunted Gannibal throughout his life. It was not a memory but an everyday fact. The landowner of Kyrkyula, Rakhula and Mikhailovskoye was inevitably a serf-owner, too. The serfs were indivisible from the land, and the owner's wealth depended on the number of 'souls' he possessed. Most foreign travel-lers who commented on the nature of serfdom equated it with slavery. Thus the Englishman William Richardson wrote, in 1784, that 'the peasants in Russia ... are in a state of abject slavery; and are reckoned the property of the nobles to whom they belong, as much as their dogs or horses'.[24]

This way of reckoning was still fairly new in Gannibal's day. The term *sobstvennost*, meaning 'property', was unknown in Russia before the time of Peter the Great. The beginning of serfdom is often dated to the reign of Ivan the Terrible, or to a law code of 1649 which bound the peasant to the estate where he lived, but it was not until 1723 that serfdom was reinforced by Peter's decree amalgamating the boyar nobility into a new service gentry, or *dvoryanstvo*, obligated to the tsar. By the reign of Elizabeth, however, Russians were beginning to use the traditional word for slavery (*rabstvo*) – the same word they applied to its American counterpart – to describe the condition of their serfs, whom they referred to as slaves (*raby*). Here it is worth noting that, in the poem 'To Yazikov', Pushkin uses the specific form *rab* to describe his great-grandfather. In print or official documents the word 'slave' could not be applied to a serf except by the serf himself. But one way of alluding to serfdom as slavery was to speak of the condition of blacks elsewhere, as Pushkin himself did in 1836 when he reviewed the autobiography of an American, John Tanner, in his journal *Sovremennik*. Tanner's story, that of a 9-year-old white boy enslaved by Native Americans in 1789, reminded the poet of his ancestor's fate. 'John Tanner was swapped for a keg of vodka,' he wrote, echoing Bulgarin's claim that a drunken sailor had bought the 6-year-old Gannibal for a bottle of rum. In his review Pushkin criticises the 'Negro President' Thomas Jefferson and the other authors of the Declaration of Independence for tolerating 'Negro slavery in the midst of freedom', while differentiating the experiences of American slaves and Russian serfs.[25] Like Tanner, the serfs were at least held on their native soil, where, despite their bondage, they could continue in many respects to live and act as their ancestors had. Slaves like Gannibal, however, were torn from their homeland and held in a new continent where inevitably, despite strenuous efforts to preserve old ways, a drastic change in lifestyle and consciousness ensued.

Historians have hardly dealt with the question of how Russians were so easily able to contradict the general rule that slaves must be outsiders. Richard Hellie plausibly suggests the importance of *kholopstvo* – state servitude – as a precedent, noting that 'Russians for centuries [had] been accustomed to enslaving their own people', and suggesting that early Russian enslavement of insiders came from a 'fundamental lack of ethnic identity and cohesion among the inhabitants of Muscovy'.[26] What appears to have been crucial in serfdom was a gradual degeneration into slavery, so that there was no point in time when Russians actually took the step of enslaving their fellow countrymen. By the time serfdom had fully developed, in the eighteenth century, nobleman and peasant seemed as different from each other as black and white, European and African. Russian noblemen were thus able to create a kind of distance between themselves and their peasants necessary for the maintenance of serfdom.

Being European perhaps as well as African, Gannibal sympathised with the fate of Russia's white slaves, though he couldn't do much about it. On one occasion, however, in 1743, he did stand up for the downtrodden peasants, in a legal case that raised complicated questions about the triangular relationship between a landowner, his tenant and the serfs.

The origins of the dispute lay in the move to Reval. His prolonged absence from Rakhula prompted Gannibal to rent out the estate for 60 roubles a year to a German aristocrat by the name of Joachim von Tiren. The African drew up a formal contract into which he inserted a clause that prohibited his tenant from exploiting the serfs. 'The present contract is null and void if a higher level of *corvée* is levied on the peasants, or they are mistreated in any way,' read the document signed by von Tiren.[27] His subsequent breach of contract was a relatively minor case of penny-pinching and abuse – some eighteenth-century landowners were notorious for beating serfs in front of guests – but its discovery gave rise, in Estonia, to a weight and passion of debate out of proportion to its gravity.

The source of Gannibal's information – and of his ire and accu-sations – must have been two serfs, Yann Esko and Hendrik Nutto, who fled to Reval seeking legal redress for their grievances against a tyrannical new master. The Moor filed a petition on their behalf only to hear von Tiren argue in court that Gannibal had given him permis-sion to mistreat the serfs. The African denied the charge and won the case. The high tribunal annulled the contract. It was a revolutionary judgment, one of the first in Russian legal history to enshrine peasants' rights in common law. Yet the outcome rankled not only with the evicted tenant but also with the new governor of Reval, Prince Peter August Friedrich von Holstein-Beck, who disliked the African as much as Löwendahl had done, and who instinctively sided with his fellow German. Thus, in defending the rights of his serfs, Gannibal made a powerful enemy.

His contemporaries shared the feeling that Gannibal's career was revolutionary in other ways, too. In the run-up to the Seven Years' War he was transferred from Reval and put in charge of artillery and forti-fication for the Russian army. His return to Saint Petersburg delighted the old guard, who saw Elizabeth's reign as a return to the principles and traditions of Peter the Great. In fact she was very different from her father in a way that affected life at court. Foreign observers spoke with approval of the sovereign's pleasant rounded figure, her blonde hair, her 'almost English face'. Gannibal applauded the way she banished the old regime's small-town German ways and set a fashion for Frenchified luxury, but he also saw and exploited her limitations. Unlike her father, Elizabeth detested hard work and 'abandoned herself to every excess of intemperance and lubricity', in the words of a contemporary, while delegating military affairs to Gannibal and the army's commander-in-chief, General Stepan Apraxin.

Known as the 'snuff-box general' because he had a *tabatière* for every day of the year, Apraxin was 'a man of most impressive stature, prodigious in his size and girth', according to the French ambassador Messelière.[28] He derived power from a wide network of contacts, including Prince Peter von Holstein-Beck and Sir Charles Hanbury-Williams, the British ambassador in Petersburg. Yet his leadership in the Seven Years' War – which saw Russia, France and Austria aligned on one side against Frederick the Great's Prussia and Britain on the other – was handicapped by court intrigue. One of those in the anti-war camp was Gannibal. 'The Prussians are a belligerent people,' he warned his friend Pyotr Shuvalov in 1756, 'and we will have to work night and day to draw level.'[29] Nevertheless, in a short time, he did oversee the transformation of Russia's chaotic militia into a professional army and even drafted plans for the 'scientific use of artillery'. These have earned the African a special place in the history of pyrotechnics. Indeed Simon Werrett, author of *Projecting Modernity: A Social History of Rocketry*, argues that Gannibal's work on the 'secret howitzer' paved the way for the development of the first military rockets by the British inventor Sir William Congreve in the early nineteenth century. 'It was called the "secret howitzer" because nobody could see the muzzle,' wrote the artillery officer Mikhail Danilov.[30]

The letters of Hanbury-Williams reveal that, in 1757, a jealous Apraxin hatched a plot to discredit Gannibal.[31] His accomplice was Prince Peter von Holstein-Beck, who accused the African of 'treasonous inactivity' and of neglecting his duties in order to spend time experimenting with fireworks. The outline of the charge is contained in a document from the archives of the department of artillery and fortification. It states that

> from the month of July 1756 until November 1757, a period of eighteen months, he [Gannibal] reported for work at his office for only 17 days in all, in addition to which ninety-three days were allegedly spent on duty elsewhere, while he claimed to be unwell the rest of the time. The paperwork was in arrears by literally thousands of documents because General Gannibal had not signed 2,755 protocols or 189 journals.[32]

The smear campaign played on the insecurities of a dying empress, as Holstein-Beck knew it would, and she launched an investigation that spent a couple of years getting nowhere: it was only terminated in 1759 when Gannibal was relieved of top-rank duties and appointed general-in-chief of sea fortresses and canal-building. He was never formally charged, so it is impossible to tell exactly what the accusations against him were. Yet they must have been serious because some of his papers were confiscated. Among them was a controversial memorandum he had commissioned from the brilliant, self-taught scientist Mikhail Lomonosov, known as the 'Leonardo da Vinci of Russia' because of his wide-ranging contributions to literature, chemistry, art, physics and mathematics.

The son of a poor fisherman who concealed his humble origins to gain admittance to the Slavonic-Greek-Latin Academy in Moscow, Lomonosov shared with Gannibal not only an interest in fireworks but also an oppositional stance.[33] Having worked together since 1755, when Gannibal helped Lomonosov to transform the Moscow academy into a fully fledged university, the two of them were among the first constituents of what nineteenth-century Russians identified as an 'intelligentsia', that is, a group defined not by social status, but by its superior education and by the content of its ideas.

The particular idea set out in Lomonosov's controversial paper, 'A Discussion of the Great Accuracy of the Maritime Route', was to revive Peter the Great's grand design for a system of inland waterways from the Baltic to the Black Sea, linking the Neva with the Volga in the north, and the Volga with the Don in the south. It was an over-ambitious project because canal-building was still in its infancy even in the west.[34] Yet Gannibal had often pondered its military advantages over the four decades since his path-breaking work on Lake Ladoga. Now, at the height of the Seven Years' War, the scheme found an enthusiastic convert in his former protégé Alexander Suvorov, a legendary soldier who felt that only by improving the supply line could Russia fight successfully in the north and south at the same time. Nevertheless, it wasn't until the middle of the twentieth century that Stalin realised the plan.[35]

Unlike Lomonosov, who arrived in the capital on foot, Suvorov came from a noble family, though he was educated at home due to ill health as a child. One day in 1740 his father Vasily had asked Gannibal, who was paying the family a visit, to dissuade the 11-year-old boy from pursuing a military career. The African spoke to the child in private about strategy and the art of war. After an hour he returned to the father and said, 'Leave him to his own devices. Let him do what he wants. He is smarter than you and me.'[36] As a result, Vasily sent his son to a military school and at the age of fifteen young Suvorov joined the Semyonovsky guards.

In 1761, still nurturing his grand scheme, Gannibal departed for the frontline in the Seven Years' War. Towards the end of the conflict a victorious Russian army led by Suvorov was occupying Berlin and East Prussia. In its capital, Königsberg, he studied the way the forked river Pregel ran through the town, flowing either side of the island of Kneiphof, with seven bridges spanning the different branches. The townspeople used to wonder if it was possible to go for a walk and cross each bridge once and once only, the famous 'Königsberg bridge problem', which Gannibal discussed with a budding young scholar, Immanuel Kant, who advertised in the local gazette to give private lessons in mathematics to Russian officers. (The Swiss mathematician Leonhard Euler invented modern graph theory by proving to the Russian Academy of Sciences that the bridge problem was insoluble.) The promise of victory over Prussia and the bold plan to engineer new waterways confirmed Gannibal's popularity in the army, but his sense of frustration was revived when Elizabeth died, leaving her throne to a German nephew, Peter III, who idolised Frederick the Great and thus immediately withdrew Russia from the war.

Unfortunately for Gannibal, in addition to having Elizabeth for an aunt, the new tsar was also a nephew of Prince Peter von Holstein-Beck, whom he promoted to the rank of special adviser. Meanwhile, the 80-year-old Count Münnich, recalled from Siberian exile, joined his fellow Germans on the Russian Council, where he fulminated against the treachery of the Negro of Peter the Great. It was clear to the African that his prospects under the new regime were bleak. He was, after all, a self-declared enemy of the house of Holstein-Gottorp which had now acquired by geography and marriage a key role in the politics of Russia. It seemed that the past had caught up with Gannibal. His rivals took great delight in observing that he owed his downfall as much as his rise to the shadow cast by Peter the Great, because the ultimate takeover of the Russian throne could be traced back to 1727, when Peter's elder daughter Anna married a duke of Holstein-Gottorp. She died the following year, three months after the birth of her son Charles Peter (later Peter III), but her sister, the Empress Elizabeth, snatched the boy from his native duchy at the age of fourteen and subjected him to a thoroughly unconvincing crashcourse in Russification as the heir apparent. There were other connections, too. In 1729 another Holstein princess gave birth to a Princess Sophia, nicknamed Figchen, who grew up to marry Peter III and become Catherine the Great.

The popular image of Catherine, the great portly nymphoma-niac cursed with flatulence and venereal disease, has overshadowed the youthful portraits of her, which reveal a slight, elegant figure, with thick, curly dark hair and blue eyes as well as the long nose and chin. If not exactly beautiful, she had at least a certain allure, being unpre-tentious and full of wit, and Gannibal was not the only disgruntled soldier who succumbed to those charms. Within months, even weeks of Peter's accession, a conspiracy had begun to form among a hotch-potch of disaffected courtiers. It gathered pace during the first half of 1762 as Peter alienated more and more of his subjects with his unsuitable conduct and ill-advised policies. He refused to declare Catherine's 7-year-old son Paul his heir because Catherine's former lover Sergei Saltykov would not admit that he was the boy's father, and thus provide Peter with grounds for divorcing his wife. Pregnant again, this time by her current lover Grigory Orlov, Catherine bided her time until the child's birth and her husband's imminent departure for an unpopular war against Denmark on behalf of Holstein.

'On the 9th of June, 1762,' writes Catherine's biographer Henri Troyat, 'Peter gave a dinner for four hundred people to celebrate the ratification of the peace treaty with Prussia.'[37] Outside the Winter Palace, Gannibal treated the royal party to a spectacular display of fireworks, converting the banks of the Neva into a mock battlefield of sparkling lights and noisy explosions.

Now a rich man, who had risen to high honours and kept company with a whole vivarium of fish big and small, Gannibal no longer expected or sought the tsar's patronage. He knew he couldn't match the influence wielded by his enemy, the prince of Holstein, and so he resigned himself to being sacked. Yet he never imagined the sacking would occur on the day of the royal fireworks. The shock lasted until the tsar stepped onto the embankment in his Prussian uniform and gazed impatiently into the twilit sky. Here was the signal. The African pocketed the letter of dismissal in his greatcoat and, facing his tormentors with the dignity of a general-in-chief reviewing troops, he lit the white touch paper. Straight away the gunpowder exploded on contact with the open flame, producing a bright flash, a loud report, dense white smoke and a sulphurous smell as a rocket burst, spluttering in darting crackles, over the water.

At the banquet the tsar made a toast to the health of the imperial family. All the guests stood up, pushing back their chairs, but Catherine remained seated. When Peter asked why she had not risen like the others, she replied that she did not have to rise because she was herself a member of the imperial family. Irritated by her deft reply, the tsar yelled, 'Fool!' across the table, looking at his wife with hatred. The only members of the imperial family whose presence he recognised in the room were himself and his two Holsteiner uncles, he said.

The angry showdown hastened Catherine's *coup d'état*, owing to the fear of imminent discovery, but its aim was soon achieved, and on 28 June 1762, with the help of a motley crew of adventurers, Catherine overthrew her husband, who died a week later in mysterious circumstances, allegedly in a drunken brawl. By then, however, Gannibal was out of Petersburg – and out of the loop– 'travelling on private affairs' to the countryside of Mikhailovskoye.

# 19

# Death of a Philosophe

Our Pskov is worse than Siberia.
—Praskovya Osipova, *Letter to Vasily Zhukovsky*

The African lingered into the reign of Catherine the Great. Yet he wasn't really 'forgotten' so much as overlooked: a bizarre relic, a throwback, a museum piece. The degree to which Gannibal accepted this situation as one in which he characteristically found himself might be suggested by the fact that the younger man who was trapped in Pernau in the 1730s was still trapped at home – restrained from extravagance while imagining what it might be like to wander – in the last two decades of his life.

It was a different home, though, and in that sense his retreat to Mikhailovskoye began a new epoch in his life. This self-conscious act of withdrawal to the Pskovan woods is described, or perhaps satirised, in *Eugene Onegin*. 'The country, where Eugene moped,/was a charming nook,' writes Pushkin at the start of chapter two:

> The manor house, hidden,
> and sheltered from the winds by a hill,
> stood above a river [...]
> and a huge neglected garden.[1]

Unlike Onegin, the African cultivated the garden at Mikhailovskoye, which he laid out himself, planting black oaks and spruces in an artificial geometric style already unfashionable in the 1760s and later to become more so. Lime trees enclosed a perfect square: hedge, garden, a vegetable patch, and beyond that, beyond the plot for ducks and geese, the two lakes Malenets and Kuchane.

He quickly turned his retirement into a desirable condition – a version of the ancient Horatian ideal of escape from the corrupting city into a small country house. Voltaire did the same at Ferney, and it was against this background of an enclosed garden and the encroaching fanatics that, in 1759, he wrote *Candide*. The hero of the book is not, as he is in Samuel Johnson's exactly contemporary *Rasselas*, a prince of Abyssinia, but he follows the trajectory of Gannibal's career in other ways. For instance, Candide undergoes the same eighteenth-century horrors. He is enslaved by the Turks, then corrupted by the French. He ends up on a remote farm not unlike Mikhailovskoye advising Dr Pangloss, who is a caricature of Leibniz, with his optimistic view of the world, that the only worthwhile thing for people to do is to cultivate their gardens. The book ends with a famous sentence: '*Il faut cultiver notre jardin.*'

Yet Voltaire's, like Onegin's, was an obvious mock hermitage. Gannibal took the famous sentence to heart. He really did become that 'eremitic sage' whom Pushkin describes in his second chapter. The old man settled into a routine of 'walks, reading, deep sleep', according to Pushkin.[2] He explored the woods, sometimes on horseback, but often on foot, tramping the countryside with a couple of wolfhounds and an iron cane. At home, he took up other solitary diversions, but particularly reading, as he wrote to his son Pyotr of that period in his life:

> At that time, it could have been said of me that I was never without a book and never without sorrow, but also never without amusement.[3]

In the spring of 1765, while staying at his house on Petersburg's Vasilevsky Island, Gannibal briefly picked up his memoirs, returning to the story of the past. The kind of work he was preparing was a 'memoir' based on his 'notes and recollections' of

Africa and of his experiences in Russia. It would include 'new facts, useful information and precise descriptions', or would have done had he not lacked a certain momentum necessary to write at length. He plunged into despondency, and said of his manuscript that he was considering 'throwing it down into the fire once and for all'. He didn't cheer up until he spent three solid weeks reading canal-builders' manuals.

Among several phantoms haunting Gannibal at the time were the mysterious canals of Vasilevsky Island that appeared on a fiftieth-anniversary map of the city in 1753. The French architect Le Blond had submitted a plan to Peter the Great to defend his new capital with a system of canals and locks. But, according to legend, when he arrived to execute the plan, the architect quarrelled with Menshikov so bitterly that the tsar halted the project. The legend was supported by another document in Gannibal's possession that showed a network of canals linking Petersburg to Moscow. Here, on Peter's instructions, Vasilevsky Island appears criss-crossed with canals, as Le Blond had designed it, even though the canals were never dug.[4]

On the death of Lomonosov in the spring of 1765, the Empress Catherine buried the scholar with great ceremony but confiscated the handwritten notes in which he outlined the 'accuracy' of Gannibal's projected waterway. The African came under suspicion too. 'The spies are busy,' wrote William Richardson. 'The suspected great men are closely watched.'[5]

Yet Gannibal was no longer a 'great man' in that public sense. He longed in retirement to forswear the world of suspicion and intrigue. Unfortunately he never lost his dread of the secret police. 'To the end of his life,' wrote Pushkin, 'he could not hear the ring of the doorbell without trepidation.'[6] As he declined physically in his hermitage, the African began to worry about the hundreds of pages of memoirs he had written during the years of rapt self-examination. He was afraid, he told Rotkirkh, that once he was dead they would fall into the wrong hands, as Lomonosov's had done. The old man, in other words, had actually forsworn nothing. He was solidly planted this side of any world elsewhere.

***

In the attic of the archaeological museum in Pskov, one of the oldest towns in Russia, a box of church documents lies on a large rectangular table. It is full of inventories, accounts, receipts, bills, memoranda, reports and old bundles of letters from other eras, other worlds. The archive at Pskov is unusually chaotic, and yet its disorder must be seen in the context of history. Until the Second World War the archive held religious icons and illuminated manuscripts as well as books and other papers. At the end of the Nazi occupation, however, on 6 February 1944, the building was comprehensively ransacked by German soldiers evacuating to Riga. Many of its treasures vanished in a day of looting, never to be seen again. 'The German fascists have stolen from Pskov everything that is of value in our museum, icons, books, manuscripts and other priceless artefacts,' wrote Ivan Mikhailov, the secretary of the town council, to his counterpart in Riga at the end of the year.[7]

One afternoon recently, while searching through the documents of the Gannibal family, I came across a brown sheet of paper that was folded in quarters – its folds, almost cracking, were see-through in daylight – and began to read a letter, dated 2 September 1765, from Catherine's summer residence at Tsarskoye Selo and signed in her inimitable hand:

> Abram Petrovich, it is not unknown to me that many manuscripts are held in your keeping, dating from the times when the Sovereign of blessed memory Peter the Great relied upon your talents in many affairs, and for that reason I think perhaps that you may have kept in your hands all the documents worthy of interest, as a souvenir of the great tsar and of your services to him at that time. And as I am aware that he planned to build a canal from Moscow to Petersburg, and also

that the plans were even drawn up, you would be doing me a great pleasure if, having found the diagram (in the event that it is in your possession), you would send it to me with all the notes and appendices, even if
they are only in draft form. But if no such thing was ever in your hands,
at least tell me where it may be sought, because I want to see it with great
urgency; alternatively, if you heard any of His Majesty's thoughts about
the project, I ask you to write and tell me what you remember. I remain
respectfully yours, Catherine.[8]

In his reply of 7 September, Gannibal promises Catherine 'to
unfold some long-forgotten details which are in my knowledge', but
only once he has received due reward for the part he played in the
overthrow of her husband. The tone is aggrieved, the writing hasty,
the syntax appalling, but the letter is full of tantalising insights into
the background of the *coup d'état*. 'Noble Empress,' he begins, 'in
response to the gracious request of Your Imperial Majesty, I would
like very humbly to make the following report:

> Although I had the honour, during the reign of that Sovereign of
> radiant and eternal memory Peter the Great, to be in charge of the
> private cabinet of His Majesty in which were kept all the plans and
> projects as well as his library; the trouble is, after so many long years
> I do not recall any more today having heard talk of the project for
> a canal between Moscow and Saint Petersburg, apart from the very
> short Perspective leading to Moscow which His Majesty always said
> he wanted to build, but after the death of the Great Sovereign, over
> a period of time I used to see his books and other memorable things
> of his Cabinet in the Academy of Sciences, and since all his projects
> and plans had been kept together, they should as a result be preserved
> there or in the Archive of the Private Cabinet.
>
> I remain Your Imperial Majesty's servant [or 'slave', that word
> *rab* again]
>
> A. Ganibal[9]

The letter ends on a note of despair, of breakdown even, though it is hardly surprising to find ambiguity here: in this play of thick shadows and rare glimmers, words can bear more than one meaning at a time. But whatever its obscurities, and possible misrepresentations, this letter is a key document. Of course it tells us nothing for certain except that Gannibal was afraid to reveal the secret plans and ruined projects hidden in the pages of the unfinished memoir. Yet it tells us enough to suggest his awkwardness in the matter. The Empress was fretful. She wanted information. 'If these plans are at the Academy, there's no point searching for them because they will probably have been stolen already,' Catherine wrote in the margin of Gannibal's letter. His silence was hardly a cover-up – you could put it down to forgetfulness – but it was definitely a tidy-up. Outside the window dark trees stretched away unto the edge of doom.

Something of the darkness visible in Gannibal's outlook at Mikhailovskoye comes across in that reply – and while there's no knowing exactly how the letter to Catherine, with its rather chilly, reclusive feel, its hint of disappointment, might be applied to Ganni-bal's psychological circumstances in the last years of his life, it is plausible that the saga of the ruined canal did apply. In old age, Gannibal lived among ruins, among superseded things, and this idea of ruin and dereliction, of out-of-placeness, was something he felt about himself: a man from another hemisphere, another back-ground, coming to rest at the end of his life on a half-neglected estate, in a province of north-west Russia, an estate full of reminders of the 'splendid promises' of the past.

His view of Catherine darkened, in 1773, after Gannibal helped to bring his old friend Denis Diderot, the cleverest man in Europe and the chief editor of the *Encyclopédie*, to Russia. Two years earlier, upon completing the 28-volume encyclopaedia, Diderot had found himself without a source of income. 'I am responsible for one of the most glorious achievements of the age [of Enlightenment], yet I am quite ruined,' he wrote sourly. The African warned Catherine of his plight and, in order to relieve Diderot of financial worry, she bought the Frenchman's library through an agent in Paris. She paid him a librarian's pension of 1,000 *livres* a year in a lump-sum advance. The following year the 60-year-old philosopher made the arduous trek to Petersburg to thank his fairy godmother for her support.

At first Catherine received Diderot with great honour and warmth three afternoons a week. In her private apartments in the Winter Palace she would sit on the imperial sofa, with a piece of needlework in her hands, while the foreigner explained his views on education, politics and the law. Soon, however, she began to consider the philosopher's ideas too impractical for real life. 'You only work on paper, where anything is possible,' she complained, 'whereas I, a poor empress, have to work on human skin.'[10] Diderot wrote to his fellow *philosophes* d'Alembert and Helvétius that the fairy godmother had turned into a witch.

Pushkin suggests that his dark-skinned ancestor also came to regard the bewitching empress as a kind of sorceress, like the Circe of Greek legend, who turned humans into wolves and swine. The first word of *Onegin*'s second chapter, quoted above, is *derevnya*, meaning 'the country'. It recurs as the title of an idyllic description that Pushkin wrote of Mikhailovskoye, in 1819, while the poet was sleuthing for information about Gannibal and his escape from the wicked city on the night of Winter Palace banquet. 'I love this dark garden,' he writes in the voice of the black rustic. 'I have exchanged the shameful court of Circe, sumptuous feasts, amusements, delusions, for the quiet whisper of oak trees, the peace of the fields.'[11]

Yet the peace of the fields is interrupted halfway through the poem when, suddenly, 'a terrible thought darkens my soul'. Gannibal's unwelcome thought mocks the distance between the Horatian ideal and Russian reality. (Pushkin's epitaph for the second chapter of *Onegin* is the happy eclogic sigh O *rus!*, meaning 'O countryside!', uttered by the urbane Roman poet Horace upon his rustication to a Sabine farm. Next to it, Pushkin inserts the phrase O *Rus!*, the old name for Russia, in a tone of wry bemusement and despair.) But his dark thought also mocks something else, that 'work on human skin'

— the slave trade, in other words — as the poet looks up from 'gloomy Russia' towards the bright sky of 'my Africa', and asks: 'Will I ever see, dear friends, my people not oppressed, and slavery [*rabstvo*] overthrown?'[12] Meanwhile, on the rooftop, a flag emblazoned with the legend FUMMO, or 'homeland', fluttered in the wind.

The old man loved his garden. He could listen to the whispering trees for hours. But he didn't always like what he heard. Take the oaks he planted, for example. He found the saplings only prompted morbid thoughts because he couldn't help reflecting that he'd never live to see them fully grown. These intimations of mortality are captured by Pushkin in a late poem, 'Mikhailovskoye Revisited', where he imagines his great-grandfather communing with nature:

> Greetings, younger
> and unknown generation! I won't
> see your powerful later growth,
> when you will outgrow my acquaintances
> and hide their old heads
> from the eye of a passer-by. But may my great-grandson
> hear your charming whisper, when,
> returning from a party with friends,
> full of happy and pleasing thoughts,
> he passes by you in the darkness of the night,
> and remembers me. [13]

It would be nice to say that Gannibal was a courageous man whom no amount of working on skin could deter. The truth is that, as his friend Ivan Cherkasov wrote sadly, he was easily terrified and often a coward. Pushkin wrote that Gannibal burned his memoir 'in a fit of panic' at Mikhailovskoye. Nabokov, who describes the scene, portrays the old man as an almost Wordsworthian figure — bent, exaggeratedly bent — in a ruined cottage with its 'two porches, one balcony, twenty doors, fourteen windows, six Dutch stoves'.[14] His 'dark thought' was a specific and contingent thing. He did not believe that there was any justice in the world. He knew that his home wasn't a castle, nor his garden a fortress. He just tried to keep the policemen off the grass.

It was a spring day in 1774. Thick ice still covered the water of Lake Malenets and had only just begun to crack on the larger Lake Kuchane, as the African looked out of one of those windows at the uniform grey of the sky. Its tint reminded him of a soldier's uniform.

A serfgirl by the name of Arina cooked a plate of grilled fish, which the old man ate in front of a pine-log fire.* At the end of the meal the African poured out a glass of vodka and summoned Rotkirkh, who carried a leather trunk to the fireside. The young Estonian picked out a sheaf of papers from the box and fed it to the red embers. For a while Gannibal just stared at the blaze, lost in thought, then slowly he got up from his chair and reached over to the logs by the hearth, setting two or three across the incandescent pile of paper. He watched impassively as if the falling scraps were no more than old newspapers. Several minutes later, when the sacrifice was over, each chapter and page burnt to ashes, the African looked at his future son-in-law with the smile of an accomplice.

Pushkin claimed that his ancestor died, aged eighty-five, 'like a *philosophe*', on his estate at Suida, a day's journey south of Petersburg. But he also described Gannibal, in a letter to his brother Lev, as a skilful meddler, '*un vieux sapajou de 18th siècle*'.[15] The 'old monkey' continued to make that journey right up until his death, and the skill was commemorated in *Onegin* where such meddling is described as a 'grand pastime/worthy of old monkeys/of our vaunted grandfathers' times'.[16]

The vaunting continued until his last sigh. On 13 May 1781, according to Rotkirkh, Christina Gannibal died at the age of seventy-six. Her death came as a fatal blow to her husband. 'We buried

---

*As Pushkin's beloved nurse, Arina Rodyonovna Yakovleva (née Matveyeva) introduced the young poet to the world of Russian legends and fairy tales, and provided the model for Tatiana's nurse in *Eugene Onegin*. She died at Mikhailovskoye in 1828, aged seventy.

Mother today,' Ivan Gannibal wrote to his brother Osip, Pushkin's grandfather. 'Father is very ill and weakens by the hour, sleeping with his eyes open and breathing short and fast, so that I fear his life is in danger and there is no hope.'[17]

The Negro of Peter the Great died the next morning, on 14 May, according to Rotkirkh, though such a date is contradicted by Pyotr Gannibal, who wrote that his father 'died on the twentieth of April, [two months] after our mother's death in February'.[18] The details are typically confusing. But perhaps it is fitting in a way that Gannibal's death should be – as his life was – somehow hidden and unclear, both true and false at the same time.

No death notice was printed. His funeral was largely ignored. Only a handful of people followed the cortège to a desolate plot in Suida where the African was buried next to his wife Christina. He had served under eight tsars and tsarinas – and two Ottoman sultans. He had survived the turmoil of slavery, exile and civil war. Now lost in provincial obscurity, his adventures all but forgotten, the dark star of Russia's enlightenment lay in a roadside grave. His true epitaph had to wait for the genius of Pushkin, whose admirers built a monument to Gannibal at the site. The tombstone pays tribute to 'a Russian mathematician, a builder of fortresses and canals', but there is no word of his military honours: the general-in-chief, the black knight.

I have suggested that Gannibal's life in Russia might have been seen – seen by him, that is – as a kind of chivalric quest, and I have shown how the image of a 'strange creature' was turned by Pushkin into a fairy tale. I am struck now by the possibility that while these 'family legends' might be part of the story – that they might indeed solve the puzzle of the black Candide, the noble savage, the jealous Moor – the story itself is very different from Othello's encounter with racism or from the adventures of Voltaire's hero. For the life of Gannibal was not a legend or a fairy tale. It was an encounter between Africa and Europe that occurred at a specific time and place, and affected the development of Russia. The African was a polymath in the Enlightenment mould, a man of eclectic skills: a linguist, a diplomat, a cryptographer, a spy, and also on occasion an able military commander. Yet his chief bent was for mathematics and the science of war. He is an important figure in the history of Russia, an intellectual pioneer, a voice of conscience, a defender of freedom. He cultivated the mind but he also cultivated a garden, and that garden, as we have seen, was deeply imbued with the struggle of African people – which is to say, ideas and actions invest Gannibal's life with far more signifi⁄ cance than that of a famous ancestor or a Negro of Peter the Great. The things he made happen still have relevance today.

Epilogue

# The Negro Poet

The Moor had entered the invisible world, the world of ghosts, of people who did not exist.

—Salman Rushdie, *The Moor's Last Sigh*

There is one final key to the mystery of Russia's black knight – a kind of negative proof which unites the various themes outlined in this book – and it takes us back to Paris, to the hallway of an elegant three-storey house where a picture hangs above the mantelpiece overlooking the Bois de Boulogne.

The oil painting is steeped in an atmosphere of a rather false kind. In the foreground a black soldier is dressed in oriental costume, with pearl earrings, a luxuriant plume of dyed ostrich feathers sprouting from his baggy white turban and a look of delicate self-satisfaction on his youthful face. Here, too, is the fur-lined cloak and half-cuirass breastplate, a dagger tucked into the waistband in a gloss of heroism, with the soldier leaning backwards slightly, his right arm akimbo, in the mock ceremonial pose favoured by court Arabs standing guard at the Winter Palace. Yet on the basis of a bronze medal dangling impractically from a chain strapped to his chest the Moor has sometimes been presumed to be Gannibal.

The history of that presumption dates back to the early 1960s when a French researcher by the name of André Meynieux discovered the painting in a storeroom at the Pavillon Sully au Pecq, in Seine-et-Oise, on the outskirts of Paris. Enthralled by its array of symbols, and the dread effects of war, Meynieux reproduced a photograph of the

African warrier in his book *Le Romantisme*, in which he argued with scholarly zeal and pictorial acumen that the subject of the portrait was a Negro sent by Peter the Great on a top-secret mission to Paris at the height of the Great Northern War.

The name of the artist is unknown, but Meynieux argued forcefully in his book that the portrait is the work of Jean-Baptiste Van Loo, a leading painter of historical subjects and of fashionable society in France and England during the first half of the eighteenth century. Significantly, Van Loo was resident in Paris between 1720 and 1722 while Gannibal was a student at the French military school at La Fère.

Yet Meynieux's identification of the black soldier as Gannibal is more speculative than his attribution of the painting to Van Loo. It owes less to the work's richly painted surface than it does to an imaginative context, a 'wealth of thought', to use Meynieux's words, that the scholar found in those Moorish eyes. His eagerness to identify the black *philosophe* led Meynieux to overemphasise circumstantial detail and also perhaps to underestimate the number of former slaves employed by Peter the Great.

Take, for example, his description of the African as the '*chef des galères* [master of the galley-slaves] *et ambassadeur de Pierre le Grand*', quoting a contemporary reference to the tsar's passage to France in 1717. The Russian word for 'galley' is *galera*, but in a letter of 1717, Peter referred to a *galyot*, which suggests it was a 'galliot', defined in the *Oxford English Dictionary* as a 'small galley used for swift navigation', and often propelled by slaves. The personality of Gannibal seems impossible to recover from such fragments of evidence. Being a slave-master is one thing. Being a 'man of the sea' is quite another, and as Gannibal explained to Alexei Makarov in 1722, while begging for permission to return to Russia overland, he was unable to stomach the 'great and awful dangers' of the deep.

One thing at least is certain: after fifteen years under the scrutiny of art historians, the Van Loo portrait left its home on the banks of the river Oise in 1977, when a private collector bought the picture at auction in Versailles for an undisclosed sum of money. Since then it has lured stray pilgrims who are fascinated by the historical opacity of Gannibal and gripped by a desire to see and touch something of his life in Paris. Most of them tend to forget, or anyway to suspend, the inconvenient fact of the matter, which is that the portrait is almost certainly not of Gannibal.

The portrait's misattribution partly came about because of a snide remark by the Saxon ambassador Georg von Helbig that 'Abraham Petrovich Gannibal was a Moor, whom Peter I brought to Russia as a ship's cabin boy'. Was it ever more than a case of mistaken identity? There were plenty of such boys in London in 1698. Peter bought several black slaves, at £30 for a female, £20 for a boy, after the Swiss mercenary Franz Lefort wrote to the tsar from Amsterdam that 'we must purchase lots of Negroes'. How many Peter ended up buying is a mystery, though his expenses ran to 'eighteen pairs of stockings for the blacks', according to one invoice.[1] One of them was called 'Petro Seichi', or so his name appeared in the Latin characters of the ship's inventory. He was a fugitive from a tobacco plantation in Spanish America. In the course of his sixteen-year service in the Russian fleet, during which the former galley slave rose to a captain's rank, and fought in all the naval battles of the Great Northern War, from Poltava to Cape Hangö, the spelling of his name changed with the alphabet, from *Seichi* to *Tsesi* and even *Desek*, until finally it settled on 'Piter Yelayev', as it was inscribed on the bronze medal presented by the tsar, in 1715, on his retirement to France.

Nothing is heard of Yelayev for over a century until his portrait began to arouse the interest of the Pushkin-haters who ultimately chased the poet to his death at Black River, outside Petersburg, where he fell mortally wounded in a duel on 27 January 1837. Seven years earlier, the police spy Faddey Bulgarin, a Pole who had fought with the French against the Russians in 1812, looked to embarrass Pushkin by misreporting Helbig's sneer. In the August issue of *Severnaya pchela* (*Northern Bee*), he lampooned the poet's black ancestry in a letter that purported to be from a correspondent in Germany. 'Byron's lordship and his aristocratic escapades,' Bulgarin noted, 'have driven many poets and rhymesters in various countries out of their minds, and they have all begun chattering about their 600-year-old nobility.' Then Bulgarin set about a hatchet job by maliciously distorting Helbig's story:

> The anecdote is told that a certain poet in Spanish America, also an imitator of Byron, whose mother or father – I can't remember which – was a Mulatto, began to claim that one of his ancestors was a Negro Prince. In the town hall of the city it was discovered that long ago there was a legal dispute between a ship's skipper and his mate. Each of them wanted to claim the Negro as his own, but the skipper contended that he had bought the Negro for a bottle of rum. Who would have thought that a versifier would acknowledge connection with that Negro?[2]

In spite of its dishonest motive Bulgarin's question remains an interesting one. Was Pushkin really a black writer? The African-American critic Dorothy Trench-Bonnett argues that *The Negro of Peter the Great* 'is the first work of fiction in modern times by a black writer, with a black hero'.[3] One of Pushkin's finest critics, Andrei Sinyavsky, notes the way he 'seized on his Negroid appearance and his African past, which he loved perhaps more dearly than he did his aristocratic [white Russian] ancestry'.[4] Unquestionably he was the descendant of a slave, though Bulgarin does not use the word. In a way, he doesn't have to: his reference to 'purchase' and 'possession' clearly implies slavery. As a rule, Bulgarin's technique was to attack his enemies using a pseudonym, and in such a crude fashion that it was often unwise to respond. On this occasion, Pushkin was unable to ignore a presumed insult to his mother. The anecdote's mention of a 'poet of Spanish America', an offspring of a mulatto, was obviously an allusion to Nadezhda Pushkina being known as the 'beautiful Creole'. In reply, the outraged poet added a postscript to his satire 'My Genealogy', in which the first word deliberately confuses the name of his persecutor with Russian slang for 'clown':

Figlyarin decided, sitting at home,
That my black granddad Gannibal
Was bought for a bottle of rum,
And fell into a skipper's hands.[5]

News of the literary bust-up spread like wildfire. It even reached the eyes and ears of Tsar Nicholas I, a subscriber to the *Northern Bee*, and also, perhaps significantly, an admirer of Pushkin's wife Natalya. The relationship between Pushkin and the tsar was a volatile one. Nicholas flattered himself with the role of censor to the wayward poet. Pushkin often felt demeaned by his official duties at court and resented being treated like a 'flunkey', which is to say, a *rab*. Yet, in 1831, he wrote to the tsar's secret police chief, Count Alexander Benckendorff, the head of the 'German' department, to explain his actions:

> About a year ago one of our journals printed a satirical article which referred to a certain man of letters, who manifested pretensions of having a noble origin, whereas he was only a bourgeois. It was added that his mother was a mulatto whose father, a poor pickaninny, had been bought by a sailor for a bottle of rum. Although Peter the Great little resembled a drunken sailor, I was the one referred to clearly enough, since no Russian man of letters except me can count a Negro among his ancestors. Since the article in question was printed in an official gazette, since indecency has been pushed to the point of speaking of my mother in a feuilleton which ought to be only literary, and since our gazetteers do not fight in duels, I believed it my duty to answer the *anonymous* satirist, which I did in verse and very sharply.

The letter to Benckendorff clearly implies that Pushkin would have challenged Bulgarin to a duel (in spite of the illegality of duelling at the time) if Bulgarin had belonged to the same class. Here the blackness of Pushkin is a case in point. The poet took his ancestor to be a black man – that much can be taken for granted; what is less clear is whether his ancestry played a direct role in the personal, literary and social struggle that ultimately ended his life.

However, a month after he wrote the letter to Benckendorff, Pushkin received a New Year's gift from his friend Pavel Nashchokin. A member of the ancient high Russian nobility, Nashchokin was aware of Pushkin's difficulty with Bulgarin. His gift was a bronze inkstand with a statuette of a black man leaning on an anchor and standing in front of two bales of cotton – two inkwells. In the letter accompanying the gift, Nashchokin wrote: 'I am sending you your ancestor with inkwells that open and reveal him to be a far-sighted person.'[6]

Pushkin loved the gift because it suggested that his 'far-sighted' black ancestor had anticipated by the inkwells that one of his descendants would be a writer: so that not only did Pushkin look backward with pride at his black great-grandfather, but that person looked forward to him. The answer to Bulgarin's question – who could have predicted that a descendant of the Negro of Peter the Great would be a writer? – was Gannibal himself. Pushkin wrote to thank Nashchokin 'for the blackamoor'. It stayed on his desk for the rest of his life.

# Notes

## 1. Hermitage

1. RGIA f. 468, op. 1, d. 4006, l. 275. Because of its extreme northerly location (59° 57' N lat. and 30° 20' E long.), Petersburg experiences very long days and short nights during the summer solstice, when a kind of eerie half-light persists between dusk and dawn.
2. RGADA 13.176.24. BL Add. 44068 f. 23.
3. APAO inv. 490, op. 2, f. 1073.
4. PSS 11:272.
5. PSS 12:313.
6. Priscilla Roosevelt discusses 'patriarchy in the provinces' in *Life on the Russian Country Estate: A Social and Cultural History* (New Haven, 1995), pp. 158–91.
7. PSS 2:288.
8. RGIA f. 468, op. 1, d. 4006, l. 275.
9. PSS 12:313.
10. Pushkin described the visit on 19 November 1824. PSS 11:395.
11. PSS 13:543.
12. L. N. Pavlushchev, *Iz semeinoi khroniki* (Moscow, 1890), p. 23.
13. PSS 6:655.

## 2. The Mask of Blackness

1. Private conversation, Saint Petersburg, 1 July 2002.
2. Vladimir Nabokov (trans.), *Eugene Onegin by Aleksandr Pushkin*, 4 vols. (London, 1964), vol. 3, p. 438.
3. D. N. Anuchin, *A. S. Pushkin: Antropologichesky eskiz* (Moscow, 1899), p. 24.
4. *Russky arkhiv* (1899), 6:355.
5. PSS 6:655.
6. Rereading (in 2002) the short stories he wrote in the 1950s and 1960s, John Updike was 'annoyed by the recurrence of the now suspect word "Negro"', which he decided not to 'correct' in a new edition, on the grounds that 'Negro' is 'at least an anthropological term ... and verbal correctness in this arena is so particularly volatile that "black", which is inaccurate, may some day be suspect in turn'.

7. A. O. Smirnova, *Zapiski 1826–45*, ed. O. N. Smirnova (St Petersburg, 1895), p. 17.

8. A. A. Olenina, *Dnevnik 1828–29*, ed. Olga Oom (Paris, 1936), p. 11.

9. PSS 3:101. The novelist Ivan Lazhechnikov described Pushkin as 'slender, not tall, with curly hair and a Negro profile' in *Znakomstvo moye s Pushkinym*, quoted in V. Veresayev, *Pushkin v zhizni*, 2 vols., 6th edn (Moscow, 1936), vol. 2, pp. 130–32.

10. Shakespeare, *Measure for Measure* II iv 79.

11. Philostratus, *Imagines* (London, 1931), 1.29.

12. APAO op. 3, inv. 1074, d. 5.

13. PSS 11:37.

14. PSS 16:208.

15. Quoted in Philip D. Curtin, *The Image of Africa: British Ideas and Action, 1780–1850* (London, 1965), p. 144.

16. Line 225, in *Ben Jonson: The Complete Masques*, ed. Stephen Orgel (New Haven, 1968).

17. See N. K. Teletova, 'O mnimom i podlinnom izobrazhenii A. P. Gannibala' in *Legendi i mifi o Pushkine* (St Petersburg, 1995), pp. 86–109.

18. *Voyennaya Entsiklopediya* (St Petersburg, 1914), 15:254.

## 3. Prince of Abissinia

1. PSS 6:654.

2. Langston Hughes, 'The Negro Artist and the Racial Mountain', *The Black Aesthetic*, ed. Addison Gayle (Garden City, NY, 1973), p. 167.

3. See Charles Verlinden, 'L'Origine de "sclavus" – esclave', *Archivum latinitatis medii aevi*, vol. 17 (1943), pp. 97–128.

4. PD 835 l. 66r.

5. PD f. 24, op. 3, d. 161, l. 34. *Othello* I ii 21–22.

6. Nabokov 3:398–99.

7. PD f. 244, op. 24, d. 19, l. 3.

8. PSS 8:25.

9. Charles Poncet, *A Voyage to Aethiopia Made in the Years 1698, 1699 and 1700* (London, 1709), p. 61.

10. James Bruce, *Travels to Discover the Source of the Nile*, 5 vols., (Edinburgh, 1790), vol. 3, p. 84.

11. A. J. Arkell, *A History of the Sudan from the Earliest Times to 1821* (London, 1961), pp. 217–20.

12. PSS 6:654–55.

13. Bruce 3:596, *Letters of William and Dorothy Wordsworth. The Middle Years*, pt 1, 1806–11, ed. E. de Selincourt, rev. Mary Moorman (Oxford, 1969), p. 129.

14. Poncet, p. 36.

15. Richard Pankhurst, *An Introduction to the Economic History of Ethiopia*, (London, 1961), p. 423. See also Solomon Ghebre-Ghiorghis, 'The Eritrean Ancestry of Alexander Pushkin (1799–1837)', unpublished thesis, University of Asmara, 2002.

16. Anuchin, p. 16.

17. Nikolai Dobrolyubov, *Selected Philosophical Essays* (Moscow, 1956), p. 88.

18. Philostratus, *Imagines*, 2.7.

19. Valentia had included Salt's 1804 account of Abyssinia in his *Voyages and Travels*, 3 vols. (London, 1809).

20. Henry Salt, *A Voyage to Abyssinia and Travels into the Interior of That Country Executed under the Orders of the British Government in the Years 1809 and 1810* (London, 1814), p. 218.

21. Salt, p. 246.

22. A. N. Vulf, *Dnevniki* (Moscow, 1929), p. 136.

23. PSS 8:27.

24. PD 837, l. 36.

## 4. Jihad

1. *Literaturnoye nasledstvo* 5868.

2. PSS 13:334.

3. *Lyubovny byt* 1:268.

4. PD 836, l. 22.

5. PD f. 244, op. 3, d. 162.

6. PSS 8:26. Adam Olearius, *The Travels of Olearius in Seventeenth-century Russia*, ed. Samuel Baron (Stanford, 1967), p. 126.

7. S. A. Vengerov, ed., *Pushkin*, 6 vols. (Petersburg, 1915), vol. 6, p. 536.

8. Arthur Rimbaud, *Oeuvres Complètes*, ed. Antoine Adam (Paris, 1972), p. 419.

9. John Laffin, *The Arabs as Master Slavers* (Englewood, N.J., 1982), p. 4.

10. Leo Africanus, *The History and Description of Africa*, trans. John Pory (1600); rpt, ed. Robert Brown, 3 vols. (London, 1896), vol. 3, pp. 833–34.

11. *Sir John Mandeville's Travels*, ed. P. Hamelius (London, 1919), pp. 103–4.

12. Hugh Thomas, *The Slave Trade: The History of the Atlantic Slave Trade 1440–1870* (London, 1997), pp. 41–42.

13. Nabokov 3:436.

14. J. F. Keane, *Six Months in Mecca* (London, 1881), pp. 94–100.

15. J. F. Schon, *Megana Hausa: Native Literature, Proverbs, Tales, Fables and Historical Fragments in the Hausa Language* (London, 1885), p. 52.

16. S. Decalo, *Historical Dictionary of Chad*, 2nd edn (Metuchen, N.J., 1987), pp. 184–85.

17. Giovanni Lorenzo Anania, *L'Universale Fabrica del Mondo, overo cosmografia*, 3rd edn (Venice, 1582), p. 350. Annie M. D. Lebeuf, 'L'origine et la constitution des principautés kotoko (Cameroun septentrional)', in *Contribution de la recherche ethnologique à l'histoire des civilisations du Cameroun*, ed. C. Tardits, i (Paris, 1981), pp. 209–18; p. 211.

18. Decalo, pp. 185–86.

19. Dixon Denham, *Narrative of Travels and Discoveries in Northern and Central Africa, in the Years 1822, 1823 and 1824, by Major Denham, Captain Clapperton and the late Doctor Oudney*, 3 vols. (London, 1826), vol. 2, pp. 429–47; p. 437.

20. Denham 2:438, 3:532.

21. Heinrich Barth, *Travels and Discoveries in North and Central Africa, being a Journal of an Expedition under the Auspices of Her Britannic Majesty in the Years 1849–55*, 3 vols. (London, 1857; rpt 1965), vol. 3, p. 125. See also Hugh Clapperton, *Journal of a Second Expedition into the Interior of Africa, from the Bight of Benin to Soccatoo* (London, 1829).

22. Barth 2:455. Maxime Rodinson, 'Généalogie royale de Logone-Birni (Cameroun)' in *Études Camerounaises*, iii (March–June 1950), pp. 29–30. Annie Lebeuf, 'Le royaume du Baguirmi', in C. Tardits, ed., *Princes et serviteurs du royaume: cinq études de monarchies africaines*, (Paris, 1987), pp. 171–225.

23. Nabokov 3:436.

24. Private conversation, Paris, 6 July 2002.

25. A. D. H. Bivar and M. Hiskett, 'The Arabic Literature of Nigeria to 1804' in *Bulletin of the School of Oriental and African Studies* (1962), p. 111. See also Humphrey J. Fisher, *Slavery in the History of Muslim Black Africa* (London, 2001), pp. 26–27.

26. Lebeuf, 'L'origine et la constitution des principautés kotoko', p. 215.

27. Gustav Nachtigal, *Sahara and Sudan*, trans. Allan G. B. and Humphrey J. Fisher, 3 vols. (London 1971–87), vol. 2, p. 233.

28. PD f. 244, op. 24, d. 19.

29. CNM MS 211 c/1975 f. 3.

## 5. The Elephant Man

1. PSS 6:7.

2. Quoted in John Hare, *Shadows across the Sahara: Travels with Camels from Lake Chad to Tripoli* (London, 2003), pp. 52–53.
3. Nachtigal 3:53–54.
4. Nachtigal 2:752. For a discussion of the slave trade between Africa and Arabia in 1960, see *Hansard Parliamentary Debates* (House of Lords), 5th ser., vol. 225 (1960), col. 335.
5. Private conversation, Logone-Birni, 7 April 2001.

## 6. Sublime Port

1. Letter to Alexei Makarov, the tsar's secretary, 5 February 1722, in Abram P. Gannibal, 'Gannibaly: Noviye danniye dlya ikh biografii', i, *Pushkin i ego sovremenniki*, xvii–xviii (Petersburg, 1913), p. 208.
2. CWV 48:255.
3. Halil Inalcik with Donald Quataert (eds.), *An Economic and Social History of the Ottoman Empire*, 1300–1914 (Cambridge, 1994), p. 285.
4. A. H. Lyber, *The Government of the Ottoman Empire in the Time of Suleyman the Magnificent* (Cambridge, Mass., 1913), p. 41
5. PD f. 244, op. 24, d. 19, l. 4. In the Ottoman army a fifth of the 500,000 troops were African.
6. BOA/Hariciye, Siyasi, no. 2878/81. See also Nestor Camariano, *Alexandre Mavrocordato le Grand Drogman: son activité diplomatique* (Thessalonica, 1970).
7. Jérome Lobo, *Voyage historique d'Abissinie du R. P. Jérome Lobo de la Compagnie de Jesus*, trans. Joachim Le Grand (Paris, 1728), pp. 417–18.
8. Bruce 2:488–89; Lobo, p. 432; Nabokov 3:414.
9. PD f. 244, op. 24, d. 19, l. 12. See also Pushkin *Rukoyu Pushkina* (Moscow, 1997), p. 54, for information concerning Ivan Gannibal's involvement in the 1771 siege of Mytilene; Alexandra Krantonelli, *Elliniki Peirateia kai Koursos* (Athens, 1998), pp. 58–59.
10. J. de Hammer, *Histoire de l'Empire Ottoman*, trans. J. J. Hellert, 18 vols. (Paris, 1835–43), vol. 8, p. 148; M. S. Anderson, *The Rise of Modern Diplomacy* (London, 1993), p. 28.
11. Montagu wrote (or 'wrote up') the letters after her return from Constantinople where she lived as the wife of the English ambassador between 1716 and 1718, *The Complete Letters of Lady Mary Wortley Montagu*, ed. Robert Halsband, 3 vols. (Oxford, 1965), vol. 1, p. 390.
12. TSMA 11286, Rahmi Mehmed Pasha, Inscha (or 'correspondence'), no. 332.
13. Tolstoy's role in Gannibal's life is sometimes overlooked by Russian historians credulously repeating a mistake made by Pushkin the amateur detective, who

wrongly believed that one of Peter's closest advisers, Dmitry Shepelev, was Russia's envoy in Turkey, not Tolstoy.

14. V. E. Vozgrin, *Istoricheskiye sudby krymskikh tatar* (Moscow, 1992), p. 240.

15. See excellent analysis in the introduction to Peter Andreyevich Tolstoy, *The Travel Diary of Peter Tolstoy*, trans. and ed. M. Okenfuss (De Kalb, Ill., 1987).

16. SIRIO 39:35.

17. See Hugh Ridsdale (ed.), *Imperial Russian Foreign Policy* (Cambridge, 1993) and Sinan Kuneralp (ed.), *Studies in Ottoman Diplomatic History*, 5 vols. (Istanbul, 1987–90).

18. PIB 2:30–34.

19. PSS 8:11.

20. J. M. Tancoigne, *Voyage à Smyrne ... suivi d'une notice sur Péra*, 2 vols. (Paris, 1817), vol. 2, p. 46.

21. N. N. Bantysh-Kamensky, *Obzor vneshnikh snoshenii Rossii (po 1800 g.)*, part 2 (Moscow, 1896), p. 242.

22. N. I. Pavlenko, *Ptentsy gnezda Petrova* (Moscow, 1989), p. 135.

23. N. G Ustryalov, *Istoriya tsarstvovaniya Petra Velikogo*, 6 vols. (St Petersburg, 1858–69), vol. 4, pt 2, p. 254.

24. Yvelise Bernard, *L'Orient du XVIe siècle à travers les récits des voyageurs français* (Paris, 1988), p. 145; Matei Cazacu, 'Projets et intrigues serbes à la cour de Solimon' in Gilles Veinstein (ed.), *Soliman le Magnifique et son temps* (Paris, 1992), p. 512.

25. PSS 10:158. See also the testimonial Peter wrote for Raguzinsky the 'Illyrian szlachtich' (a Polish word, meaning 'gentleman'), 'Zhalovannaya gramota Savvi Lukichu-Raguzinskomu', dated 6 July 1703, which is both a merchant's charter and a licence to spy, in PIB 2:552; it was renewed on 2 April 1705, see PIB 3:307–10.

26. See Metin I. Kunt, 'The Koprulu Years: 1656–1661', unpublished Ph.D dissertation, Princeton University, 1971.

27. Lord Byron, *Don Juan*, canto v, lines 201–2, in *Complete Poetical Works*, ed. Jerome McGann, 7 vols. (Oxford, 1980–93), vol. 5, p. 248.

28. Charles White, *Three Years in Constantinople*, 3 vols. (London, 1845), vol. 1, p. 266; Molly Mackenzie, *Turkish Athens* (London, 1992), pp. 30–32.

29. Philip Mansel, *Constantinople: City of the World's Desire, 1453–1924* (London, 1995), p. 81.

30. The term 'sultanate of women' (*kadinlar saltanatii*) was coined by an early twentieth-century historian, Ahmed Refik, whose analysis has been criticised for its misogynist undertones. Lesley P. Peirce prefers the term 'age of the

Queen Mother' in *The Imperial Harem: Women and Sovereignty in the Ottoman Empire* (Oxford, 1993), pp. 91–112. Between 1578 and 1625, power fell into the grasp of the chief Janissary officers, the agas.

31. Paul Rycaut, *The Present State of the Ottoman Empire* (London, 1675), p. 46.
32. Barnette Miller, *Beyond the Sublime Porte* (New Haven, 1931), p. 116.
33. See also Donald Quataert, *The Ottoman Empire, 1700–1922* (Cambridge, 2000), pp. 37–51.
34. Demetrius Cantemir, *History of the Growth and Decay of the Othman Empire*, parts 1–2, trans. N. Tindal (London, 1734–35), p. 429.
35. Lord Byron, *Letters and Journals*, ed. Leslie Marchand, 13 vols. (London, 1973–94), vol. 3, p. 180. Byron visited Constantinople in the summer of 1810.
36. Hammer 13:128.
37. Cantemir, p. 456.
38. Hammer 13:151. On the Russian involvement in the uprising, see Mehmed Aga Silihdar, our main contemporary witness to the Edirne Event, in *Nusretname*, trans. Ismet Parmak⁄Sizoglu, 2 vols. (Istanbul, 1962–69), vol. 1, pp. 344–47. Also Abou⁄El⁄Haj Rifaat, *The 1703 Rebellion and the Structure of Ottoman Politics* (Istanbul, 1984), pp. 135–40; Vicomte de la Jonquière, *Histoire de l'Empire Ottoman*, 2 vols. (Paris, 1914), vol. 2, pp. 280–82.
39. The mufti's petition to the valide sultan and her reply are reproduced in Pars Tuglaci, *Osmanli Saray Kadinlari* (Istanbul, 1985), pp. 321–23.
40. Hammer 13:129.
41. Cantemir, p. 438.

## 7. Escape from the Seraglio

1. Eugene Schuyler, *Peter the Great*, 2 vols. (New York, 1884), vol. 2, p. 173.
2. See B. H. Sumner, *Peter the Great and the Ottoman Empire* (Oxford, 1949), pp. 63–64.
3. Marquis de Ferriol, *Correspondance* (Paris, 1870), p. 116; E. Miller, 'Alexandre Mavrocordato', *Journal des Savants* (May, 1879), p. 229.
4. Robert Sutton, *The Despatches of Sir Robert Sutton, Ambassador to Constantinople 1710–14*, ed. Akdes Nimat Kurat (London, 1953), p. 29.
5. Vladimir Putin, a proud native of Petersburg, rehabilitated the tsar's two⁄headed eagle in 2000 as a fitting emblem for the ambiguous Russian presidency. For an expert view of Peter's stealing of Roman thunder from Moscow, see Yu. M. Lotman (with B. A. Uspensky), 'Otzvuki kontseptsii 'Moskva – tretii Rim' v ideologii Petra Pervogo' (1982), in Lotman, *Istoriya i typologiya russkoi kulturi* (St Petersburg, 2002), pp. 349–61.

6. Hammer 13:142.

7. The letter to Peter, dated 13 Safer 1115, or roughly the end of August 1703, is in TSMA 11286, Rahmi Mehmed Pasha, *Inscha* (or 'correspondence'), no. 42; Hammer 13:151.

8. Cantemir, p. 440.

9. Hammer 13:141.

10. A. L. F. Alix, *Précis de l'Histoire de l'Empire Ottoman*, 3 vols. (Paris, 1824), vol. 2, pp. 319–27.

11. RGADA f. 160 (Letters from miscellaneous individuals, 1704) no. 11, l. 4.

12. Pushkin, *Rukoyu Pushkina*, pp. 34–35.

13. RGADA f. 89 (Relations between Russia and Turkey), op. 1 1704, d. 2, l. 314.

14. PD f. 24, op. 3, d. 161, l. 34.

15. PD f. 244, op. 3, d. 162, l. 32.

16. Ferriol, *Correspondance*, p. 190.

17. Mansel, p.131.

18. Georg von Helbig, *Russische Günstlinge* (Tübingen, 1809), p. 135.

19. F. A. Bulgarin, 'Vtoroye pismo iz Karlova na Kamenny Ostrov' in *Severnaya pchela (Northern Bee)*, 1830, no. 104. According to Nikolai Grech, a fellow spy, Bulgarin heard the anecdote from Count S. S. Uvarov in the home of Alexei Olenin, whose daughter's beauty Pushkin contrasts to his own 'blackamoor profile' in 'To Dawe, Esq.' – as discussed earlier – see Veresayev (1936) 2:121.

20. RGADA f. 160, d.11, ll. 11–11ob.

21. Cantemir, p. 442.

22. RGADA f. 89 (Relations between Russia and Turkey), op. 1 1704, d. 2, l. 179–80. Raguzinsky's reference to 'Constantin Cantacuzene' elides two ruling dynasties of Moldavia and Wallachia, in the persons of Constantin Cantemir and Serban Cantacuzene.

23. As above, ll. 314–18.

24. N. K. Teletova, *Zabytye rodstvennye svyazi A. S. Pushkina* (Leningrad, 1981), pp. 115–58; pp. 124–25.

25. Bantysh-Kamensky, p. 243.

26. Johann Georg Korb, *Diary of an Austrian Secretary of Legation at the Court of Tsar Peter the Great*, trans. Count MacDonnel, 2 vols. in one (London, 1968), vol. 1, p. 208; see also Robert K. Massie, *Peter the Great: His Life and World* (London, 1981), p. 271.

27. RGADA f. 248, op. 3, d. 43.

28. PIB 1:390.

## 8. Old Muscovy

1. PSS 8:14.

2. E. Shmurlo, *Pyotr Veliky v otsenke sovremennikov i potomstva* (St Petersburg, 1912), p. 25.

3. G. V. Yesipov, *Raskolnichi dela XVIII stoletiya*, 2 vols. (St Petersburg, 1861), vol. 1, p. 168.

4. Eugene Schuyler, *Peter the Great*, 2 vols. (New York, 1884), vol. 1, p. 285. Lindsey Hughes provides the best analysis of Peter's quirks, and Russian responses to them, in her magisterial *Russia in the Age of Peter the Great* (New Haven, 1998), pp. 357–89 and 445–61.

5. Balatri lived in Moscow from 1698 to 1701. For his 'Vita e viaggi di F. B., nativo di Pisa', written 1725–32, see Yu. Gerasimova, 'Vospominaniya Filippo Balatri. Novy inostranny istochnik po istorii Petrovskoi Rossii (1698–1701)' in *Zapiski otdela rukopisei* 27 (1965), pp. 164–90.

6. Quoted in Hughes, p. 357.

7. PSS 6:522.

8. Arden Reed discusses the English and French gods of meteorology in *Romantic Weather: The Climates of Coleridge and Baudelaire* (Hanover, R.I., 1983).

9. V. G. Belinsky, *Polnoye sobraniye sochineny*, 13 vols. (Moscow, 1953–59), vol. 8, p. 391.

10. PSS 6:98–99. The real-life Vyazemsky, whom Pushkin introduces to his fictional heroine in *Onegin* 7 xlix, line 10, criticised the poem's Moscow scenes in a letter to his wife, dated 23 January 1828: 'Pushkin's description of Moscow does not quite live up to his talent. It is limp and frigid, although, of course, containing many nice things. The joker put me in, too.'

11. K. N. Batyushkov, *Sochineniya* (Moscow, 1955), p. 309.

12. Paul of Aleppo, *The Travels of Macarius: Extracts from the Diary of the Travels of Macarius, Patriarch of Antioch, Written by his son, Paul, Archdeacon of Aleppo, 1652–60*, trans. F. C. Balfour (London, 1936), p. 26.

13. *Poltava*, canto 3, lines 183–87, see PSS 5:56.

14. Just Juel, 'Iz zapisok datskogo poslannika Iusta Iulia', *Russky arkhiv* 30 (1892), nos. 1:273–304; 2:35–74, 319–33, 495–518; 3:5–48, 113–50, 241–62; 3:45–46.

15. O. Belyayev, *Kabinet Petra Velikogo*, 3 vols. (St Petersburg, 1800), vol. 1, p. 123–24.

16. A. Babkin, 'Pisma Frantsa i Petra Lefortov o "Velikom posolstve"' in *Voprosy istorii*, no. 4 (1976), pp. 120–32; p. 130.

17. I. L. Feynberg, '*Abram Petrovich Gannibal, Praded Pushkina: Razyskaniya i Materialy* (Moscow, 1983), p. 29.

18. Yet Peter stuck with the old-fashioned Julian calendar. By the eighteenth century it had fallen eleven days behind the Gregorian calendar, which Russia only adopted in 1918. PSZ 3 no. 1735, pp. 680–81; no. 1736, pp. 681–82.

19. Pushkin, *Rukoyu Pushkina*, p. 34.

20. Cornelius de Bruyn, *Travels into Muscovy, Persia and Part of the East Indies: Containing an Accurate Description of What is Most Remarkable in Those Countries*, 2 vols. (London, 1737), vol. 1, p. 46.

21. Biblioteka RAN, Pb 24/1, t. 1, l. 3.

22. PSS 8:11.

23. Korb 1:222, 255.

24. Letter of 24 January 1706. BL Stafford Papers, Add. MS 31128, f. 34.

25. Juel, 3:30.

26. N. B. Golikova, *Politicheskiye protsessy pri Petre I* (Moscow, 1957), pp. 131–32, quoted in Hughes, p. 450.

27. F. C. Weber, *The Present State of Russia*, 2 vols. (London, 1722–23), vol. 1, pp. 90–91.

28. Victor Erofeyev, 'Dirty Words', trans. Andrew Bromfield, *New Yorker* (15 September 2003) pp. 42–46; p. 48. For Peter's even-handedness in mocking Catholic Rome and the Russian Patriarchate, see Yu. M. Lotman, *Istoriya i typologiya russkoi kulturi* (St Petersburg, 2002), p. 357.

29. Pushkin, *Rukoyu Pushkina*, p. 35.

30. *Polnoye sobraniye zakonov rossiskoi imperii*, 5: no. 3159 (13 February 1718).

31. Hughes, p. 316. See also O. Neverov, '"His Majesty's Cabinet" and Peter I's Kunstkammer', in O. Impey and A. McGregor (eds.) *The Origins of Museums: The Cabinet of Curiosities in 16th–17th-century Europe* (Oxford, 1985), p. 54.

32. PSS 8:5.

33. Nabokov 3:423.

34. E. Schmurlo, 'Gannibal', in F. A. Brokgauz and I. A. Efron (eds.), *Entsiklopedichesky slovar*, 82 vols. (St Petersburg, 1904), vol. 8, p. 137.

35. M. Vegner, *Predki Pushkina* (Moscow, 1937), p. 23.

36. PSS 8:25.

37. V. P. Grebenyuk (ed.), *Panegiricheskaya literatura petrovskogo vremeni* (Moscow, 1979), p. 298.

38. Teletova (1981), pp. 126–27. See also V. Kozlov, 'Kogda rodilsya praded Pushkina Gannibal?', *Nedelya*, no. 44 (1969), p. 19.

39. Pushkin, *Rukoyu Pushkina*, p. 35.

40. Zenaïde A. Ragozin, 'Pushkin and His Work', *Cosmopolitan*, no. 28 (January 1900), pp. 307–14.

41. Quoted in N. A. Malevanov, 'Petra Pitomets A. P. Gannibal' in *Neva*, no. 2 (1972), p. 192. See also *Pokhodnye zhurnaly Petra I 1695–1726* (St Petersburg, 1853–55), 1705, p. 2.

42. PD f. 24, op. 3, d. 161, l. 34.

43. M. A. Alekseyeva, *Gravyura Petrovskogo vremeni* (Leningrad, 1990), p. 19; V. K. Makarov, *Russkaya svetskaya gravyura pervoi chetverti XVIII v.* (Leningrad, 1973), pp. 213, 235–36.

44. A. E. Viktorov, *Opisaniye zapisnykh knig i bumag starinnykh dvortsovykh prikazov, 1613–1725* (Moscow, 1883), vol. 2, p. 481.

45. V. V. Stassov, *Arap Petra I i kalmyk Yekaterini II* (St Petersburg, 1861), pp. 68–69; Nabokov 3:428. See also Teletova (1995), pp. 100–103.

## 9. Baptism of Fire

1. Charles Whitworth, 'Dispatches 1704–8', in SIRIO 50:61–62.

2. Adam Mickiewicz, *Pan Tadeusz*, trans. Kenneth Mackenzie (London, 1964), l. 1.

3. PSS 12:312.

4. PSS 6:654.

5. PSS 8:82.

6. Whitworth quoted in T. Mackiv, *English Reports on Mazepa 1687–1709* (New York, 1983); PRO SP 91 vol. 4 (1705); Korb 2:142–43.

7. Whitworth, *An Account of Russia as it was in the Year 1710* (Moscow and Leningrad, 1988), p. 72.

8. PIB 3:346.

9. Ustryalov 4:374.

10. Biblioteka RAN, PB 24/1, t. 1, l. 3.

11. PD f. 24, op. 3, d. 161, l. 34.

12. Pushkin, *Rukoyu Pushkina*, p. 36.

13. PD f. 244, op. 3, l. 162.

14. Schuyler 2:44.

15. Nabokov 3:424–25.

16. *Rukoyu Pushkina*, p. 36.

17. Tsvetaeva's Russian phrase is *gigantova krestnika pravnuk* in 'Stikhi k Pushkinu', *Stikhotvoreniya i poemy* (Moscow, 1996), p. 279. For Pushkin's description of the baptism, see PSS 12:312. Gannibal's son Pyotr wrote that his father 'was given the name Peter, but as he cried like an infant whenever he was called by

that name, the tsar agreed to call him by his former name – which is to say, the name he had until his baptism: Abram', PD f. 244, op. 3, l. 162.

18. PD f. 244, op. 3, l. 162.

19. V. O. Klyuchevsky, *Kurs russkoi istorii*, 2nd edn, 5 vols. (Moscow, 1923), vol. 4, p. 77.

20. PSS 12:157.

21. B. A. Kurakin, *Rossiyu podnyal na dyby*, vol. 2, p. 6.

22. RGVIA f. 846, op. 15, ed. khr. 1–7.

23. Whitworth, *Account of Russia*, p. 64.

24. S. Baehr, *The Paradise Myth in Eighteenth-century Russia* (Stanford, 1991), pp. 31, 69.

25. PIB 4:27, 11:242.

## 10. Peter's Paradise

1. The phrase occurs in 'Veshnee teplo' (or 'Spring Warmth') by the court poet Vasily Tredyakovsky, who struck up a friendship with Gannibal after following the African to Paris, where he studied at the Sorbonne. 'What gardens are these/Planted by the great father?' Tredyakovsky asks of Saint Petersburg in 'Veshnee teplo' before answering his own question: 'Cry out, "the Northern Eden"!'. See V. K. Tredyakovsky, *Izbrannye proizvedeniya* (Moscow and Leningrad, 1963), pp. 261–62.

2. RGADA f. 9, otd. 1, kn. 57, l. 39.

3. Gavrila Afanasyevich's sister refers to the *skazka*, or 'fairy tale', in *The Negro of Peter the Great*, PSS 8:25. 'People who love Saint Petersburg will return time and time again to the genius of Peter I. After all, he created the city. He began to build it. He put the city on its feet – and he made it great. It wasn't just government buildings and palaces that immediately appeared in Petersburg. Almost at the same time, as if in a fairy tale, appeared majestic places of worship, plants, factories, fortifications, hospitals, universities and theatres. And it was all done with imperial splendour and verve. This was worthy of a city laying claim to global importance,' said Putin in remarks broadcast on Channel One News, 2 p.m., 30 May (O. S. 16 May) 2003.

4. The historical basis for the legend is doubtful. There are no relevant entries in the court journals, and it is possible that the tsar was not even there on the day in question, see *Pokhodnye zhurnaly Petra I 1695–1726*, 1703, p. 4, and A. Sharymov, 'Byl li Petr I osnovatelyem Sankt-Peterburga?', *Avrora*, nos 1/8 (1992), pp. 108–65.

5. PSS 5:131. The poem was not published in full during Pushkin's lifetime, owing to problems with the imperial censorship. It seems Nicholas I took

a dim view of the city's talisman, the famous bronze equestrian statue of Peter cast by Etienne Falconet, coming to life and terrorising a Petersburger who dared to indict the works of the tsar. The *Bronze Horseman*'s prologue, however, appeared in the December 1834 issue of the journal *Biblioteka dlya chteniya* ('Library for Reading') under the title 'Petersburg: an excerpt from a poem'.

6. PIB 4:209.

7. V. O. Klyuchevsky, *Sochineniya v vosmi tomakh* (Moscow, 1958), vol. 4, p. 125.

8. Whitworth, *Account of Russia*, p. 44.

9. Count Francesco Algarotti, *Lettres du Comte Algarotti sur la Russie* (London and Paris, 1769), p. 64. See also Yu. M. Lotman, 'Simvolika Peterburga i problemy semiotiki goroda' (1984), in Lotman, *Istoriya i typologiya russkoi kulturi* (St Petersburg, 2002), pp. 208–20.

10. Helbig, p. 135.

11. Grigory Kaganov, *Images of Space: St Petersburg in the Visual and Verbal Arts*, trans. Sidney Monas (Stanford, 1997), p. 4.

12. PSS 8:10.

13. Romans 5:14.

14. Helbig, p. 135.

15. PIB 4:369.

16. *Russky arkhiv* (1877) 3:284.

17. 'The Czar was once advised to abolish Slavery, and to introduce a moderate Liberty, which would encourage his Subjects, and promote his own Interest at the same time; but the wild Temper of the Russians, who are not governed without Constraint, was a sufficient Reason for rejecting the Proposition at that Time', F. C. Weber, *Present State of Russia*, 2 vols. (London, 1722–23), vol. 1, p. 49.

18. Adam Olearius, *The Travels of Olearius in Seventeenth-century Russia*, ed. Samuel Baron (Stanford, 1967), p. 126. See also Marshall Poe, 'What did Russians mean when they called themselves "Slaves of the Tsar"?' in *Slavic Review* 57 (1998), pp. 585–608.

19. J. Perry, *The State of Russia* (1716; rpt London, 1967), p. 237.

20. Weber 1:4.

21. Marquis de Custine, *Letters from Russia*, trans. Robin Buss (Harmondsworth, 1991), pp. 47, 151.

22. RGADA 13.176.25.

23. Pyotr Kozlovsky is the dissident and garrulous Prince K— who accosts Custine on the boat from Travemünde to Kronstadt, see *Letters from Russia*, p. 20.

24. PIB 9:231.

25. PIB 9:246.

26. Lines 5–7, in Byron, *Complete Poetical Works*, vol. 4.

27. RAN PB 24/1, t. 2, ll. 42–44.

28. Daniel Defoe, *Review of the State of the British Nation*, 18–20 August 1709. See also *An Impartial History of the Life and Actions of Peter Alexowitz, the Present Czar of Muscovy* (London, 1723), p. 208.

29. PSS 13:143. Mazepa's nephew, Andrei Voynarovsky, was arrested by Russian agents in Hamburg and sent to Yakutsk in Siberia, where he died in exile.

30. N. K. Teletova, *Gannibal – predki Pushkina* (Leningrad, 1978), p. 271.

## 11. Secret Sharer

1. Recent discussion of Heathcliff's African origins has cast new light on the impact of the slave trade on northern England, and suggested that Emily Brontë may have got the idea for Heathcliff's character from watching a performance in the title role of *Othello* by the black American actor Ira Aldridge at Bradford in 1841. Christopher Heywood describes Brontë's hero as 'a child of Africa from the world's largest slave port [Liverpool]' in *Wuthering Heights*, ed. Heywood (Toronto, 2002), p. 42. Russian enthusiasm for Aldridge's Shakespearean roles during his first visit to Petersburg in 1858 soon turned to guarded suspicion, and the actor was reduced to touring Moscow and the remote provinces from 1861 to 1866 after he was banned from the capital, see 'The Impact of Ira Aldridge' in Allison Blakely, *Russia and the Negro: Blacks in Russian History and Thought* (Washington D.C., 1986), pp. 62–70.

2. Dieudonné Gnammankou, *Abraham Hannibal: l'aïeul noir de Pouchkine* (Paris and Dakar, 1996), p. 44. See chapter two of Pushkin's *Arap Petra Velikogo* for Gannibal's youthful familiarity with Catherine and Elizabeth, PSS 8:11.

3. PSS 8:4–5.

4. Georg Grund, *Doklad o Rossii v 1705–1710 gg*, trans. from the German (*Bericht über Russland in den Jahren 1705–1710*) by Yu. N. Bespyatykh (St Petersburg, 1992), pp. 131–32.

5. V. E. Vozgrin, *Istoricheskiye sudby krymskikh tatar* (Moscow, 1992), p. 243.

6. 'Reskripty i ukazy Petra I k liflyandskim general-gubernatoram: Polonskomu, kn. Golitsynu i kn. Repninu', in *Osmnadtsaty vek.*, ed. Pyotr Bartenev, 4 vols. (Moscow, 1869), vol. 4, p. 22. (29 June 1714, to Prince Golitsyn in Reval).

7. Peter I, *Pokhodny zhurnal za 1714 god* (Petersburg, 1854), p. 110.

8. Pavlenko, *Ptentsy gnezda Petrova*, p. 247.

9. P. A. Vyazemsky, *Polnoye sobraniye sochineny*, 10 vols. (Petersburg, 1878–86), 8:68.

10. Gannibal, 'Gannibaly', p. 210.

11. Aeneas Tacitus, *How to Survive Under Siege*, trans. David Whitehead (Oxford, 1990), pp. 147–65.

12. RAN PB 24/1, t. 1, ll. 137–42.

13. N. Malevanov, 'Praded poeta', *Zvezda* (1974), no. 6, p. 157. Münnich wrote the memorandum to Anna in 1733. Dobroye (29 August 1708) was a minor skirmish in the run-up to the battle of Lesnaya.

14. Pushkin, *Rukoyu Pushkina*, p. 44.

15. PSS 3:187.

16. *Othello* I ii 11, I iii 228. PSS 8:27.

17. Teletova (1981), pp. 126–27. See also V. Kozlov, p. 19. There is a document in the Moscow Central Archives with the heading 'Received by the tsar's household', which apparently records a payment for the 'sale' of Alexei to Golitsyn.

18. PIB 5:252 (13 May 1707).

19. I. I. Golikov, *Deyaniya Petra Velikogo, mudrogo preobrazitelya Rossii, sobrannye iz dostovernykh istochnikov i raspolozhennye po godam*, 2nd edn, vol. 15 (Moscow, 1843), pp. 156–57.

20. P. Dolgoruky, *Mémoires de Prince Pierre Dolgoroukow*, 2 vols. (Geneva, 1867), vol. 1, p. 244. See also J. Cracraft, 'Feofan Prokopovich', in J. Garrard (ed.), *The Eighteenth Century in Russia* (Oxford, 1973), p. 75.

21. Dolgoruky 1:246.

22. As above, p. 247. See also Willem Bartjens, *De Vernieuwde Cyfferinge* (Amsterdam, 1637; rpt 1708), p. 184.

23. Stephen Butterfield sees black consciousness in white societies as 'divided and estranged because it succeeds in the white world by virtue of its outstanding abilities [yet is] more and more removed from the black masses', in *Black Autobiography in America* (Amherst, 1974), p. 93.

24. Kozlov, p. 19.

25. PSS 6:26.

26. PD f. 244, op. 24, d. 19, ll. 4–5.

27. Nabokov 3:427.

28. Ustryalov 6:366 ff.

## 12. Nègre du Czar

1. PSS 8:4.

2. Louis de Rouvroy, duc de Saint-Simon, *Mémoires*, 43 vols. (Paris, 1879–1930) 11:85.

3. PSS 8:3.

4. Kurakin 1:295.

5. RAN PB 24/1, t. 1, l.3*ob*. As well as being first cousins, the two rivals were also brothers-in-law, since the duc d'Orléans had married Maine's sister, another bastard. The duchesse du Maine, on the other hand, was the granddaughter of the Great Condé, Louis II de Bourbon, and hence, as a princess of the blood, occupied a higher rank than her husband, who was in principle 'diminished' by his illegitimacy.

6. Richer d'Aubé, 'Réflexions sur le Gouvernement de France' BNP, Manuscrits français, Nouvelles acquisitions françaises, 9511–16, fol. 57. Peter was impressed by Law's wizardry, by what the economist J. K. Galbraith has called 'the miracle of banking': the discovery of credit. Law understood that if money was lodged in a bank vault for safekeeping, the person who owned it could take away a piece of paper testifying to his ownership of the sum. He founded a bank with the authority to issue such notes and a promise to reduce the public debt. But then, in the summer of 1717, he merged the bank with the Louisiana Company, which had exclusive privileges to develop the vast French territories in the Mississippi river valley of North America. By forming a stock company, he was able to sell shares to the general public, more or less floating the national debt. Law's plan worked well for a few years but ran afoul of speculative and political intrigue, neither of which was directly attributable to Law. As the author of the scheme popularly known as the 'Mississippi Bubble', he was forced to flee France in 1720. Peter offered Law 2,000 peasants and the order of Saint Andrei to encourage him to build towns and villages and factories on the Caspian Sea, but nothing came of the project.

7. Colin Jones, in *The Great Nation: France from Louis XV to Napoleon* (London, 2002), p. 47, echoes Cardinal de Retz's verdict on the Great Condé's brother, the ineffectual prince de Conti – 'un zéro'. Retz supported the brothers in the Fronde, a series of civil wars (1648–53) during the minority of Louis XIV. Named after the 'sling' of a children's game played in the streets of Paris, the Fronde was a reaction to the policies of Cardinal Richelieu.

8. Madame de Staal-Delaunay, *Mémoires*, ed. G. Doscot (Paris, 1970), pp. 85, 239.

9. RAN PB 24/1, t.1, l. 3*ob*.

10. Staal-Delaunay, p.111.

11. As above, p. 96.

12. PSS 8:5.

13. Musée du Louvre, Paris, PM 730.

14. BML, MS 857, f. 653.

15. Montagu, *Letters*, 1:442.

16. Nabokov 3:423.

17. Janet Gleeson, *The Moneymaker* (London, 1999), p. 67.

18. PSS 8:4. The origin of Voltaire as a *nom de plume* remains doubtful, perhaps an anagram of *Arouet le jeune* (i.e., the younger).

19. Nabokov 3:430.

20. Charles-Louis de Secondat Montesquieu, *Persian Letters*, trans. C. J. Betts (Harmondsworth, 1973), pp. 226–27.

21. CWV 36:14.

22. Saint-Simon 30:98.

23. *Anecdotes sur le Czar Pierre le Grand* (1748), ed. Michel Mervaud, CWV 46:78. *Veritable vie privée du maréchal de Richelieu* (Paris, 1791), p. 86.

24. Letter of 15 May 1717, BML MS 857, f.753. Bazin, an assistant police officer, wrote to the marquis d'Argenson on 16 May 1717: 'I have the honour to inform you that I have taken M. Harrouet to the Bastille, in accordance with His Majesty's wishes, which you communicated to me,' BAP 10633, ff. 453–54.

25. Schuyler 2:305.

26. RAN PB 24/1, t. 1, l. 3*ob*.

27. Alexei Yurov, a fellow student, recalled the warning in a letter to Peter from Paris, dated 1 November 1718, quoted in P. P. Pekarsky, *Nauka i Literatura v Rossii pri Petre Velikom*, 2 vols. (St Petersburg, 1862), vol. 1, pp. 164–65.

28. CWV 85:70.

29. M. D. Khmyrov, *Istoricheskiye stati* (St Petersburg, 1873), p. 10.

30. Marcel Pollitzer, *Le Maréchal Galant: Louis François Armand, duc de Richelieu* (Paris, 1952), pp. 81–82. See also R. L. de Voyer de Paulmy, marquis d'Argenson, *Journal et mémoires*, ed. E. J. B. Rathery, 9 vols. (Paris, 1859–67). J. Buvat, *Journal de la Régence*, 1715–23, ed. E. Campardon, 2 vols. (Paris, 1865), and the unpublished memoirs of the duke d'Antin, in the Bibliothèque Nationale, Paris, Manuscrits français. Nouvelles acquisitions français, 23729–37.

31. Gannibal, 'Gannibaly', p. 27.

## 13. Man of Parts

1. RAN PB 24/1, t. 1, l. 3*ob*.

2. RAN PB 24/1, t. 1, l. 4.

3. As above.

4. As above.

5. A. Bolotov, *Zhizn i priklyucheniya Andreya Timofeyevicha Bolotova*, 4 vols., (Moscow, 1873), vol. 1, p. 223.

6. RAN PB 24/1, t. 2, l. 143. Wellington adopted exactly the same procedure when he besieged San Sebastian ninety-four years later. Perhaps he, like Bolotov's uncle, had read *Geometry and Fortification*.

7. Georg Leyets, *Abram Petrovich Gannibal: Biograficheskoye-Issledovaniye* (Tallinn, 1984), p. 42.

8. 'In his baggage, for the benefit of the [French] foreign ministry, was a map of the Black Sea, heaven knows how procured, marking the site of Russian fortresses still to be built at the mouth of the Don,' writes P. N. Furbank in *Diderot: A Critical Biography* (London, 1992), p. 389. Presumably, as the former general-in-chief in charge of fortress construction, the Moor of Petersburg was a likely source.

9. Gannibal, 'Gannibaly', p. 210.

10. As above, pp. 211–12.

11. PSS 8:8.

12. 'Gannibaly' 1:208.

13. Pekarsky 1:242.

14. Bantysh-Kamensky 1:93–94.

## 14. Regime Change

1. PSS 8:10.

2. PD f. 244, op. 24, d. 19, l. 8.

3. PSS 9:437, 441.

4. Bantysh-Kamensky 1:93–94.

5. N. Ya. Eydelman, *Tvoi 18-i vek: Prekrasen nash soyuz* (Moscow, 1991), pp. 28–29.

6. Anatoly Lanshchikov, 'Imperator-bolshevik', *Rodina*, 1992, no. 3, pp. 86–92. *Gulag* is an acronym formed from the official Soviet designation of its system of prisons and labour camps.

7. Hughes, p. 465.

8. PSS 8:11.

9. Weber 1:15–16.

10. Frontispiece to Ivan Nestouranoi [G. Rousset de Missy], *Mémoires du règne de Pierre le Grand* (Amsterdam, 1729–37), reproduced in J. Cracraft, *The Petrine Revolution in Russian Architecture* (Chicago, 1988), fig. 141.

11. *Literaturnaya Rossiya*, 10 September 1976, p. 16.

12. Gannibal, 'Gannibaly', 1:234.

13. S. P. Luppov, *Kniga v Rossii v pervoi chetverti XVIII veka* (Leningrad, 1973), p. 245.

14. Vegner, p. 34.

15. 'Gannibaly' 1:217.

16. S. N. Shubinsky, 'Knyaginiya Volkonskaya i ee druzhya', *Istorichesky vestnik* 98 (1904), p. 931.

17. *Othello* I ii 18–19. The 'signory' was the Venetian government.

18. PD f. 244, op. 24, d. 19, l. 9.

19. F. Prokopovich, *Kratkaya povest o smerti Petra Velikogo Imperatora i Samoderzhtsa Vserossiskogo* (St Petersburg, 1831), p. 22.

20. Hughes, p. 263.

21. PSS 8:27.

22. A. A. Golombyevsky, *Sotrudniki Petra Velikogo* (Moscow, 1903), p. 114.

23. S. G. Nelipovich, 'Positsiya B. Kh. fon Myunnikha v diskussii 1725 goda o sokrashennii armii i voyennogo byudzheta Rossii', *Voyenno-istorichesky zhurnal*, no. 8 (1990), pp. 3–7.

24. Khmyrov, pp. 18–19.

25. *Istoriya l.-gv. Preobrazhenskogo polka*, vol. 4 (St Petersburg, 1883), p. 169.

## 15. The Arab of Siberia

1. PD f. 244, op. 24, d. 19, l. 10.

2. PSS 12:312.

3. G. Semin, *Sevastopol: istorichesky ocherk* (Moscow, 1954), p. 24.

4. Khmyrov, pp. 18–19.

5. Anton Chekhov, *Polnoye sobraniye sochineny i pisem* (Moscow, 1924–68), vols. 14–15, p. 28.

6. M. D. Sergeyev, *Zhizn i zloklyucheniya Abrama Petrova, Arapa Petrova Velikogo* (Irkutsk, 1988), p.20.

7. Khmyrov, p. 19.

8. RGADA, 'Snosheniya Rossii s Kitayem', f. 62, 1728, d. 12, l. 15.

9. GAIO f. 142, op. 2, d. 26, l. 37.

10. NARB f. 174, op. 15, d. 12, l. 5.

11. PSS 6:655.

12. Nabokov 3:434.

13. PSS 6:655.

14. RGIA f. 1329, op. 3, d. 64, l. 125.

15. S. M. Solovyev, *Istoriya Rossii s drevneishikh vremen* (Moscow, 1963), bk 10, p. 259.

## 16. Fortress Mentality

1. Veresayev 1:338.
2. SOAS, MS 380624, f. 2.
3. BL Add. MSS 475639, f. 27.

## 17. The Othello Music

1. C. H. Manstein, *Mémoires historiques, politiques et militaires sur la Russie*, 3 vols. (Paris, 1860), vol. 7, p. 298 and vol. 2, p. 366.
2. P. Dolgoruky 1:246.
3. PSS 12:313.
4. *Othello* I iii 220–23.
5. As above, III 3 ii 5.
6. RGIA f. 1329, op. 3, d. 64, l. 125.
7. *Othello* I i 19.
8. See 'The Othello Music' in G. Wilson Knight, *The Wheel of Fire*, (London, 1930; rpt 1970), pp. 97–119.
9. PSS 8:5.
10. Khmyrov, p. 47.
11. PSS 11:164.
12. PSS 8:27.
13. Leyets, p. 74.
14. PSS 8:30.
15. PSS 12:157.
16. PSS 2:300.
17. ADA, op. 96, d. 87, l. 350.
18. S. I. Opatovich, 'Yevdokiya Andreyevna Gannibal', *Russkaya Starina* (1877), vol. xviii, pp. 69–78.
19. Khmyrov, p. 28.
20. PSS 8:6–7. Pushkin tells a similar story, 'About the Negro of Count C**' in *Table Talk*. The count's daughter gave birth to a black child, see PSS 12:159.
21. Khmyrov, p. 29.
22. Opatovich, p. 71.
23. As above.
24. Cited in Richard Stites, *The Women's Liberation Movement in Russia* (Princeton, 1978), pp. 6–7.
25. Opatovich, p. 76.

## 18. Unmoored

1. CSHA f. 854, op. A, ed. khr. 96, l. 6.

2. *Sbornik Mukhanova*, 2nd edn (St Petersburg, 1866), p. 251.

3. PD f. 244, op. 24, d. 19, l. 11.

4. *Don Juan*, canto x, lines 459–60, where Byron pokes fun at 'the graceless name of Biron', and adds in a footnote: 'In the Empress Anne's time, Biren her favourite assumed the name and arms of the "Birons" of France, which families are yet extant with that of England. There are still the daughters of Courland of that name; one of them I remember seeing in England in the blessed year of the Allies [1814] – (the Duchess of S.) – to whom the English Duchess of S[omerse]t presented me as a namesake.' *Complete Poetical Works* 5:745.

5. PSS 6:655.

6. PSS 2:218, 12:313.

7. R. Wittram, *Baltische Geschichte: die Ostseelande, Livland, Estland, Kurland, 1180–1918* (Munich, 1954), pp. 128–34.

8. A. Bayov, *Russkaya armiya v tsarstvovaniye Imperatritsi Anni Ioannovni*, 2 vols. (St Petersburg, 1906), vol. 1, p. 199.

9. TCA f. 230, op. 1, ed. khr. BR 22, n. 30.

10. Khmyrov, pp. 32–33.

11. PD f. 24, op. 3, d. 161, l. 34r.

12. The alleged martyrdom of the African soldier in the year 286 is recorded in the *Passio martyrum Acaunensium* (*The Passion of the Martyrs of Agaunum*) by the fifth-century French bishop Saint Eucherius, who describes a legion of Egyptian Christians serving in the Roman army under the command of Maurice (in Latin, Mauritius). Ironically, they were sent by Maximian, who later became Roman emperor, to help quash a revolt of Christian peasants in Gaul. The legion met Maximian at Octodurum (now Martigny, in Switzerland), but they refused to fight against their brethren and withdrew in protest to Agaunum, where Maximian had them put to death.

13. Letter dated 22 November 1742 in Abram P. Gannibal, *Pisma Abrama Ganibala*, ed. N. Gastfreynd (St Petersburg, 1904), p. 39.

14. Hans Rogger, *National Consciousness in Eighteenth-century Russia* (Cambridge, Mass., 1960), pp. 30–32.

15. V. V. Vasilyev, *Starinnye feiyerverki v Rossii* (Leningrad 1960), pp. 18–19.

16. Note to the History of the Swedish War, quoted in T. S. Maykov, 'Petr I i "Gistoriya Sveiskoi voini"', in N. I. Pavlenko, ed., *Rossiya v period reform Petra I* (Moscow, 1973), p. 117. See also M. A. Alekseyeva, *Feiyerverki i illuminatsii v grafike XVIII veke. Katalog vystavki* (Leningrad, 1978).

17. PD f. 244, op. 24, d. 19, l. 11. The words come from Luke's gospel, chapter 23, verse 42, where they are spoken by the thief on the cross next to Jesus.

18. PD f. 244, op. 24, d. 19, l. 11.

19. PSS 8:11.

20. PSS 2:218

21. PD f. 244, op. 24, d. 1.

22. Manstein 2:222–23.

23. TGA f. 230, op. 1, ed. khr. BR 21, l. 42.

24. William Richardson, *Anecdotes of the Russian Empire* (London, 1784), p. 193.

25. PSS 12:104. John Tanner, *A Narrative of the Captivity and Adventures of John Tanner, during Thirty Years Residence Among the Indians*, ed. Edwin James (New York, 1830). Pushkin read the French translation, *Mémoires de John Tanner, ou trente années dans les déserts de l'Amérique du Nord*, trans. Ernest de Blosseville (Paris, 1835), 2 vols. The term 'Negro President' might have been interpreted to mean that Jefferson was a pro-Negro president, an *ami des noirs*, and the lover of his own slave, Sally Hemmings. In fact, as David Brion Davis notes in *The Problem of Slavery in the Age of Revolution, 1770–1823* (Ithaca, 1975), p. 94, Jefferson declined, while in Paris, an invitation to join the Société des Amis des Noirs. In fact, the term 'Negro President' was coined by his Federalist opponents after Jefferson defeated the incumbent John Adams in the 1800 presidential election with a margin of Electoral College votes based not on the citizenry that could express its will but on the blacks owned by Southern masters. It galled the Federalists that Jefferson hailed his victory as a triumph of democracy and majority rule when, as one newspaper in Boston said, he had made his 'ride into the TEMPLE OF LIBERTY on the shoulders of slaves' (*Mercury and New-England Palladium*, January 20 1801). See also J. Thomas Shaw, 'Pushkin on America: His 'John Tanner'' in *Orbis Scriptus: Dmitrij Tschizewskij zum 70. Geburtstag*, ed. Dietrich Gerhardt *et al.* (Munich, 1966), pp. 739–56; and Garry Wills, *'Negro President': Jefferson and the Slave Power* (New York, 2003).

26. Richard Hellie, *Slavery in Russia 1450–1725* (Chicago, 1982), pp. 390, 711; and Peter Kolchin, *Unfree Labor: American Slavery and Russian Serfdom* (Cambridge, Mass., 1987), p. 233. Orlando Patterson has described an 'extrusive' concept of slave as 'insider who had fallen', as well as the more familiar model, in *Slavery and Social Death* (Cambridge, Mass., 1982), pp. 38–44. See also Herbert Leventer, 'Comments on Richard Hellie's "Recent Soviet Historiography on Medieval and Early Modern Russian Slavery"', *Russian Review* 36 (January 1977), pp. 64–67; and Hellie's persuasive rebuttal in 'A Reply', *Russian Review* 36, pp. 68–75. Also Hellie's original article, *Russian Review* 35 (January 1976), pp. 1–32.

27. Leyets, p. 144.

28. M. Messelière, *Voyage à Petersbourg* (Paris, 1803), p. 113.

29. H. Kaplan, *Russia and the Outbreak of the Seven Years' War* (Berkeley, 1968), pp. 103, 106, n. 13.

30. M. V. Danilov, *Zapiski artillerii Mikhaila Vasilyevicha Danilova* (Moscow, 1842), pp. 80–81.

31. [Catherine II], *Correspondence of Catherine the Great with Sir Charles Hanbury-Williams*, ed. the Earl of Ilchester, (London, 1928), p. 177.

32. D. D. Blagoi, 'Abram Petrovich Gannibal – arap Petra Velikogo', *Molodoye Gvardiya* 3 (March, 1937), pp. 72–89; p. 85.

33. See Ian Chesley, 'Writing Fire with Fire: Lomonosov as Pyrotechnician' (paper delivered to the American Association of Teachers of Slavic and Eastern European Languages, San Diego, 28 December 2003) for a useful discussion of the analogy between fireworks and politics; also Barbara Widenor Maggs, 'Firework Art and Literature: Eighteenth-century Pyrotechnical Tradition in Russia and Western Europe', *Slavonic and East European Review* 54 (January 1976). Roehling, 'Illustrated Publications on Fireworks and Illuminations', in A.G. Cross (ed.), *Russia and the West in the Eighteenth Century* (Newtonville, Mass., 1983), pp. 94–100.

34. The Don–Volga canal was never completed, and the shorter, northern section only in the nineteenth century; see A. J. Rieber, 'Politics and Technology in Eighteenth-century Russia' in *Science in Context* 8 (1995) pp. 342–43; also A. Voskresensky, *Zakonodatelnye akty Petra I* (Moscow and Leningrad, 1945), vol. 1, p. 129.

35. Alex de Jonge, *Stalin and the Reshaping of the Soviet Union* (London, 1986), p. 514.

36. *Russky arkhiv* (1882) 1: 209–10.

37. Henri Troyat, *Catherine the Great*, trans. Emily Read (rpt London, 2000), pp. 130–31.

## 19. Death of a Philosophe

1. PSS 6:263.

2. PSS 6:371.

3. AG f. 3, d. 3.

4. Kyril Zinovieff and Jenny Hughes, *The Companion Guide to Saint Petersburg* (Woodbridge, Suffolk, 2003), p. 316.

5. William Richardson, *Anecdotes of the Russian Empire* (London, 1784), pp. 103–4.

6. PSS 12:313.

7. Letter of 25 December 1944, GANIPO f. 1048, op. 2, d. 8, l. 3.

8. APAO inv. 490, op. 5, f. 3.

9. *Pisma Abrama Ganibala*, p. 13.

10. Louis Philippe, comte de Ségur, *Mémoires, souvenirs ou anecdotes*, 3 vols. (Paris, 1827), vol. 3, p. 37. See also Diderot's *Mémoires pour Catherine II*, ed. P. Vernière (Paris, 1966).

11. PSS 2:89.

12. PSS 2:91.

13. PSS 3:400.

14. Nabokov 2:207.

15. September–October 1822, from Kishinev, PSS 13:50.

16. PSS 6:75.

17. Gannibal, 'Gannibaly', p. 289.

18. PD f. 244, op. 24, d. 19, l. 12; f. 244, op. 3, d. 162, l. 32.

## Epilogue: The Negro Poet

1. Lindsey Hughes, *Peter the Great: A Biography* (New Haven, 2002), p. 50. See also S. Dixon et al., eds., *Britain and Russia in the Age of Peter the Great: Historical Documents* (London, 1998), p. 16.

2. F. A. Bulgarin, 'Vtoroye pismo iz Karlova na Kamenny Ostrov', in *Severnaya pchela (Northern Bee)* 1830, no. 104.

3. Dorothy Trench-Bonnett, 'Alexander Pushkin – Black Russian Poet', *Black Scholar* 2 (March/April 1989), p. 5.

4. Abram Tertz (Andrei Sinyavsky), *Strolls with Pushkin*, trans. Catharine Theimer Nepomnyashchy and Slava I. Yastremski (New Haven, 1993), p. 120.

5. PSS 3:187.

6. PSS 14:250. See J. Thomas Shaw, 'Pushkin on His African Heritage: Publications during His Lifetime' in *Puškin Today*, ed. David M. Bethea (Bloomington, 1993), pp. 121–35.

# Sources

## Archives, Periodicals and Abbreviations

| | |
|---|---|
| ADA | Arkhiv Dela Artillerii, Moscow |
| AG | Arkhiv Gannibalov, Vserossiiskogo Muzeya A.S. Pushkina, St Petersburg |
| APAO | Arkhiv Pskovskogo Arkheologicheskogo Obshchestva |
| BAP | Bibliothèque de l'Arsenal, Paris |
| BL | British Library |
| BML | Bibliothèque Municipale, Lille |
| BNP | Bibliothèque Nationale, Paris |
| BOA | Ottoman Archive, Istanbul |
| CNM | Chad National Museum, N'Djamena |
| CSHA | Central State Historical Archive of Estonia, Tallinn |
| CWV | Complete Works of Voltaire |
| GAIO | Gosudarstvenny Arkhiv Irkutskoi Oblasti |
| GANIPO | Gosudarstvenny Arkhiv Noveishei Istorii Pskovskoi Oblasti |
| GAPO | Gosudarstvenny Arkhiv Pskovskoi Oblasti |
| GARF | Gosudarstvenny Arkhiv Rossiskoi Federatsii, Moscow |
| GATO | Gosudarstvenny Arkhiv Tomskoi Oblasti |
| IDDMID | Istoriko-Dokumentalny Departament Ministerstva Inostrannikh Del RF |
| NARB | Natsionalny Arkhiv Respubliki Buryatiya |
| NART | Natsionalny Arkhiv Respubliki Tatarstan |
| PD | Pushkinsky Dom, St Petersburg |
| PIB | Pisma i bumagi Imperatora Petra Velikogo |
| PRO | Public Record Office, London |
| PSS | Polnoye Sobraniye Sochineny |
| PSZ | Polnoye sobraniye zakonov rossiiskoi imperii, St Petersburg, 1830 |
| RAN | Russian Academy of Sciences |
| RGADA | Rossiisky Gosudarstvenny Arkhiv Drevnikh Aktov, Moscow |

RGIA        Rossiisky Gosudarstvenny Istorichesky Arkhiv, St Petersburg
RGVA        Rossiisky Gosudarstvenny Voyenny Arkhiv
RGVIA       Rossiisky Gosudarstvenny Voyenno-Istorichesky Arkhiv, Moscow
SIRIO       Sbornik imperatorskogo rossiiskogo istoricheskogo obshchestva
SOAS        School of Oriental and African Studies, London
TCA         Tallinn City Arkhiv
TsGASPb     Tsentralny Gosudarstvenny Arkhiv Sankt-Peterburga
TsGIASPb    Tsentralny Gosudarstvenny Istorichesky Arkhiv Sankt-Peterburga
TSMA        Topkapi Saray Muzesi Arshivi

*Archivum latinitatis medii aevi*
*Black Scholar*
*Hansard Parliamentary Debates*
*Journal des Savants*
*Literaturnoye nasledstvo*
*Lyubovny byt*
*Nedelya*
*Pushkin i ego sovremenniki*
*Russkaya Starina*
*Russky arkhiv*
*Sbornik imperatorskogo rossiiskogo istoricheskogo obshchestva* (SIRIO)
*Sbornik Mukhanova*, 2nd edn, St Petersburg, 1866
*Voprosy istorii*
*Voyennaya Entsiklopediya*, St Petersburg, 1914
*Zapiski otdela rukopisei*

# Bibliography

AENEAS TACITUS, *How to Survive Under Siege*, trans. David Whitehead, Oxford, 1990.

AFRICANUS, Leo, *The History and Description of Africa*, trans. John Pory, 1600; rpt, ed. Robert Brown, 3 vols., London, 1896.

AGEYEVA, O. G., *Obshchestvennaya kulturnaya zhizn Peterburga 1. chetverti XVIII v.*, Moscow, 1991.

AKSYONOV, Vasily, *Volteryantsy i Volteryanki*, Moscow, 2004.

ALEKSEYEVA, M. A., *Feiyerverki i illuminatsii v grafike XVIII veke. Katalog vystavki*, Leningrad, 1978.

— *Gravyura Petrovskogo vremeni*, Leningrad, 1990.

ALGAROTTI, Count Francesco, *Lettres du comte Algarotti sur la Russie*, London and Paris, 1769.

ANANIA, Giovanni Lorenzo, *L'Universale Fabrica del Mondo, overo cosmografia*, 3rd edn, Venice, 1582.

ANDERSON, M. S., *The Rise of Modern Diplomacy*, London, 1993.

ANUCHIN, Dmitry, 'A. S. Pushkin: Antropologichesky eskiz', *Russkiye Vedomosti*, Moscow, 1899, pp. 1–44.

ARGENSON, R. L. de Voyer de Paulmy, marquis d', *Journal et mémoires*, ed. E. J. B. Rathery, 9 vols., Paris, 1859–67.

ARKELL, A. J., *A History of the Sudan from the Earliest Times to 1821*, London, 1961.

AROGUNDADE, Ben, *Black Beauty*, London, 2002.

BAEHR, S., *The Paradise Myth in Eighteenth-century Russia*, Stanford, Calif., 1991.

BANTYSH-KAMENSKY, N. N., *Obzor vneshnikh snoshenii Rossii (po 1800 g.)*, part 2, Moscow, 1896.

BARTH, Heinrich, *Travels and Discoveries in North and Central Africa, being a Journal of an Expedition under the Auspices of Her Britannic Majesty in the Years 1849–55*, London, 1857; rpt 1965.

BARTJENS, Willem, *De Vernieuwde Cyfferinge*, Amsterdam, 1637; rpt 1708.

BATYUSHKOV, K. N., *Sochineniya*, Moscow, 1955.

BAYOV, A., *Russkaya armiya v tsarstvovaniye Imperatritsi Anni Ioannovni*, 2 vols., St Petersburg, 1906.

BELINSKY, V. G., *Polnoye sobraniye sochineny*, 13 vols., Moscow, 1953–9.

BELYAYEV, O., *Kabinet Petra Velikogo*, 3 vols., St Petersburg, 1800.

BERNARD, Yvelise, *L'Orient du XVIe siècle à travers les récits des voyageurs français*, Paris, 1988.

BETHEA, David M., ed., *Puškin Today*, Bloomington, 1993.

BIVAR, A. D. H., and HISKETT, M., 'The Arabic Literature of Nigeria to 1804' in *Bulletin of the School of Oriental and African Studies*, 1962.

BLAGOI, D. D., 'Abram Petrovich Gannibal— arap Petra Velikogo' in *Molodoye Gvardiya* 3 (March, 1937), pp. 72–89.

BLAKELY, Allison, *Russia and the Negro: Blacks in Russian History and Thought*, Washington D.C., 1986.

BOLOTOV, Andrei, *Zhizn i priklyucheniya Andreya Timofeyevicha Bolotova*, 4 vols., Moscow, 1873.

BREDIN, Miles, *The Pale Abyssinian: A Life of James Bruce*, London, 2000.

BROKGAUZ, F. A. and EFRON, I. A., eds., *Entsiklopedichesky slovar*, St Petersburg, 1904.

BRONTË, Emily, *Wuthering Heights*, ed. Christopher Heywood, Toronto, 2002.

BRUCE, James, *Travels to Discover the Source of the Nile in the Years 1768, 1769, 1771, 1772 and 1773*, 5 vols., Edinburgh, 1790.

BRUYN, Cornelius de, *Travels into Muscovy, Persia and Part of the East Indies: Containing an Accurate Description of What is Most Remarkable in Those Countries*, 2 vols., London, 1737.

BRYER, Anthony, and URSINUS, Michael, eds., *From Manzikert to Lepanto: The Byzantine World and the Turks, 1071–1571*, Byzantinische Forschungen, no. 16, Amsterdam, 1991.

BULYGIN, I. A., *Monastyrskiye krestyane Rossii v pervoi cht. XVIII v.*, Moscow, 1977.

BUTTERFIELD, Stephen, *Black Autobiography in America*, Amherst, 1974.

BUVAT, J., *Journal de la Régence*, 1715–23, ed. E. Campardon, 2 vols., Paris, 1865.

BYRON, George Gordon, Lord, *Complete Poetical Works*, ed. Jerome McGann, 7 vols., Oxford, 1980–93.

—— *Byron's Letters & Journals*, ed. Leslie Marchand, 13 vols., London, 1973–94.

CAMARIANO, Nestor, *Alexandre Mavrocordato le Grand Drogman: son activité diplomatique*, Thessalonica, 1970.

CANTEMIR, Demetrius, *History of the Growth and Decay of the Othman Empire*, parts 1–2, trans. N. Tindal, London, 1734–35.

[CATHERINE II], *Correspondence of Catherine the Great with Sir Charles Hanbury-Williams*, ed. the Earl of Ilchester, London, 1928.

CHEKHOV, Anton, *Polnoye sobraniye sochineny i pisem*, Moscow, 1924–68.

CLAPPERTON, Hugh, *Journal of a Second Expedition into the Interior of Africa, from the Bight of Benin to Soccatoo*, London, 1829.

CRACRAFT, J., *The Church Reform of Peter the Great*, London, 1971.

CROSS, A. G., ed., *Russia and the West in the Eighteenth Century*, Newtonville, Mass., 1983.

CURTIN, Philip D., *The Image of Africa: British Ideas and Action, 1780–1850*, London, 1965.

CUSTINE, Marquis de, *Letters from Russia*, trans. Robin Buss, Harmondsworth, 1991.

DANILOV, M. V., *Zapiski artillerii Mikhaila Vasilyevicha Danilova*, Moscow, 1842.

DAVIS, David Brion, *Slavery and Human Progress*, Oxford, 1984.

— *The Problem of Slavery in the Age of Revolution, 1770–1823*, Ithaca, 1975.

DE BEER, Gavin R., *Alps and Elephants: Hannibal's March*, London, 1955.

DE JONGE, Alex, *Stalin and the Reshaping of the Soviet Union*, London, 1986.

DE LA CROIX, Horst, *Military Considerations in City Planning: Fortifications*, New York, 1972.

DECALO, S., *Historical Dictionary of Chad*, 2nd edn, Metuchen, N.J., 1987.

DEFOE, Daniel, *An Impartial History of the Life and Actions of Peter Alexowitz, the present Czar of Muscovy*, London, 1723.

DENHAM, Dixon, *Narrative of Travels and Discoveries in Northern and Central Africa, in the Years 1822, 1823 and 1824, by Major Denham, Captain Clapperton and the Late Doctor Oudney*, 3 vols., London, 1826.

DIDEROT, Denis, *Mémoires pour Catherine II*, ed. P. Vernière, Paris, 1966.

DIXON, S., et al., eds., *Britain and Russia in the Age of Peter the Great: Historical Documents*, London, 1998.

DOBROLYUBOV, Nikolai, *Selected Philosophical Essays*, Moscow, 1956.

DOLGORUKY, P., *Mémoires de Prince Pierre Dolgoroukow*, 2 vols., Geneva, 1867.

DUFFY, Christopher, *Fire and Stone: The Science of Fortress Warfare, 1660–1860*, Newton Abbot, 1975.

— *Siege Warfare*, vol. 1: *The Fortress in the Early Modern World, 1494–1660*; and vol. 2: *The Fortress in the Age of Vauban and Frederick the Great, 1680–1789*, London, 1979–85.

— *Russia's Military Road to the West: The Origins and Nature of Russian Military Power 1700–1800*, London, 1981.

EAGLETON, Terry, *Heathcliff and the Great Hunger: Studies in Irish Culture*, London, 1995.

EFENDI, Mehmed, *Le Paradis des infidels: Un ambassadeur ottoman en France sous la Régence,* Paris, 1981.

EROFEYEV, Victor, 'Dirty Words', trans. Andrew Bromfield, *New Yorker* (15 September 2003), pp. 42–48.

EYDELMAN, N. Ya., *Tvoi 18-i vek: Prekrasen nash soyuz,* Moscow, 1991.

FANON, Franz, *Black Skins, White Masks,* trans. Charles Lam Markmann, New York, 1967.

FERRIOL, Marquis de, *Correspondance,* Paris, 1870.

FEYNBERG, I. L., *Abram Petrovich Gannibal, Praded Pushkina: Razyskaniya i Materialy,* Moscow, 1983.

FISHER, Allan G.B., and FISHER, Humphrey J., *Slavery and Muslim Society in Africa: The Institution in Saharan and Sudanic Africa, and the Trans-Saharan Trade,* London, 1970.

FISHER, Humphrey J., *Slavery in the History of Muslim Black Africa,* London, 2001.

FURBANK, P. N., *Diderot: A Critical Biography,* London, 1992.

GANNIBAL, Abram P., *Pisma Abrama Ganibala,* ed. N. Gastfreynd, St Petersburg, 1904.

— 'Gannibaly: Noviye danniye dlya ikh biografii', i, *Pushkin i ego sovremenniki,* xvii–xviii, St Petersburg, 1913.

GARRARD, J., ed., *The Eighteenth Century in Russia,* Oxford, 1973.

GAYLE, Addison, ed., *The Black Aesthetic,* Garden City, New York, 1973.

GERHARDT, Dietrich, et al., eds., *Orbis Scriptus: Dmitrij Tschizewskij zum 70. Geburtstag,* Munich, 1966.

GHEBRE-GHIORGHIS, Solomon, 'The Eritrean Ancestry of Alexander Pushkin (1799–1837)', unpublished thesis, University of Asmara, 2002.

GLEESON, Janet, *The Moneymaker,* London, 1999.

GNAMMANKOU, Dieudonné, *Abraham Hannibal: l'aïeul noir de Pouchkine,* Paris and Dakar, 1996.

GOLIKOVA, N. B., *Politicheskiye protsessy pri Petre I,* Moscow, 1957.

GOLOMBYEVSKY, A. A., *Sotrudniki Petra Velikogo,* Moscow, 1903.

GOODWIN, Godfrey, *The Janissaries,* London, 1994.

GRABAR, I., *V. A. Serov: zhizn i tvorchestvo,* Moscow, 1913.

GREBENYUK, V. P., ed., *Panegiricheskaya literatura petrovskogo vremeni,* Moscow, 1979.

GRUND, Georg, *Doklad o Rossii v 1705–1710 gg,* trans. from the German (*Bericht über Russland in den Jahren 1705*) by Yu. N. Bespyatykh, St Petersburg, 1992.

HAMMER, J. de, *Histoire de l'Empire Ottoman,* trans. J. J. Hellert, 18 vols., Paris, 1835–43.

HARE, John, *Shadows across the Sahara: Travels with Camels from Lake Chad to Tripoli*, London, 2003.

HELBIG, Georg, *Russische Günstlinge*, Tübingen, 1809.

HELLIE, Richard, *Slavery in Russia, 1450–1725*, Chicago, 1982.

HOGG, Ian V., *Fortress: A History of Military Defence*, London, 1975.

HUGHES, Lindsey, *Russia in the Age of Peter the Great*, New Haven, 1998.

— *Peter the Great: A Biography*, New Haven, 2002.

IMPEY, O., and McGREGOR, A., eds., *The Origins of Museums: The Cabinet of Curiosities in 16th–17th-century Europe*, Oxford, 1985.

INALCIK, Halil, with QUATAERT, Donald, eds., *An Economic and Social History of the Ottoman Empire, 1300–1914*, Cambridge, 1994.

JONES, Colin, *The Great Nation: France from Louis XV to Napoleon*, London, 2002.

JONQUIÈRE, Vicomte de la, *Histoire de l'Empire Ottoman*, 2 vols., Paris, 1914.

JONSON, Ben, *The Complete Masques*, ed. Stephen Orgel, New Haven, 1968.

KAGANOV, Grigor, *Images of Space: St Petersburg in the Visual and Verbal Arts*, trans. Sidney Monas, Stanford, 1997.

KAPLAN, H., *Russia and the Outbreak of the Seven Years' War*, Berkeley, 1968.

KEANE, J. F., *Six Months in Mecca*, London, 1881.

KHMYROV, M. D., *Istoricheskiye stati*, St Petersburg, 1873.

KLYUCHEVSKY, V. O., *Kurs russkoi istorii*, 2nd edn, Moscow, 1923.

— *Sochineniya v vosmi tomakh*, Moscow, 1958.

KOLCHIN, Peter, *Unfree Labor: American Slavery and Russian Serfdom*, Cambridge, Mass., 1987.

KORB, Johann Georg, *Diary of an Austrian Secretary of Legation at the Court of Tsar Peter the Great*, trans. Count MacDonnel, 2 vols. in one, London, 1968.

KRANTONELLI, Alexandra, *Elliniki Peirateia kai Koursos*, Athens 1998.

KUNERALP, Sinan, ed., *Studies in Ottoman Diplomatic History*, 5 vols., Istanbul, 1987–90.

KUNT, Metin I., 'The Koprulu Years: 1656–1661', unpublished PhD dissertation, Princeton University, 1971.

KURAKIN, B. A., *Rossiyu podnyal na dyby*, 2 vols., Moscow, 1987.

LADURIE, Emmanuel Le Roy, with the collaboration of Jean-François Fitou, *Saint-Simon and the Court of Louis XIV*, trans. Arthur Goldhammer, Chicago, 2001.

LAFFIN, John, *The Arabs as Master Slavers*, Englewood, N. J., 1982.

LANGE, D., *Le Diwan des sultans du [Kanem-] Bornu, chronologie et histoire d'un royaume africain (de la fin du Xe siècle jusqu'à 1808)*, Wiesbaden 1977.

—— 'The Kingdoms and Peoples of Chad', in D. T. Niane, ed., *General History of Africa*, vol. 4: *Africa from the Twelfth to the Sixteenth Century*, London, 1984, pp. 238–65.

—— trans. *A Sudanic Chronicle: The Borno Expeditions of Idris Alauma (1564–76), according to the account of Ahmad b. Furtu*, Stuttgart, 1987.

—— 'The Chad Region as a Crossroads', in M. El Fasi, ed., *General History of Africa*, vol. 3, *Africa from the Seventh to the Eleventh Century*, London, 1988, pp. 436–60.

—— 'Preliminaires pour une histoire des Sao', *Journal of African History* 30 (1989), pp. 189–210.

LANGE, D., and BERTHOUD, S., 'L'intérieur de l'Afrique Occidentale d'après Giovanni Lorenzo Anania (XVIième siècle)', *Cahiers d'Histoire Mondiale* 16 (2) (1972), pp. 299–351.

LAZARD, P., *Vauban, 1633–1707*, Paris, 1934.

LEBEUF, Annie M. D., 'L'histoire d'un empire: le Baguirmi' in *Balafon* 37 (1977), pp. 3–11.

—— 'L'ancien royaume du Baguirmi' in *Mondes et Cultures*, xxxviii, 3 (1978), pp. 437–43.

—— 'L'origine et la constitution des principautés kotoko (Cameroun septentrional): essai de chronologie relative' in C. Tardits, ed., *Contribution de la recherche ethnologique à l'histoire des civilisations du Cameroun*, i, Paris, 1981, pp. 209–18.

—— 'Recherches archéologiques dans les basses vallées du Chari et du Logone (Cameroun septentrional)' in *Recherche, Pédagogie et Culture* 55 (1981), pp. 42–46.

—— 'La justice répressive chez les Kotoko du Nord-Cameroun' in *Droit et Culture* 9 (1986), pp. 169–70.

—— 'Sauvetage d'un dépôt archéologique à Logone-Birni' in *Ethnologiques: Hommage à Marcel Griaule*, Paris, 1987, pp. 199–216.

—— 'Un nom, un rôle: l'identité sociale chez les Lagouané (Nord-Cameroun)' in *Singularités: Les voies d'émergence individuelle*, Paris, 1989, pp. 421–34.

LEBEUF, J.-P., 'La circoncision chez les Kotoko, dans l'ancien pays sao', *Journal de la Société des Africanistes* 8 (1938), pp. 1–9.

—— 'Sao et Kotoko du Tchad', *Zaire* (March 1947), pp. 297–311.

—— 'Bibliographie Sao et Kotoko', *Études Camerounaises* 21–22 (1948), pp. 121–37.

—— *Archéologie tchadienne, Les Sao du Cameroun et du Tchad*, Paris, 1962.

—— 'Foulles archéologiques dans le butte Sao de Mdaga (Tchad) (Ve siècle avant J.-C. - milieu du XIXe après J.-C.)', *Bollettino del Centro Camuno di Studi Preistorici* 17 (1979), pp. 120–26.

LEBEUF, J.-P., and LEBEUF, A., *Les arts des Sao, Cameroun, Tchad, Nigeria*, Paris, 1977.

LEYETS, Georg, *Abram Petrovich Gannibal: Biograficheskoye Issledovaniye*, Tallinn, 1984.

LOBO, Jérome, *Voyage historique d'Abissinie du R. P. Jerome Lobo de la Compagnie de Jesus*, trans. Joachim Le Grand, Paris, 1728.

LOTMAN, Yu. M., *Istoriya i typologiya russkoi kulturi*, St Petersburg, 2002.

LOVEJOY, Paul E., 'Indigenous African Slavery' in *Historical Reflections*, 6(1) (1979), pp. 19–61.

— ed., *The Ideology of Slavery in Africa*, London, 1981.

— *Transformations in Slavery: A History of Slavery in Africa*, Cambridge, 1983.

— ed., *Africans in Bondage: Studies in Slavery and the Slave Trade*, Madison, 1986.

LUPPOV, S. P., *Kniga v Rossii v pervoi chetverti XVIII veka*, Leningrad, 1973.

LYBER, A. H., *The Government of the Ottoman Empire in the Time of Suleyman the Magnificent*, Cambridge, Mass., 1913.

MACKIV, T., *English Reports on Mazepa 1687–1709*, New York, 1983.

MACKENZIE, Molly, *Turkish Athens*, London, 1992.

McMANNERS, John, *Church and Society in Eighteenth-century France*, 2 vols., Oxford, 1998.

MADARIAGA, Isabel de, *Russia in the Age of Catherine the Great*, London, 1981.

MAKAROV, V. K., *Russkaya svetskaya gravyura pervoi chetverti XVIII v.*, Leningrad, 1973.

MALTSEVA, T. Yu., *Gannibaly i Pushkiny na Pskovshchine*, ed. G. N. Dubichin, Moscow, 1999.

MANDEVILLE, Sir John, *Mandeville's Travels*, ed. P. Hamelius, London, 1919.

MANSEL, Philip, *Constantinople: City of the World's Desire, 1453–1924*, London, 1995.

MANSTEIN, C. H., *Mémoires historiques, politiques et militaires sur la Russie*, 3 vols., Paris, 1860.

MASSIE, Robert K., *Peter the Great: His Life and World*, London, 1981.

MATAR, Nabil, *Turks, Moors and Englishmen in the Age of Discovery*, New York, 2000.

MEILLASSOUX, Claude, ed., *L'Esclavage en Afrique précoloniale*, Paris, 1975.

MESSELIÈRE, M., *Voyage à Petersbourg*, Paris, 1803.

MICKIEWICZ, Adam, *Pan Tadeusz*, trans. Kenneth Mackenzie, London, 1964.

MIERS, Suzanne, and KOPYTOFF, Igor, eds., *Slavery in Africa: Historical and Anthropological Perspectives*, Madison, 1977.

MILLER, Barnette, *Beyond the Sublime Porte*, New Haven, 1931.

MONTAGU, Lady Mary Wortley, *The Complete Letters of Lady Mary Wortley Montagu*, ed. Robert Halsband, 3 vols., London, 1965–67.

MONTESQUIEU, Charles-Louis de Secondat, baron de, *Persian Letters*, trans. C. J. Betts, Harmondsworth, 1973.

NABOKOV, Vladimir, 'Pushkin and Gannibal: A Footnote' in *Encounter* (1962), vol. 19, no. 1, pp. 11–26.

— trans., with a commentary, *Eugene Onegin by Aleksandr Pushkin*, 4 vols., London, 1964.

NACHTIGAL, Gustav, *Sahara and Sudan*, trans. G. B. Allan and Humphrey J. Fisher, 3 vols., London 1971–87.

OLEARIUS, Adam, *The Travels of Olearius in Seventeenth-century Russia*, ed. Samuel Baron, Stanford, 1967.

OLENINA, A. A., *Dnevnik 1828–29*, ed. Olga Oom, Paris, 1936.

PANKHURST, Richard, *An Introduction to the Economic History of Ethiopia*, London, 1961.

PATTERSON, Orlando, *Slavery and Social Death*, Cambridge, Mass., 1982.

PAUL OF ALEPPO, *The Travels of Macarius: Extracts from the Diary of the Travels of Macarius, Patriarch of Antioch, Written by his Son, Paul, Archdeacon of Aleppo, 1652–60*, trans. F. C. Balfour, London, 1936.

PAVLENKO, N. I., *Ptentsy gnezda Petrova*, Moscow, 1989.

— ed., *Rossiya v period reform Petra I*, Moscow, 1973.

PAVLUSHCHEV, L. N., *Iz semeinoi khroniki*, Moscow, 1890.

PEIRCE, Lesley P., *The Imperial Harem: Women and Sovereignty in the Ottoman Empire*, Oxford, 1993.

PEKARSKY, P. P., *Nauka i literatura v Rossii pri Petre Velikom*, 2 vols., Moscow, 1862.

PERRY, J, *The State of Russia Under the Present Czar*, London 1716; rpt London, 1967.

PETER I, *Pisma i bumagi Imperatora Petra Velikogo*, 13 vols., St Petersburg and Moscow, 1887–1992.

— *Pokhodnye zhurnaly Petra I 1695–1726*, St Petersburg, 1853–55.

PHILOSTRATUS, *Imagines*, London, 1931.

PIKE, Burton, *The Image of the City in Modern Literature*, Princeton, 1981.

POLLITZER, Marcel, *Le Maréchal Galant: Louis François Armand, duc de Richelieu*, Paris, 1952.

PONCET, Charles, *A Voyage to Aethiopia made in the Years 1698, 1699 and 1700*, London, 1709.

PROCTOR, Dennis, *Hannibal's March in History*, Oxford, 1971.

PROKOPOVICH, F., *Kratkaya povest o smerti Petra Velikogo Imperatora i Samoderzhtsa Vserossiskogo*, St Petersburg, 1831.

PURCHAS, Samuel, *Purchas, His Pilgrimage*, London, 1613.

PUSHKIN, Alexander, *Polnoye sobraniye sochineny*, 16 vols., Leningrad, 1937–59.

— *Pisma*, eds. B. L. and L. B. Modzalevsky, 3 vols., Moscow–Leningrad, 1926–35.

— *Rukoyu Pushkina*, revised edition, Moscow, 1997.

QUATAERT, Donald, *The Ottoman Empire, 1700–1922*, Cambridge, 2000.

REED, Arden, *Romantic Weather: The Climates of Coleridge and Baudelaire*, Hanover, R. I., 1983.

RICHARDSON, William, *Anecdotes of the Russian Empire*, London, 1784.

RIDSDALE, Hugh, ed., *Imperial Russian Foreign Policy*, Cambridge, 1993.

RIEBER, A. J., 'Politics and Technology in Eighteenth-century Russia' in *Science in Context* 8 (1995), pp. 342–43.

RIFAAT, Abou-El-Haj, *The 1703 Rebellion and the Structure of Ottoman Politics*, Istanbul, 1984.

RIMBAUD, Arthur, *Oeuvres Complètes*, ed. Antoine Adam, Paris, 1972.

RODINSON, Maxime, 'Généalogie royale de Logone-Birni (Cameroun)' in *Études Camerounaises*, iii (March–June 1950), 29–30, pp. 75–82.

ROGGER, Hans, *National Consciousness in Eighteenth-century Russia*, Cambridge, Mass., 1960.

ROIDER, Karl A., Jr, *Austria's Eastern Question*, Princeton, 1982.

ROOSEVELT, Priscilla, *Life on the Russian Country Estate: A Social and Cultural History*, New Haven, 1995.

RYCAUT, Paul, *The Present State of the Ottoman Empire*, London, 1675.

SAINT-SIMON, Louis de Rouvroy, duc de, *Mémoires*, 43 vols., Paris, 1879–1930.

SALT, Henry, *Voyages and Travels*, 3 vols., London, 1809.

— *A Voyage to Abyssinia and Travels into the Interior of That Country Executed under the Orders of the British Government in the Years 1809 and 1810*, London, 1814.

SCHAMA, Simon, *Landscape and Memory*, London, 1995.

SCHON, J. F., *Megana Hausa: Native Literature, Proverbs, Tales, Fables and Historical Fragments in the Hausa Language*, London, 1885.

SCHUYLER, Eugene, *Peter the Great*, 2 vols., New York, 1884.

SCULLARD, Howard H., *A History of the Roman World: 753 to 146 BC*, 4th edn, 1980.

SEBAG MONTEFIORE, Simon, *Prince of Princes: The Life of Potemkin*, London, 2000.

SÉGUR, Louis Philippe, comte de, *Mémoires, Souvenirs ou Anecdotes*, 3 vols., Paris, 1827.

SEMIN, G., *Sevastopol: istorichesky ocherk*, Moscow, 1954.

SERGEYEV, M. D., *Zhizn i zloklyucheniya Abrama Petrova, Arapa Petrova Velikogo*, Irkutsk, 1988.

SHMURLO, E., *Pyotr Veliky v otsenke sovremennikov i potomstva*, St Petersburg, 1912.

SILIHDAR, Mehmed Aga, *Nusretname*, trans. Ismet Parmak-Sizoglu, 2 vols., Istanbul, 1962–69.

SMIRNOVA, A. O., *Zapiski 1826–45*, ed. O. N. Smirnova, St Petersburg, 1895.

SOLOVYEV, S. M., *Istoriya Rossii c drevneishikh vremen*, bk 10, Moscow, 1963.

STAAL-DELAUNAY, Madame de, *Mémoires*, ed. G. Doscot, Paris, 1970.

STASSOV, V. V., *Arap Petra I i kalmyk Yekaterini II*, St Petersburg, 1861.

STITES, Richard, *The Women's Liberation Movement in Russia*, Princeton, 1978.

SUMNER, B. H., *Peter the Great and the Ottoman Empire*, Oxford, 1949.

SUTTON, Robert, *The Despatches of Sir Robert Sutton, Ambassador to Constantinople 1710–14*, ed. Akdes Nimat Kurat, London, 1953.

TANCOIGNE, J. M., *Voyage à Smyrne…suivi d'une notice sur Péra*, 2 vols., Paris, 1817.

TANNER, John, *A Narrative of the Captivity and Adventures of John Tanner, During Thirty Years' Residence among the Indians*, ed. Edwin James, New York, 1830.

—— *Mémoires de John Tanner, ou trente années dans les déserts de l'Amérique du Nord*, trans. Ernest de Blosseville, 2 vols., Paris, 1835.

TARDITS, C., ed., *Princes et serviteurs du royaume: cinq études de monarchies africaines*, Paris, 1987.

TELETOVA, N. K., *Gannibaly – predki Pushkina*, Leningrad, 1978.

—— *Zabytye rodstvennye svyazi A. S. Pushkina*, Leningrad, 1981.

—— *Legendi i mifi o Pushkine*, St Petersburg, 1995.

TERTZ, Abram (Andrei Sinyavsky), *Strolls with Pushkin*, trans. Catharine Theimer Nepomnyashchy and Slava I. Yastremski, New Haven, 1993.

THOMAS, Hugh, *The Slave Trade: The History of the Atlantic Slave Trade 1440–1870*, London, 1997.

TOLSTOY, Peter Andreyevich, *The Travel Diary of Peter Tolstoy*, trans. and ed. M.Okenfuss, De Kalb, Ill., 1987.

—— *Sostoyaniye Naroda Turetskogo v 1703 godu*, Simferopol, 1914.

TREDYAKOVSKY, Vasily, *Izbrannye proizvedeniya*, Moscow and Leningrad, 1963.

TROYAT, Henri, *Catherine the Great*, trans. Emily Read, rpt, London, 2000.

TSVETAEVA, Marina, *Stikhotvoreniya i poemy*, Moscow, 1996.

TUGLACI, Pars, *Osmanli Saray Kadinlari*, Istanbul, 1985.

USTRYALOV, N. G., *Istoriya tsarstvovaniya Petra Velikogo*, 6 vols., St Petersburg, 1858–69.

VASILYEV, V. V., *Starinnye feierverki v Rossii*, Leningrad, 1960.

VEGNER, M., *Predki Pushkina*, Moscow, 1937.

VEINSTEIN, Gilles, ed., *Soliman le Magnifique et son temps*, Paris, 1992.

VENGEROV, S. A., ed., *Pushkin*, Petersburg, 1915.

VERESAYEV, V., *Pushkin v zhizni*, 2 vols., 6th edn, Moscow, 1936.

VERLINDEN, Charles, 'L'Origine de "sclavus" – esclave' in *Archivum latinitatis medii aevi*, vol. 17 (1943), pp. 97–128.

— *L'Esclavage dans l'Europe médiévale*, Paris, 1955.

VIKTOROV, A. E., *Opisaniye zapisnykh knig i bumag starinnykh dvortsovykh prikazov, 1613–1725*, Moscow, 1883.

VOLTAIRE, *Complete Works of Voltaire*, eds. Theodore Besterman et al., Geneva, 1968 – .

VOSKRESENSKY, A., *Zakonodatelnye akty Petra I*, Moscow and Leningrad, 1945.

VOZGRIN, V. E., *Istoricheskiye sudby krymskikh tatar*, Moscow, 1992.

VULF, A. N., *Dnevniki*, Moscow, 1929.

VYAZEMSKY, P. A., *Polnoye sobraniye sochineny*, 10 vols., St Petersburg, 1878–86.

WEBER, F. C., *The Present State of Russia*, 2 vols., London, 1722–23.

WHITE, Charles, *Three Years in Constantinople*, 3 vols., London, 1845.

WHITWORTH, Charles, *An Account of Russia as it was in the Year 1710*, Moscow and Leningrad, 1988.

WILLS, Garry, *'Negro President': Jefferson and the Slave Power*, New York, 2003.

WILSON KNIGHT, G., *The Wheel of Fire*, 1930; rpt London, 1970.

WITTRAM, R., *Baltische Geschichte: die Ostseelande, Livland, Estland, Kurland, 1180–1918*, Munich, 1954.

WORDSWORTH, William, *Poems*, ed. John O. Hayden, 2 vols., Harmondsworth, 1977.

— and WORDSWORTH, Dorothy, *Letters of William and Dorothy Wordsworth: The Middle Years*. Part 1, 1806–11, ed. E. de Selincourt, rev. Mary Moorman, Oxford, 1969.

YESIPOV, G. V., *Raskolnichi dela XVIII stoletiya*, 2 vols., St Petersburg, 1861.

ZINOVIEFF, Kyril, and HUGHES, Jenny, *The Companion Guide to Saint Petersburg*, Woodbridge, Suffolk, 2003.

# Index